Don't Be Quiet, Start a Riot!
Essays on Feminism and Performance

Tiina Rosenberg

Published by
Stockholm University Press
Stockholm University
SE-106 91 Stockholm, Sweden
www.stockholmuniversitypress.se

Text © Tiina Rosenberg 2016
License CC-BY
ORCID: Tiina Rosenberg: 0000-0002-7012-2543

Supporting Agency (funding): The Swedish Research Council

First published 2016
Cover Illustration: *Le nozze di Figaro* (W.A. Mozart). Johanna Rudström (Cherubino) and Susanna Stern (Countess Almaviva), Royal Opera, Stockholm, 2015. Photographer: Mats Bäcker.
Cover designed by Karl Edqvist, SUP

Stockholm Studies in Culture and Aesthetics (Online) ISSN: 2002-3227

ISBN (Paperback): 978-91-7635-023-2
ISBN (PDF): 978-91-7635-020-1
ISBN (EPUB): 978-91-7635-021-8
ISBN (Kindle): 978-91-7635-022-5

DOI: http://dx.doi.org/10.16993/baf

This work is licensed under the Creative Commons Attribution 4.0 Unported License. To view a copy of this license, visit creativecommons.org/licenses/by/4.0/ or send a letter to Creative Commons, 444 Castro Street, Suite 900, Mountain View, California, 94041, USA. This license allows for copying any part of the work for personal and commercial use, providing author attribution is clearly stated.

Suggested citation:
Rosenberg, Tiina 2016 *Don't Be Quiet, Start a Riot! Essays on Feminism and Performance*. Stockholm: Stockholm University Press. DOI: http://dx.doi.org/10.16993/baf. License CC-BY 4.0

 To read the free, open access version of this book online, visit http://dx.doi.org/10.16993/baf or scan this QR code with your mobile device.

Stockholm Studies in Culture and Aesthetics

Stockholm Studies in Culture and Aesthetics (SiCA) is a peer-reviewed series of monographs and edited volumes published by Stockholm University Press. SiCA strives to provide a broad forum for research on culture and aesthetics, including the disciplines of Art History, Heritage Studies, Curating Art, History of Ideas, Literary Studies, Musicology, and Performance and Dance Studies. In terms of subjects and methods, the orientation is wide: critical theory, cultural studies and historiography, modernism and modernity, materiality and mediality, performativity and visual culture, children's literature and children's theatre, queer and gender studies. It is the ambition of SiCA to place equally high demands on the academic quality of the manuscripts it accepts as those applied by refereed international journals and academic publishers of a similar orientation. SiCA accepts manuscripts in English, Swedish, Danish, and Norwegian.

Editorial Board

Staffan Bergwik, Associate Professor of History of Ideas at the Department of Culture and Aesthetics at Stockholm University
Jørgen Bruhn, Professor of Comparative Literature at the Centre for Intermedial and Multimodal Studies at Linnaeus University in Växjö
Elina Druker, Associate Professor of Literature at the Department of Culture and Aesthetics at Stockholm University
Johanna Ethnersson Pontara, Associate Professor of Musicology at the Department of Culture and Aesthetics at Stockholm University
Kristina Fjelkestam, Professor of Gender Studies at the Department of Ethnology, History of Religions and Gender Studies at Stockholm University

Malin Hedlin Hayden, Associate Professor of Art History at the Department of Culture and Aesthetics at Stockholm University
Christer Johansson (coordination and communication), PhD Literature, Research Officer at the Department of Culture and Aesthetics at Stockholm University
Jacob Lund, Associate Professor of Aesthetics and Culture at the School of Communication and Culture – Aesthetics and Culture, Aarhus University
Catharina Nolin, Associate Professor of Art History at the Department of Culture and Aesthetics at Stockholm University
Ulf Olsson (chairperson), Professor of Literature at the Department of Culture and Aesthetics at Stockholm University
Meike Wagner, Professor of Theatre Studies at the Department of Culture and Aesthetics at Stockholm University

Titles in the series

1. Rosenberg, Tiina 2016. *Don't Be Quiet, Start a Riot! Essays on Feminism and Performance.* Stockholm: Stockholm University Press. DOI: http://dx.doi.org/10.16993/baf. License: CC-BY 4.0

Contents

Illustrations   vii
Acknowledgments   ix
Introduction   xi

PART I: ENVOICING GENDER AND SEXUALITY

1. The Touch of Opera, or, Can A Feminist Forgive Anything for a Good Tune?   3
2. No Questions Asked: Wagnerian Love Ban in *Lohengrin*   23
3. Who's Who Underneath the Kimono? Queer Mysteries of *M. Butterfly*   53
4. Queer Feelings: Zarah Leander, Sentimentality, and the Gay Diva Worship   81
5. The Soundtrack of Revolution: Memory, Affect, and the Power of Protest Songs   101

PART 2: SCANDINAVIAN CLASSICS

6. Queer Tintomara: Ephemeral and Elusive Gender(s) in *The Queen's Diadem*   119
7. AGAINST LOVE: Nora and Hedda on the Contemporary Scandinavian Stage   151
8. From Here to Eternity: Miss Julie Strikes Back and Refuses to Die   167

PART 3: ON FEMINIST ACTIVIST AESTHETICS

9. Still Angry After All These Years, or Valerie Solanas Under My Skin   177
10. Solidarity Lost and Found. Reflections on Contemporary Feminist Performance   185

11. Against Tolerance: Thoughts on Contemporary Scandinavian Racism   207
12. Don't Be Quiet, Start a Riot! On Feminist Activist Performance   219

Index of Persons   239

Illustrations

Cover image: *Le nozze di Figaro* (W.A. Mozart). Johanna Rudström (Cherubino) and Susanna Stern (Countess Almaviva), Royal Opera, Stockholm, 2015. Photographer: Mats Bäcker. Copyright CC-BY-NC-ND, Royal Opera, Stockholm.

1. *Le nozze di Figaro* (W.A. Mozart). Frida Österberg (Cherubino) and Madeleine Ulrici Jostedt (Countess Almaviva), Folkoperan, Stockholm, 2011. Photographer: Mats Bäcker. Copyright CC-BY-NC-ND: Folkoperan, Stockholm. 2

2. *Der Rosenkavalier* (Richard Strauss). Malin Byström (Marschallin) and Anna Stéphany (Octavian), Royal Opera, Stockholm, 2015. Photographer: Alexander Kenney. Copyright CC-BY-NC-ND, Royal Opera, Stockholm. 6

3. *Der Rosenkavalier* (Richard Strauss). Anna Stéphany (Octavian) and Elin Rombo (Sophie), Royal Opera, Stockholm, 2015. Photographer: Alexander Kenney. Copyright CC-BY-NC-ND, Royal Opera, Stockholm. 8

4. *Lohengrin* (Richard Wagner). Emma Vetter (Elsa) and Michael Weinius (Lohengrin), Royal Opera, Stockholm, 2012. Photographer: Alexander Kenney. Copyright CC-BY-NC-ND, Royal Opera, Stockholm. 22

5. *Madama Butterfly* (Giacomo Puccini). Asmik Grigorian (Butterfly), Royal Opera, Stockholm, 2014. Photographer: Marcus Gårder. Copyright CC-BY-NC-ND, Royal Opera, Stockholm. 52

6. Zarah Leander after a concert at Waldbühne in Berlin, July 1957. Archiv Paul Seiler Berlin, http://www.zarah-leander.de. Photographer: Georg Ebert. Copyright CC-BY-NC-ND: Paul Seiler, Sammlung Seiler Berlin. www.zarah-leander.de 80

7. *Guerrillero Heroico*. Ernesto Che Guevara at the funeral for victims of the La Coubre explosion, 1960. Photographer: Alberto Diaz Gutierrez (Alberto Korda). Public domain / Museo Che Guevara (Centro de Estudios Che Guevara en La Habana, Cuba).

https://en.wikipedia.org/wiki/Guerrillero_Heroico#/media/File:Heroico1.jpg   100

8   *The Queen's Diadem* (Carl Jonas Love Almqvist). Elin Klinga (Tintomara) and Anja Lundquist (Adolfine). Royal Dramatic Theatre, Stockholm, 2008. Photographer: Roger Stenberg. Copyright CC-BY-NC-ND, Royal Dramatic Theatre, Stockholm.   118

9   *Hedda Gabler* (Henrik Ibsen). Sonja Richter (Hedda) and Paprika Steen (Tesman). Betty Nansen Teatret, Copenhagen, 2005. Photographer: Thomas Petri. Copyright CC-BY-NC-ND: Thomas Petri, Betty Nansen Teatret, Copenhagen.   150

10   Alexandra Dahlström rehearsing her role as Alexandra/Julie at The Schoolhouse Theater, Croton Falls, New York. Still from Fia-Stina Sandlund's film *She's Staging It*, 2012. Photographer: Marius Dybwad Brandrud. Copyright CC-BY-NC-ND.   166

11   *Valerie Solanas for President of the United States* (Sara Stridsberg). Ingela Olsson (Valerie Solanas) and Noomi Rapace (Cosmogirl). Royal Dramatic Theatre, Stockholm, 2006. Photographer: Roger Stenberg. Copyright CC-BY-NC-ND, Royal Dramatic Theatre, Stockholm.   176

12   D Muttant (Maya Hald) and Y Puss (Åse Fougner) performing D Muttant's Mission in 2005. Photographer: José Figueroa. Copyright CC-BY-NC-ND.   184

13   Makode Linde at a demonstration in support of endangered artists and writers at the Kulturhuset City Theatre in Stockholm, 14 February, 2015. Photographer: Frankie Fouganthin. Copyright Creative Commons Attribution-Share Alike 4.0 International license, CC-BY-SA. https://sv.wikipedia.org/wiki/Makode_Linde#/media/File:Makode_Linde_in_Feb_2015.jpg   206

14   Pussy Riot, Moscow, 2012. Photographer: Igor Mukhin. Copyright Creative Commons Attribution-Share Alike 3.0 Unported license, CC-BY-SA. https://en.wikipedia.org/wiki/Pussy_Riot#/media/File:Pussy_Riot_by_Igor_Mukhin.jpg   218

Acknowledgments

The author and the publisher gratefully acknowledge permission to reproduce copyrighted material in this book:

1. "The Touch of Opera, or, Can a Feminist Forgive Anything for a Good Tune?" *Journal of Theatre and Drama*, 4 (1998), 23–36.
2. "Kuka on kukin hameen alla? Queer – ja postkolonialistinen näkökulma M. *Butterflyihin*" ("Who Is Who Under the Kimono? Queer and Post-Colonial Views on *M. Butterfly*"). In *Dramaturgioita. Näkokulmia draamateoriaan, dramaturgiaan ja draama-analyysin ongelmiin* (Dramaturgies. Perspectives on Drama Theory, Dramaturgy, and Drama Analysis), edited by Heta Reitala and Timo Heinonen, 159–186. Helsinki: Palmenia, 2001.
3. "'Elsa, hast du mich wohl verstanden?' Feministinen analyysi Wagnerin *Lohengrinista*" ("Elsa, Have You Not Understood Me? A Feminist Analysis of Wagner's *Lohengrin*"). In *Dramaturgioita. Näkokulmia draamateoriaan, dramaturgiaan ja draama-analyysin ongelmiin* (Dramaturgies. Perspectives on Drama Theory, Dramaturgy, and Drama Analysis), edited by Heta Reitala and Timo Heinonen, 131–158. Helsinki: Palmenia, 2001.
4. "Queer Feelings: Zarah Leander, Sentimentality, and the Gay Diva Worship." *Nordic Theatre Studies* 21 (2009), 114–128.
5. "The Soundtrack of Revolution: Memory, Affect, and the Power of Protest Songs." *Culture Unbound* 5 (2013), 175–188.
6. "Tintomara. Queerteatraalinen luenta C.L.J.Almqvistin romaanista Kuningattaren jalokivikoru" ("Tintomara: A Queer-Theatrical Reading of C.J.L. Almqvist's Novel *The Queen's Diadem*"). In *Pervot pidot. Homo-, lesbo- ja queernäkökulmia*

kirjallisuudentutkimukseen (Queer Symposion. Gay, Lesbian, and Queer Perspectives on Literature), edited by Kaisa Ilmonen and Lasse Kekki, 93–122. Helsinki: Like, 2004.

7. "Against Love: Nora and Hedda on the Contemporary Scandinavian Stage." In *Global Ibsen: Performing Multiple Modernities*, edited by Erika Fischer-Lichte, Barbara Gronau, and Christel Weiler, 89–101. London: Routledge, 2010.

8. "From Here to Eternity: Miss Julie Strikes Back and Refuses to Die." *Western European Stages* 24 (2012), 79–84.

9. "Still Angry After All These Years, or Valerie Solanas Under My Skin." *Theatre Journal, Special Issue on Contemporary Women Playwrights* 62 (2010), 529–534.

10. "Solidarity Lost and Found. Reflections on Contemporary Feminist Performance." In *The Politics of Being on Stage*, edited by Anja Klöck, 205–228. Hildesheim: Olms Verlag, 2012.

11. "Against Tolerance: Thoughts on Contemporary Scandinavian Racism." In *Fiebach. Theater, Wissen, Machen*, edited by Antje Budde, 58–66. Berlin: Theater der Zeit, 2014.

12. "Don't Be Quiet, Start a Riot. Tankar kring feministisk konstaktivism" ("Don't Be Quiet, Start a Riot. Thoughts on Feminist Art Activism"). In *Kritiska gemenskaper: Att skriva feministisk och postcolonial vetenskap* (Critical Communities. Writing Feminist and Postcolonial Scholarship), edited by Kerstin Sandell, Maja Sager, and Nora Räthzel, 237–246. Lund: Lund University, 2014.

Introduction

Gender, sexuality, and live performance are powerful forces that operate bodily and physically in unexpected ways. Affects are inscribed on our emotional and memory-based soundtracks early in life. The emotional connections are complex and we are not always in control of how our internal soundboard resonates when played upon by certain melodies. Such memories are archived and may appear when least expected. Affects and live performance represent both pleasure and a foretaste of utopia.

As Richard Dyer, writing about entertainment, comments, "Entertainment does not, however, present models of utopian worlds, as in the classic utopias of Thomas More, William Morris, et al. Rather, the utopianism is contained in the feelings it embodies. It presents, head-on as it were, what utopia would feel like, rather than how it would be organized. It thus works at the level of sensibility, by which I mean an affective code that is characteristic of, and largely specific to, a given mode of cultural production."[1]

Live performance is one guiding principle in the making and receiving of culture. The notion of performance is a broad one, including both art practices and performances of everyday life. Theatre as *performed genre* can be defined as any classic verbal or musical text that exists in live execution by performers. The work does not come into being until it is made actual by performers. The body of the performer is the authorial voice of any performed genre. Roland Barthes points out that "the erotic function of the theatre is not accessory, for the theatre alone of all the figurative arts (cinema, painting) presents the bodies and not their representation."[2] Presentation is the bodily presence on stage and the representation of its embeddedness in cultural forms, "its unequal but not monolithic relations of production and reception, its tense and unfinished, unfinishable relation to the reality to which it refers."[3]

The essays collected in this volume address some of the meanings and implications of gender and sexuality in performance, whereby those elements may not always be pleasurable. Critical feminist analysis often differs from queer approaches that are far more pleasure oriented. Queer (especially gay male) studies have been particularly concerned with pleasure. The queer feminist combination allows us to analyze the ramifications and costs of pleasure while we remain attentive to queer methodologies, for they may capture a wide range of impulses beyond fixed and normative categories of gender and sexuality.

Staying alive

The chapters in this book have appeared elsewhere over time, but certain themes keep coming back. First, how does one relate to dead women's opera and theatre? "Going to the theatre is like going to one's own funeral," as Hélène Cixous once put it, a quotation that recurs in these essays.[4] The phrase summarizes the feminist frustration with a tradition as old as ancient Greek tragedy in which women are routinely murdered or sacrificed. In Western classical drama and opera it seems that the best woman on stage is a dead woman; it is part of the pleasure of the performance. Those women who are especially revolting are sacrificed. Western theatre perpetuates a social order that requires either the death, domestication, or sacrifice of the female protagonist.[5]

Second, being a queer feminist academic means writing about performances by women and queers who survive. Recurring themes in these chapters are affect, androgyny, body genres, cross-dressing, desire, emotion, gender, kitsch, love, sentimentality, sexuality, travesti roles, utopia, and voice – the singing, talking, and screaming voice; but also the metaphorical voice of women and queers in theatre and opera history. One of the guiding historiographical challenges has been how to write about things we are critical of but still cannot help loving. In "Der Fall Wagner" Nietzsche says of Wagner's music that it does not only attack the listener, but persuades the nerves as well (*die Nerven überreden*).[6] It is a part of a feminist's task to analyze and explain the meaning of being attacked and persuaded by canonized art.

According to Sara Ahmed, the feminist concern with the future must be bound up with the legacy of the feminist past. "For feminists, a political and strategic question remains: When should we let go? And what should we let go of? Such a question has no immediate resolution: we must decide, always, what to do, as a decision that must be made again, and again, in each present we find ourselves in."[7] A canon is a body of work consolidated in a continuous process until it is generally accepted. It not only defines public taste, but also epitomizes scholars' views on what constitutes proper art and history – and in so doing has long excluded women and minorities.[8]

About this book

As its title suggests, the articles in this volume are linked to ongoing discussions within the field of queer feminist performance studies. They were written over a period of some twenty years, and are therefore disparate in both topic and tone. What unites them is a quest to understand feminist and queer performance on its own terms. One might define the theoretical project behind them all as the development of a queer feminist political engagement with the performing arts.

The first part of the collection investigates the affective dimensions of the human voice and performance, and their implications for gender and sexuality. While it is about the singing voice inside of the listener, it is also about affect, affection, pleasure, and memory in the enjoyment of musical performance. Chapters 1 and 2 contrast the discourse of women as victims against the envoicing of women in opera. Trouser roles and the figure of Elsa in Wagner's *Lohengrin* are used as examples. Chapter 3 discusses a forbidden love affair based on sexual misconception in David Henry Hwang's play *M Butterfly*, taking Puccini's *Madama Butterfly* as its intertext. Chapter 4 moves away from the opera discourse and analyzes the use of voice in gay male diva culture, as exemplified by Zarah Leander. Chapter 5 concludes the section with a meditation on the hunting memory of a long forgotten protest song.

The second part analyzes four examples of classical Scandinavian theatre and their feminist and queer interpretation: *The Queen's Diadem* by Carl Jonas Love Almqvist, a nineteenth-century gender classic of Swedish literature that is in the form of a theatricalized novel, and feminist theatre productions of Strindberg's *Miss Julie*, and Ibsen's *Hedda Gabler* and *A Doll's House*.

The third part concerns feminist activist aesthetics and political agency. It examines contemporary feminist performance in Sweden, focusing on Sara Stridsberg's project on Valerie Solanas, anti-racist interventions, and the feminist activist groups Pussy Riot and Femen.

The essays have been revised, correcting errors and adding new references, but the arguments themselves have not been altered. There has been an immense growth in feminist and queer theatre and performance studies in the last two decades, and I am aware of gaps in coverage. The examples chosen as topics for these essays are themes I have been interested in. They should be taken as points of entry into the investigation of complex issues.

Two of the texts, "No Questions Asked: Wagnerian Love Ban in *Lohengrin*" and "Queer Tintomara: Ephemeral and Elusive Gender(s) in *The Queen's Diadem*" also have new titles. For those interested, the texts and their origins are listed in the Acknowledgments as they originally appeared. Three are translations from Finnish to English. "Don't Be Quiet, Start a Riot. Tankar kring feministisk konstaktivism" was written in Swedish. The English version included here differs somewhat from the Swedish original. The others were all written in English.

Thanks

I would like to thank the publishers for welcoming the idea of reprinting the essays in this volume. I also want to thank Folkoperan, the Royal Opera, and the Royal Dramatic Theatre in Stockholm, as well as the Betty Nansen Teatret in Copenhagen, Paul Seiler at the Zarah Leander Archive in Berlin, Fia-Stina Sandlund in New York, and José Fiqueroa in Stockholm for permission to reprint photographs from their collections. Heartfelt thanks also to Christina Lenz, Jonas Holm, and Karl Edqvist at Stockholm University Press. I am very grateful to Anni Wessman and Toni Snellman for help in translating the *M. Butterfly*, Tintomara, and *Lohengrin* essays. I also want to thank my colleagues and friends in Finland, Sweden, and elsewhere, especially the Feminist Working Group at the International Federation for Theatre Research. Sharing ideas with you has always been fruitful, and I look forward to continuing it. Finally, my sincere appreciation to the Swedish Research Council for several grants awarded to me over the years that have provided me with the opportunity to think and write.

Stockholm, May 2016

Tiina Rosenberg

Notes

1. Dyer, "Entertainment and Utopia," 20.
2. Barthes, *Roland Barthes*, 83–84.
3. Dyer, *The Matter of Things*, 4.
4. Cixious, "Aller à la mer." See also Case, *Feminism and Theatre*; Diamond, *Unmaking Mimesis*.
5. Clément, *Opera*.
6. Nietzsche, *Der Fall Wagner*.
7. Ahmed, *The Cultural Politics of Emotion*, 188.
8. Freeland, *But Is It Art?* 122–147.

Works Cited

Ahmed, Sara. *The Cultural Politics of Emotion*. New York: Routledge, 2004.

Barthes, Roland. *Roland Barthes*. Paris: Éditions du Seuil, 1975; English translation by Richard Howard. London: Macmillan, 1995.

Cixous, Hélène. "Aller à la mer." In *Twentieth Century Theatre: A Sourcebook*, edited with translations by Richard Drain, 133–135. London: Routledge, 1995. Originally published in *Le Monde*, 28 April 1977.

Dyer, Richard. "Entertainment and Utopia." In *Only Entertainment*, 19–36. London: Routledge, 2002 [1992].

———. *Matter of Things. Essays on Representation*. London: Routledge, 2002 [1993].

Freeland, Cynthia. *But Is It Art? Introduction to Art Theory*. New York: Oxford University Press, 2001.

Nietzsche, Friedrich. *Der Fall Wagner: Schriften und Aufzeichnungen über Richard Wagner*. Frankfurt: Insel Verlag, 1983 [1888].

PART I:
ENVOICING GENDER AND SEXUALITY

Le nozze di Figaro (W.A. Mozart). Frida Österberg (Cherubino) and Madeleine Ulrici Jostedt (Countess Almaviva), Folkoperan, Stockholm, 2011. Photographer: Mats Bäcker. Copyright CC-BY-NC-ND: Folkoperan, Stockholm.

1. The Touch of Opera, or, Can a Feminist Forgive Anything for a Good Tune?

> I hear the high mezzo voice of the Enigma.
> Because it is the Enigma, it doesn't explain itself;
> It makes itself heard.
>
> Hélène Cixous, *Tancredi Continues*

"Still, the fact alone that people of different sexes are brought together in a glamorous auditorium that's the last word in worldly luxury – and then the heathenish disguises, the painted faces, the footlights, the effeminate voices – it all can't help encouraging a certain licentiousness and inducing evil thoughts and impure temptations," Abbé Bournisien bursts out in Flaubert's *Madame Bovary*.[1] Of course, he is right! Since Plato, the sensual and passionate has been a threat for those hostile to the seductiveness of the performing arts. But neither philosophers nor "les Péres" such as Augustine have prevented opera lovers like Emma Bovary from taking pleasure in the opera when "she gave herself up to the lullaby of the melodies, and felt all her being vibrate as if the violin bows were drawn over her nerves."[2]

What then exactly are these mysterious vibrations, the *jouissance* that the operatic experience evokes? Susan McClary cites Michel Foucault's remark in his *History of Sexuality* that during the seventeenth century, when opera was established as a public performing art, the West radically started to alter its attitudes toward human erotic behavior. Music is often concerned with stimulating and channeling desire through the medium of sound by using patterns that resemble those of sexuality.[3] "To a greater

---

How to cite this book chapter:
Rosenberg, Tiina 2016. The Touch of Opera, or, Can a Feminist Forgive Anything for a Good Tune? In: Rosenberg, Tiina *Don't Be Quiet, Start a Riot! Essays on Feminism and Performance*. Pp. 2–21. Stockholm: Stockholm University Press. DOI: http://dx.doi.org/10.16993/baf.a. License: CC-BY 4.0

extent than ever before, gender and sexuality become central concerns of Western culture in the seventeenth century," McClary writes, "and the new public arts all develop techniques for arousing and manipulating desire, for 'hooking' the spectator."[4] In opera, the dramaturgical movement – from a seductive overture through an interval of building tension, leading to one or more climactic moments, then a repetition of the cycle – seems self-evident. But according to McClary tonal compositions from Bach's organ fugues to Brahms's symphonies "whip up torrents of libidinal energy that are variously thwarted or permitted to gush."[5]

Joseph Kerman's *Opera as Drama* (1952) analyzed opera as a performed physical exchange between singer and audience. Catherine Clément's *Opera, or the Undoing of Women* (1979) and Susan McClary's *Feminine Endings: Music, Gender, and Sexuality* (1991) are the most influential early feminist studies in the field. In *Angel's Cry: Beyond the Pleasure Principle of Opera* (1992) Michael Poizat used Lacanian psychoanalysis to ask why opera awakens such passionate desire in its audience. He concludes that opera is a quest for jouissance, the rare and orgasm-like instant of eroticized pleasure induced by the climactic moment of an aria.

Opera research that takes the queer approach celebrates the exuberant qualities of opera and shares Emma Bovary's vibrations. Wayne Koestenbaum's *The Queen's Throat: Opera, Homosexuality and the Mystery of Desire* (1993) and Sam Abel's *Opera in the Flesh: Sexuality in Operatic Performance* (1997) analyze opera from a gay male perspective, although the queerness of opera is not confined to gay male desire. Corinne E. Blackmer and Patricia Juliana Smith's anthology, *En Travesti: Women, Gender Subversion, Opera* (1995), is an attempt to write women's lesbian/queer opera history. Heather Hadlock's "The Career of Cherubino, or The Trouser Role Grows Up" (2000), Naomi André's *Voicing Gender: Castrati, Travesti, and the Second Woman in Early Nineteenth-Century Italian Opera* (2006), and Judith A. Peraino's *Listening to the Sirens: Musical Technologies of Queer Identity from Homer to Hedwig* (2006) are all examples of a continued interest in trouser roles and queer musicology in more recent opera studies.[6]

This chapter discusses gender and desire in trouser roles and the relationship between the overabundance that characterizes opera and feminist aesthetics. Inspired by Sam Abel's statement, "I can forgive anything for a good tune," it asks if a feminist can forgive anything for a good tune.[7]

Better in pants

The enduring presence of cross-dressing in Western history and its specific high- and subcultural articulations have been an important part of the discourse of gender studies since the 1980s.[8] Women in classic Western narratives cross-dress for different reasons: to rescue or punish their husbands, to become soldiers, to pose as criminals and outlaws, or to stand up as emancipated, bisexual, or lesbian women. The mystery of androgyny, which is closely connected with the history of bisexuality, is also one of the attractions of cross-dressing. Through the centuries opera has repeatedly made use of cross-dressing in parts originally created for castrati, a repertoire later taken over by female (and male) singers; or performed in trouser roles where a woman sings the part of a man; or in trouser roles where a woman plays a woman who, in accordance with the plot, disguises herself as a man.[9]

Not surprisingly, recent opera studies have focused on trouser roles as opera's lesbian or more broadly *queer* (in this context meaning unspecified non-heterosexual) heroines. In a trouser role, a woman *en travesti* (literally "across dress") sings as and looks like (in theory at least) a man, but sounds like, and in fact is, a woman.[10] The pants, however, do not very convincingly root the female performer's "male" status in a man's genital and libidinal economy. The mimetic function of trouser roles is a masculine one: the cross-dressing woman is only thinkable in relation to the masculinity she represents. Male characters in opera (and representations in general) are universal precisely because they are male. The only way a female character can achieve universality is to transcend her gender. Put simply, men can be men but women, in order to become significant, have to become something more than women.

Blackmer and Smith point out that the trouser role tradition leads to a number of questions that many have contemplated but

Der Rosenkavalier (Richard Strauss). Malin Byström (Marschallin) and Anna Stéphany (Octavian), Royal Opera, Stockholm, 2015. Photographer: Alexander Kenney. Copyright CC-BY-NC-ND, Royal Opera, Stockholm.

few have dared to answer. Whether operatic cross-dressing is merely another layer of disguise, or whether it is a revelation of what some audience members and performers have known all along is an open question.[11] Gertrud Lehnert, who has written on cross-dressing women in literature, states that the cross-dressing disguise activates the myth of androgyny as human perfection, makes same-sex desire visible, and heightens male pleasure by temporarily lifting a woman up to the level of a man, but in the end dropping her back into her "proper" place.[12] The desire for a cross-dressing woman depends on what the spectator wants to see: a woman, a man, or an androgynous, gender-unspecific character. The trousers are, however, a powerful phallic sign, and the audience and performers are all asked to suspend disbelief and accept the gender signal of the clothing for "all-male" trouser roles like Cherubino (*Le nozze di Figaro*) and Octavian (*Der Rosenkavalier*). The underlying cultural imperative, as Teresa de Lauretis observes, is that the hero must be male, regardless of the gender of the text-image.[13]

Opera and sexuality

Abbé Bourisien's moral qualms about effeminate voices in the quotation from *Madame Bovary* cited earlier, suggests the potential gender elasticity of opera. Emma Bovary is still safely heterosexual; the priest can be certain of this. But as far as opera is concerned, he has reason to be worried. Through the castrati and trouser roles, the opera expresses a gender-flexible eroticism. Opera is, in Eve Kosofsky Sedgwick's view, *queer* – not necessarily homosexual per se, but standing in opposition to mainstream, normalized constructions of desire. This queerness is constituted by "the open mesh of possibilities, gaps, overlaps, dissonances and resonances, lapses and excesses of meaning when the constituent elements of anyone's gender, of anyone's sexuality aren't made (or *can't be* made) to signify monolithically."[14]

In the tradition of trouser roles, the dissonant juxtaposition between the signifier and the signified, and the sexual tension that it generates, is what constitutes the object of desire. The tradition, which reads trouser roles as male, and definitely straight, may not be as hard for audiences – and performers – to swallow as one might at first think. In fact, the transgressive, conspicuous act of cross-dressing has long been completely "normalized" on stage. Even in operas like *Der Rosenkavalier* (1911) and *Ariadne auf Naxos* (1916), in which trouser roles are distinctly presented as bisexual/lesbian, the audience is supposed to read the singers as "men."[15] Octavian in *Rosenkavalier* and the Composer in *Ariadne*, both cross-dressed mezzo-sopranos, make use of the female voice and act out the narrative in trousers, hardly disguising the female body and voice. The *queerness* of these operas is so explicit that, compared to most classic narratives where audiences are unlikely to get a glimpse of anything queer, those viewing *Rosenkavalier* and *Ariadne* have a hard time heterosexualizing an obviously queer narrative.[16]

Kurt Pahlen, editor of the complete text edition of *Der Rosenkavalier*, gives the standard explanation of Octavian's gender: "Many a person unschooled in music who comes to see *Rosenkavalier* may find it strange that the title role of the young Octavian is sung by a female voice."[17] In other words, the eye and body of the musically uneducated (read: a queer person) catches

Der Rosenkavalier (Richard Strauss). Anna Stéphany (Octavian) and Elin Rombo (Sophie), Royal Opera, Stockholm, 2015. Photographer: Alexander Kenney. Copyright CC-BY-NC-ND, Royal Opera, Stockholm.

the essential presentation of the body – the female – while the musically educated (read: non-queer) eye catches the "correct" gender – the male. Does gender matter, and who now has the ideological power to decide it?

Opera as body genre

The aspect of music that is most difficult to explain, according to McClary, is its "uncanny ability to make us experience our bodies in accordance with its gestures and rhythms."[18] As stated in the Introduction to this volume, theatre as *performed genre* can be defined as any classic verbal or musical text that exists in live execution by performers. The work does not come into being until it is made actual by performers. The body of the performer is the authorial voice of any performed genre. Roland Barthes points out that "the erotic function of the theatre is not accessory, for the theatre alone of all the figurative arts (cinema, painting) presents the bodies and not their representation."[19] Theatrical bodily presentation, the performer's aura, in Walter Benjamin's words, has the authorial power over the narrative. The story tells you one thing, the body something else. Barthes's distinction reminds us that logos is not in command on stage.

Theatrical presentation eroticizes the body of the performer, but the spectator never perceives the body through visuals alone. Opera intensifies this experience through vocality. Opera audiences are not only fascinated by voices but also actively participate in the performance through their physical presence in the same auditorium with the singers and by their applause and cheers. Opera performers are not primarily engaging with each other; they are directly addressing the audience. This might be explained as a practical necessity, as their voices might otherwise not carry over the orchestra. However, opera lovers do not think of it that way. They feel caressed, even penetrated, by the voices. Emma Bovary imagines that the tenor on stage really is gazing at her – as he well may be. Her passion is so great that she longs to rush into his arms. Historically, she is right. Actors and singers have always primarily faced the audience. The realistic acting style in which characters focus on each other dates from the nineteenth century theatre.

"Why does an opera performance feel so much like sex?" asks Abel. His answer is that opera feels like a sexual act because it *is* a sexual act. He is not thinking of Freud's notion of sublimation as metaphorical or vicarious sex, an intellectual reenactment or contemplation of pleasurable sensations.[20] There is nothing vicarious about opera's sensuality, Abel states. The erotics of opera do not necessarily take place between the characters on stage but between the singers and the audience, mediated by the voice, as the example of Emma Bovary shows.

The term *body genre* is used by Linda Williams to describe films whose excessive displays of emotion generate physical sensations in the audience.[21] She sees body genre as a subcategory of melodrama, a "filmic mode of stylistic and/or emotional excess that stands in contrast to more 'dominant' modes of realistic, goal-oriented narrative."[22] Williams's notion of melodrama and body genres seems, as Judith A. Peraino has written, almost tailor-made for opera.[23] The *melo(s)* in melodrama indicates the excess of melody – a result of emotional expression so extreme as to exceed the bounds of speech and enter the realm of song. Williams is referring to the specific form of excess which opera lovers crave from their preferred art form: elements of direct or indirect sexual excitement and rapture that even infuse the pathos of melodrama.

Women and opera: Victims or envoicing?

The feeling of being seduced and carried away from every critical discourse is an uneasy one for a feminist. But sometimes even a feminist needs a break from *Verfremdung*, and in this regard the feminist discourse about women and opera offers two possibilities. The first sees women as victims of the opera, and the second views opera as envoicing women.[24]

Opera is an art form with many gender-related anxieties. Women are the victims of the opera, argues Catherine Clément. She analyzes opera as a ritual of sacrifice staged by male librettists, composers, directors, conductors, and opera managers. "Opera is not forbidden to women," Clément writes. "Women are its jewels, the ornament indispensable for every festival. No prima donna, no opera. But the role of the jewel, a decorative object, is not the deciding role; and on the opera stage women perpetually sing their eternal undoing. The emotion is never more poignant than at the moment when the voice is lifted to die."[25] Opera is a male paradigm par excellence. The women, however independent and active they may seem, play a male game and are finally sacrificed. Clément lists an array of plots taken from what she calls "the dead women's opera," an unbroken litany of women punished for daring to desire and to act. McClary has stated that if Clément's catalogue is depressingly redundant, so are the schemata of dominant opera narratives.[26]

The phallic power of the gaze has been extensively commented upon in feminist criticism and theory. Women on stage do not represent the subject position – their desire is not symbolized in patriarchal culture, nor do the dynamics of their desires operate within the theatrical experience. "The audience becomes the male subject, exiled in the system of theatrical representation and driven by unfulfilled desire," writes Sue-Ellen Case.[27]

The rather discouraging view taken by Clément and other feminists is founded on strong evidence. Clément, however, is categorical. She discusses the female characters in so-called "serious opera," but neglects comic operas and does not see the gender-crossing potential of trouser roles. Female characters in comic operas and many women in trouser roles take matters into their own hands, managing to end up with a partner whom they have freely chosen, rather than one assigned to them by someone else.[28]

Carolyn Abbate presents the envoicing discourse: a woman, through the power of her voice, transcends her gender.[29] The castrato voice and, later, women's voices have been essentials of opera since its beginnings, and have served to envoice the marginalized. Abbate is inspired by Barthes's essay "The Grain of the Voice" in which he proposes the rebirth of the author "inside" of the work of art. Barthes eliminates a specifically male position (the author logos), supplanting it with an overtly female and musical force (the voice).[30] The experience of the voice, not the musical notation, transcends its "masculinity." The distinction Barthes makes between the presentation and the representation of the body in performance strongly suggests that all performance is characterized by corporeality and instability – something a narrative cannot entirely control.

For Barthes, listening is an active erotic act, not a passive receptive one. "The voice is that space which can hardly be placed, in which body and language come together, yet without becoming one," comments Doris Kolesch.[31] In this combination of the abstract and corporeal, Barthes locates an art form without the system of signifier/signified. The grain of the voice is the materiality of the body speaking its mother tongue.[32]

Barthes's alignment of the female with discursive language and with music sounds familiar. As Abbate points out, associating music with the feminine is pervasive in feminist theory, as in Julia Kristeva's notion of the *chora* as an enveloping but non-linguistic sound. This is so much so that many writers take for granted that what is spoken by the pre-linguistic female or maternal voice is "music."[33] This French poststructuralist position – what Alice Jardine has called "the-woman-in-effect" – does not clearly express what is actually meant by feminine.[34]

Luce Irigaray sees the feminine of the philosophers as an attempt at colonization that once more pushes women from cultural space;

male theorists have become better at being women than women are. Abbate asks if a feminine voice within a work of art can ever be defined, other than as something negative that can only be heard to sing after a real "author" is methodically eliminated from what we read or hear.[35] Barthes would probably respond that the body speaking its mother tongue is rather a metaphor for the other meaning-creating locations for which he is looking. The voice is something specific in itself, a vibration beyond the classic linguistic sign, deeply rooted in the human body.[36] Nevertheless, the body is still a gendered one.

The caressing touch of the voice

Michel Foucault and Judith Butler address the body and its pleasures as the target of technologies of surveillance and control, but both have almost nothing to say about those bodies, or the pleasures, that are being controlled. As their critics complain, this creates a disembodied, unstable, or empty space around which to frame any alternative understandings or politics.[37]

In her extravagant poetics of the 1970s, Irigaray sought to embrace all the metaphors of the feminine in order to construct a language for the feminine body, that is, to explore the "distinction of the sexes in terms of the way they inhabit or are inhabited by language."[38] Lynne Segal observes that Butler's thoughts are in some ways reminiscent of those of Irigaray who, in declaring the unrepresentability – and hence repudiation – of women in phallogocentric discourse, proposes a strategy of "disruptive excess."[39] Irigaray argues that by deliberately taking on the feminine role, women "convert a form of subordination into an affirmation, and thus begin to thwart it."[40] However, Butler is critical of Irigaray because she does not use this strategy as a type of parody, a subversive mimesis. Irigaray dares to metaphorically characterize a specifically feminine pleasure, most memorably in the essays "This Sex Which Is Not One" and "When Our Lips Speak Together."[41] Her formulation of a positive theory of femininity is not an aberration, as Naomi Schor claims in her essay "This Essentialism Which Is Not One."[42] It is rather the logical extension of her deconstruction of the specular logic of saming.

According to Irigaray, the predominance of the visual, and the discrimination and individualization of form, is particularly foreign to female eroticism. Women take far more pleasure in touching than looking, Irigaray states, and her entry into a dominant scopic economy again signifies her consignment to passivity. But the voice is not limited to iconic models of mimesis. The voice, not the gaze, has the quality of touching someone (*toucher de la caresse*). The female voice replaces the male author in a single cutting stroke, filling it not by an androgynous voice but with a female who has been artificially constructed for this purpose by the one who is singing, the performer.

Women's paired like-voices, "two equal voices rubbing up against each other," produce in Elizabeth Wood's words a border crossing, a bivocal Sapphonic effect primarily in travesty and transvestic duets formerly sung by castrati.[43] The castrato, argues musicologist Joke Dame, voiced sexual difference by going against the grain of a dominant oppositional female-male pairing.[44] The modern substitution of male tenors and female sopranos cannot match the interchange and interweaving of body, timbre, and pitch produced by castrati because their registers are too far apart. McClary points out that when we listen to two female like-voices, we experience female desire differently. This notion comes very close to Irigaray's account of women's eroticism in terms of "two lips in continuous contact."[45]

Could female sexuality, then, be positively represented by the metaphor of these "two lips," as Irigaray suggests? The two lips, while never one, are also never strictly two. They are simultaneously one and two. Where one identity ends and another begins remains unclear. This paradoxical image defies binary categories and forms of classification, being both inside and outside, one and two, genital and oral. The icon of two lips is not a truthful image of female anatomy but a new emblem by which female sexuality can be positively represented.[46] For Irigaray the problem is not the experience or recognition of female pleasure, but its representation, which actively constructs women's experience of their corporeality and pleasures.

Many trouser roles for both mezzos and sopranos, as Wood finds, are relatively free of warm "womanly vibrato." The extreme range in one female voice, from richly dark deep chest tones to piercingly clear high falsetto, and its break at the crossing of registers, is the effect she calls sonic cross-dressing, "a merging rather than splitting of *butch* authority and *femme* ambiguity, an acceptance and integration of female and male."[47] Wayne Koestenbaum suggests that the break between registers (fancifully called *il ponticello*, the little bridge) is the place within one voice where the split between male and female occurs, and that failure to disguise this gendered break is, like falsetto, fatal to the art of 'natural' voice production. "The register line, like the color line, the gender line, or the hetero/homo line," he writes, "can be crossed only if the transgressor pretends that no journey has taken place."[48]

According to Wood, the Sapphonic voice is a transvestic enigma, belonging to neither female nor male as constructed – a synthesis, not a split. Thus, 'Sapphonic voice' becomes a metaphor for the inclusive role-playing entity proposed by Case in her essay "Towards a Butch-Femme Aesthetic."[49] Wood calls this voice a challenge to the polarities of both gender and sexuality as these have been socially constructed in the form of a stable binary symmetry. The Sapphonic voice suggests that both gender and sexuality are transferable. Since it is a combination of registers, its acoustic effect resists vocal categories and (un)natural polarities. It also confounds simplistic messages about female desire and relationships defined by class, age, sexual status, and identity, both in music and operatic roles conventionally assigned to specific female voices. For listeners, the Sapphonic voice is a destabilizing agent of fantasy and desire. "The woman with this voice," Wood reflects, "this capacity to embody and traverse a range of sonic possibilities and overflow sonic boundaries, may vocalize inadmissible sexualities and a thrilling readiness to go beyond so-called natural limits, an erotics of risk and defiance, a desire for desire itself."[50]

Another layer of disguise, or, whose mimesis is this anyway?

Is the power of musical desire to mimic sympathy precisely the danger Clément has warned against? Historically, women have been denied power in the theatrical apparatus, yet signs of female sexuality have been crucial to the functioning of that sphere. Is mimesis, then, once and for all masculine? Elin Diamond points out that mimesis denotes both the activity of representing and its result. It is the impossible double, simultaneously the stake and the shifting sands, order and potential disorder, reason and madness.[51] Irigaray writes that women should make use of mimesis and mimicry in order to put phallogocentric discourse in motion. Therefore, to play with mimesis is one strategy through which women may take possession of the place of their exploitation through discourse, without allowing themselves to be simply reduced to it. Disruptive excess is one way of doing so.

Opera, being too much of everything, is not a part of theatre realism, or what Diamond calls "mimesis's positivist movement."[52] The excessive engagement of opera problematizes both mimesis and identification because it offers too much with which to identify.[53] Since excess is that which overflows boundaries, it has been seen as the space of transvestite desire.[54] The emphasis on performance, according to the distinction Barthes makes between representation and presentation of bodies, is one element in the undoing of opera's masculinity. The ear is a culpable organ, a symbol of emasculation.[55] The tradition of despising pleasure received through the ear, and condemning it as "tickling," is ancient. "A singer is queer," Koestenbaum writes, "because she presents the ear with unexpected bounty."[56]

When it comes to trouser roles, it may be as simple as Terry Castle has stated: the male persona is only that and no more in narrative fiction. The fact that the body is female and the sound is a woman's voice remains undeniable.[57] "Bravo! What a fine voice. I didn't know you sang so well!" the Countess says after Cherubino's thrilling arietta "Voi, che sapete che cosa è amor" (You who know what love is) in *Figaro*. She does not say, "What a beautiful pair of pants you wore!" Even if women cannot be seen, they obviously can be heard.

Notes

1. Flaubert, *Madame Bovary*, 255.
2. Ibid., 319.
3. McClary, *Feminine Endings*, 8.
4. Ibid., 36.

5. Ibid., 12–13.

6. Abel, *Opera in the Flesh*; André, *Voicing Gender*; Blackmer & Smith, *En Travesti*; Clément, *Opera*; Hadlock, "The Career of Cherubino, or The Trouser Role Grows Up"; Kerman, *Opera as Drama*; Koestenbaum, *The Queen's Throat*; Poizat, *Angel's Cry*; Peraino, *Listening to the Sirens*.

7. Abel, *Opera in the Flesh*, 35.

8. Dekker & van de Pol, *Tradition of Female Transvestism*.

9. Blackmer & Smith, *En Travesti*, 133.

10. Strauss, *Rosenkavalier*, 401. For this definition of the trouser role syndrome, see Blackmer & Smith, *En Travesti*, 5.

11. Blackmer & Smith, *En Travesti*, 11. The term *en travesti* (often *jouer en travesti* in French), meaning 'disguised,' comes from the Italian *travestire* (to disguise), a word that goes back to the Latin *trans* (across, beyond) + *vestire* (clothe): to clothe oneself in the garments of the opposite sex. *Trouser roles/breeches parts, Hosenrolle, byxroll, housurooli* are national terms for *travesti* roles for women in male clothing.

12. Lehnert, *Maskeraden und Metamorphosen*, 243. See also the same author's *Wenn Frauen Männerkleider tragen*.

13. de Lauretis, *Alice Doesn't*, 118–119.

14. Sedgwick, *Tendencies*. See also Abel, *Opera in the Flesh*, 65.

15. Blackmer & Smith, *En Travesti*, 14.

16. The word *queer* is here used in the sense of non-heterosexual, following the definition of the term as developed by queer theorists of the 1990s. It includes different kinds of sexual possibilities and border crossings between 'normal' and 'pathological,' 'heterosexual' and 'homosexual,' and 'feminine' and 'masculine.'

17. Strauss, *Rosenkavalier*, 401.

18. McClary, *Feminine Endings*, 23.

19. Barthes, *Roland Barthes*, 83.

20. Abel, *Opera in the Flesh*, 23.

21. Williams, "Film Bodies," 3.

22. Ibid.

23. Peraino; "I am an Opera" in Blackmer and Smith, *En Travesti*, 127.

24. See Clément, *Opera*, 3–23; Abbate, "Opera;" Abbate, *In search of Opera*.

25. Clément, *Opera*, 5.

26. McClary, *Feminine Endings*, 171.

27. Case, *Feminism and Theatre*, 120.

28. Blackmer & Smith, *En Travesti*, 62.

29. Abbate, "Opera." See also Koestenbaum, *The Queen's Throat*.

30. Roland Barthes, "Le grain de la voix," 238.

31. Kolesch, *Roland Barthes*, 124.

32. Ibid.

33. Abbate, "Opera," 232.

34. Jardine, *Gynesis*, 31–49.

35. Abbate, "Opera," 232.

36. Kolesch, *Roland Barthes*, 117–129.

37. Segal, *Straight Sex*, 183.

38. Ibid., 191; Irigaray, *This Sex*, 78.

39. Irigaray, *This Sex*, 78; Segal, *Straight Sex*, 191. See also Butler, *Gender Trouble*, 25–26.

40. Irigaray, *This Sex*, 76.

41. Ibid., 205–218.

42. Schor, "This Essentialism," 66.

43. Wood, "Sapphonics."

44. Dame, "Unveiled Voices."

45. McClary, *Feminine Endings*, 37.

46. Wood, "Sapphonics," 31. The voice has been described as the duplicate of the vagina. In 1756 Jean Blanchet called the glottis "a

horizontal cleft terminated by two lips." Robert Lawrence Weer in 1948 called the vocal cords "two thick membranes," "two lips," and "little shutters." See Koestenbaum, *The Queen's Throat*, 160.

47. Wood, "Sapphonics," 32.
48. Koestenbaum, *The Queen's Throat*, 167.
49. Case, "Towards a Butch-Femme Aesthetic."
50. Wood, "Sapphonics," 33.
51. Diamond, *Unmaking Mimesis*, v.
52. Ibid., vii.
53. Abel, *Opera in the Flesh*, 33.
54. Garber, *Vested Interests*, 28.
55. Koestenbaum, *The Queen's Throat*, 183.
56. Ibid., 98.
57. Castle, *The Apparitional Lesbian*, 230.

Works Cited

Abbate, Carolyn. "Opera; or, the Envoicing of Women." In *Musicology and Difference: Gender, Sexuality and Music Scholarship*, edited by Ruth E. Solie, 225–258. Berkeley: University of California Press, 1993.

———. *In Search of Opera*. Princeton: Princeton University Press, 2001.

Abel, Sam. *Opera in the Flesh: Sexuality in Operatic Performance*. Boulder, CO: Westview Press, 1996.

André, Naomi. *Voicing Gender: Castrati, Travesti, and the Second Woman in Early Nineteenth-Century Italian Opera*. Bloomington: Indiana University Press, 2006.

Barthes, Roland. *Roland Barthes*. Paris: Éditions du Seuil, 1975; English translation by Richard Howard. London: Macmillan, 1995.

———. "Le grain de la voix." In *Entretiens 1962–1980*. Paris: Éditions de Seuil, 1981.

Blackmer, Corinne E. and Patricia Juliana Smith, eds. *En Travesti: Women, Gender Subversion, Opera*. New York: Columbia University Press, 1995.

Butler, Judith. *Gender Trouble: Feminism and the Subversion of Identity*. New York: Routledge, 1990.

Case, Sue-Ellen. *Feminism and Theatre*. New York: Routledge, 1988.

———. "Towards a Butch-Femme Aesthetic." *Discourse* 11 (1998): 55–73.

Castle, Terry. *The Apparitional Lesbian: Female Homosexuality and Modern Culture*. New York: Columbia University Press, 1993.

Clément, Catherine. *Opera, or the Undoing of Women*. Translated by Betsy Wing with a forward by Susan McClary. London: Tauris Publishers, 1997.

Dame, Joke. "Unveiled Voices: Sexual Difference and the Castrato." In *Queering the Pitch: The New Gay and Lesbian Musicology*, edited by Philip Brett, Elizabeth Wood, and Gary C. Thomas, 139–154. New York: Routledge, 1994.

Dekker, Rudolf, and Lotte van de Pol. *The Tradition of the Female Transvestism in Early Modern Europe*. New York: St Martin's Press, 1989.

de Lauretis, Teresa. *Alice Doesn't: Feminism, Semiotics, Cinema*. Bloomington: Indiana University Press, 1984.

Diamond, Elin. *Unmaking Mimesis*. London: Routledge, 1997.

Flaubert, Gustave. *Madame Bovary*. Paris: Éditions Rombaldi, 1968 [1875]; English translation by Francis Steegmuller. New York: Vintage, 1992.

Garber, Marjorie. *Vested Interests: Cross-Dressing and Cultural Anxiety*. New York: Harper, 1993.

Hadlock, Heather. "The Career of Cherubino, or The Trouser Role Grows Up." In *Siren Songs. Representations of Gender and Sexuality in Opera*, edited by Mary Ann Smart, 67–92. Princeton: Princeton University Press, 2000.

Irigaray, Luce. *This Sex Which Is Not One*. Ithaca: Cornell University Press, 1985.

Jardine, Alice A. *Gynesis: Configurations of Woman and Modernity*. Ithaca: Cornell University Press, 1985.

Kerman, Joseph. *Opera as Drama*. New York: Vintage, 1956.

Koestenbaum, Wayne. *The Queen's Throat: Opera, Homosexuality and the Mystery of Desire*. London: Penguin, 1993.

Kolesch, Doris. *Roland Barthes*. Frankfurt: Campus Verlag, 1997.

Lehnert, Gertrud. *Maskeraden und Metamorphosen. Als Männer verkleidete Frauen in der Literatur*. Würzburg: Königshausen and Neumann, 1994.

———. *Wenn Frauen Männerkleider tragen. Geschlecht und Maskerade in Literatur und Geschichte*. Munich: Deutscher Taschenbuchverlag, 1997.

McClary, Susan. *Feminine Endings: Music, Gender, and Sexuality*. Minneapolis: University of Minnesota Press, 1991.

Peraino, Judith A. *Listening to the Sirens: Musical Technologies of Queer Identity from Homer to Hedwig,* Berkeley: University of California Press, 2006.

———."I am on Opera: Identifying with Henry Purcell's Dido and Aeneas." In *En Travesti: Women, Gender Subversion, Opera*, edited by Blackmer, Corinne E. and Patricia Juliana Smith, 99–131. New York: Columbia University Press, 1995.

Poizat, Michael. *Angel's Cry: Beyond the Pleasure Principle of Opera*. Ithaca: Cornell University Press, 1992.

Schor, Naomi. "This Essentialism Which Is Not One." In *Engaging With Irigaray: Feminist Philosophy and Modern European Thought*, edited by Carolyn Burke, Naomi Schor, and Margaret Whitford, 57–78. New York: Columbia University Press, 1994.

Sedgwick, Eve Kosofsky. *Tendencies*. Durham, NC: Duke University Press, 1993.

Segal, Lynne. *Straight Sex: The Politics of Pleasure*. London: Virago Press, 1994.

Smart, Mary Ann, ed. *Siren Songs: Representations of Gender and Sexuality in Opera*. Princeton: Princeton University Press, 2000.

Strauss, Richard. *Der Rosenkavalier*. Edited by Kurt Palen. Munich: Goldmann Verlag, 1980 [1911].

Williams, Linda. "Film Bodies: Gender, Genre, and Excess." *Film Quarterly* 44 (1991): 2–13.

Wood, Elizabeth. "Sapphonics." In *Queering the Pitch: The New Gay and Lesbian Musicology*, edited by Philip Brett, Elizabeth Wood and Gary C. Thomas, 27–66. New York: Routledge, 1994.

Lohengrin (Richard Wagner). Emma Vetter (Elsa) and Michael Weinius (Lohengrin), Royal Opera, Stockholm, 2012. Photographer: Alexander Kenney. Copyright CC-BY-NC-ND, Royal Opera, Stockholm.

2. No Questions Asked: Wagnerian Love Ban in *Lohengrin*

The fascination of operatic art resides in its abundance. Liberated from the constraints of realism and probability, the spectator can surrender to it or to turn away entirely, and enjoy it like an oyster: either swallowed whole or not at all.[1] The critical operagoer, particularly a feminist one, has many challenging positions to negotiate. Will the confrontation lead to a rejection of the entire genre?

Susan McClary observes that the aspect of music that is most difficult to account for is its almost frightening ability to make our entire body respond to its rhythms.[2] What, then, would opera be without music? What would remain if the music were stripped away and all that were left was the libretto? Could it stand on its own? The text of an opera or musical drama represents a unique genre. Unlike other dramatic texts, an opera's libretto is made whole only by the musical accompaniment and the events that accompany it on stage. A libretto is generally shorter and more fragmentary than any other type of dramatic text because it takes at least three times longer to sing a piece than to recite it. One needs to leave room for the music: the form demands it.[3]

Nevertheless, it should be possible to carry out a dispassionate reading of a libretto, as we shall here attempt with Richard Wagner's *Lohengrin* (1848). It seems impossible to consider *Lohengrin* without its music; however, the reverse is also true. Wagner wished to unite the verbal with the musical in order to create a *Ton-Wort-Drama*. Combined with the score and the spectacle that unfolds on stage, this new form of drama was supposed to be a *Gesamtkunstwerk* (unified work of art) that Wagner hoped would establish stagecraft as a hyper-art.

How to cite this book chapter:
Rosenberg, Tiina 2016. No Questions Asked: Wagnerian Love Ban in *Lohengrin*. In: Rosenberg, Tiina *Don't Be Quiet, Start a Riot! Essays on Feminism and Performance*. Pp. 22–50. Stockholm: Stockholm University Press. DOI: http://dx.doi.org/10.16993/baf.b. License: CC-BY 4.0

In order to examine the fate of *Lohengrin's* female lead Elsa from a feminist perspective we first should consider what that perspective means. Gayle Austin defines it as follows:

> A feminist approach to anything means paying attention to women. It means paying attention when women appear as characters and noticing when they do not. It means making some 'invisible' mechanisms visible and pointing out, when necessary, that while the emperor has no clothes, the empress has no body. It means paying attention to women as writers and as readers or audience members. It means taking nothing for granted because the things we take for granted are usually those that were constructed from the most powerful point of view in the culture, and that is not the point of view of women.[4]

One of the basic principles that feminist theory shares with other theories of cultural criticism is that seeing/reading/listening can never be neutral. It is always bound up with a specific historical context and is expressed from a particular cultural perspective. A woman has a dual focus (what has been called a sidelong glance), looking simultaneously in two directions.[5] Thus, feminist aesthetic analysis must begin with the fact that a woman is defined – to use Simone de Beauvoir's terminology – as "the other" and is taught to regard herself as such. However, "other" here must not be confused with *otherness*, which is a potentially positive marker of gender difference denoting the ordinal position of being second, that is, coming after the first, masculine gender.

The basic rule for a feminist reading of dramatic texts is that the reader must resist the canonized masterpieces of dramatic literature.[6] The same principle may be applied to their traditional interpretations. A feminist reading is here combined with an empathetic approach, assuming that the assessment of any work must be contextual. The feminist viewpoint clashes undeniably with Wagner's notion of women, whereas a patient, less single-minded reading may help us understand and enjoy *Lohengrin* more fully.

Woman as outsider

A patriarchally constructed and managed theatrical institution assigns women a special position. The long tradition of women appearing on stage has them dancing, singing, undressing, and dressing in front of the relentless, often admiring gaze of the audience. As Ann Kaplan writes, "Men do not simply look; their gaze carries with it the power of action and of possession that is lacking in the female gaze. Women receive and return a gaze, but cannot act on it."[7] Not being in possession of a subject position and gaze is concomitant with the more general exclusion of women from the sphere of the arts.

Mimesis, as defined by Aristotle, characterizes not only poetry, but encompasses theatre as well. In the fourth chapter of his *Poetics*, he identifies mimesis as an aspect of human nature, and uses the concept to express the step from the social world into the realm of poetry.[8] According to Aristotle, imitation is a fundamental human need. Although he was probably referring to both women and men, mimesis in ancient Greek theatre excludes women. The concept is a masculine one, defined by and for men. In *Feminism and Theatre*, Sue-Ellen Case points out that mimesis also bars women from the sphere of aesthetic experience in general. She finds the definitions in the *Poetics* based on a combination of social reality and aesthetic rules that render women outsiders in both areas.[9]

Not only are women excluded from the aesthetic system in general; according to Case their function in drama is to set boundaries for the masculine subject in order to facilitate the plastic definition of his outline, or, alternatively, illustrate ways in which women differ from men. Such a gender difference is expressed by clarifying male characteristics at the expense of women's. Case concludes that the woman is made invisible, and this invisibility creates an empty space that turns our attention to the masculine subject. The effect is that women are shown as subjects only insofar as they contribute to the definition of the male character.[10]

In her 1978 feminist theatre manifesto "Aller à la mer," Hélène Cixous proclaims that going to the theatre for a woman is like going to her own funeral. The key issue for Cixous is how women can attend the theatre without being complicit in the institutional sadism directed against them. The female spectator occupies the victim's position within the patriarchal family structure that is repeated ad nauseum in the theatre. Who is this female victim? As examples of women victimized in drama Cixous lists Electra, Antigone, Ophelia, and Cordelia. "In every man," Cixous writes, "there is a dethroned King Lear who requires his daughter to idealize him: 'Tell me that I am the greatest, the me-est, the most like a king, or I'll kill you!'"[11]

Women and opera

As stated in Chapter 1, the discourse on women and opera is dominated by two approaches. The first sees women as victims of operatic art – victims who have no voice and no subject position. Catherine Clément analyzes opera as a sacrificial rite in which the entire operation is in the hands of men. Women, however independent or active they may appear, are sacrificed, particularly if they are rebellious women. According to Clément, what is relevant is not that women in operas die (men die, too), but *how* they die. And there are so many ways to die. Carmen, Gilda, Butterfly, and a number of others die from a stab wound, some by their own hand. Violetta and Mimi die of tuberculosis. Norma, Brünnhilde, and Jeanne d'Arc are burned at the stake. Senta and Tosca leap to their deaths. Some drown or are poisoned, others die of a variety of causes, like Antonia, Isolde, and Mélisande.[12]

Carolyn Abbate offers another perspective on women in opera. In contrast to Clément she claims that opera actually gives voice to women. While librettists provide relatively little character leeway for women, vocally the opera offers them much greater latitude than the classical theatre.[13] It is not the score, but the experience of a voice that has the capacity to overcome the "masculinity" of a piece of music. The voice is able to vibrate and convey new and unexpected meanings.

Wagner's intense female voices represent a turning point in the history of the theatre. In contrast to the young dramatic *spinto* sopranos in bel canto, Wagner's women generate a larger volume of sound than any female operatic heroines had done before. The unusually deep orchestra pit in Wagner's Festspielhaus in Bayreuth also has the effect of amplifying the singers' voices, carrying them over and above the sounds of the orchestra. This serves Wagner's aim of creating a vocal style in which music and language merge, so that the declamation of the dramatic text is enunciated clearly.

Abbate's idea of opera as an opportunity to give voice to women is based on the musicological texts of Roland Barthes in which he discusses what he calls, *le grain de la voix,* the grain of the voice.[14] Barthes conceives of the voice as a new kind of author, singing inside every text. Music and voice both take something that is linguistically unarticulated and raise until it becomes a new entity. That articulation resounds in the listener, who is charmed by it. Voice is that elusive element in which body and language meet without merging completely.

In the musical fusion of the abstract and the concrete/corporeal we can glimpse Barthes's dream of an art form that lacks any system of signifier/signified.[15] Questioning the hierarchical and gendered subject–object positions of traditional aesthetics is one way to search for alternative modes of understanding. Barthes, who seldom uses the terms of gender theory in his arguments, ascribes to the voice the power of femininity. According to him, the "grain" of the voice is the materiality of the body speaking in its mother tongue. Setting the voice in opposition to the masculine logos is a common device in French psychoanalytic and feminist theory, which often emphasizes the prelinguistic stage as one of femininity and maternity.

Set against this background, Barthes's arguments can be seen as approaching the Western cliché of the "femininity" of music. In fact, Wagner, in an essay entitled "Oper und Drama," writes that music is a woman.[16] Voice is a singular phenomenon, a non-category. In its vibration it goes beyond the classical linguistic signifier and becomes a throbbing that rises from the depths of the human body. The singer's voice conjures up another realm, a realm of meaning beyond language. Enraptured listening is a path that takes us to this space; but in addition to direct experience, it requires of us knowledge of aesthetic structures that are both gendered and hierarchical.

Women in Wagner's oeuvre

Wagner's writings, his operas in particular, demonstrate a considerable interest in women and femininity. The notion of women that appears in his texts is essentialist: men are active, woman are passive. A woman not only receives a man's sperm and bears his children, but her soul and will are completely dependent on him. A woman loves because she must, Wagner declares in an essay on "Oper und Drama."[17] Without love, a woman is nothing.

Impossible and irreconcilable love is a recurring Wagnerian theme. Nearly all the women in his operas take great risks in trying to integrate their loves and their lives; it belongs to their utopian potential. That is why a woman's fall is so profound and her tragedy so great. A good woman is a loving woman, and most heroines in Wagner's operas are good according to his standards of loving and suffering. The only evil woman in Wagner's operas is Ortrud, Elsa's rival in *Lohengrin*. She represents a demonic woman who only has her own interests at heart and does not shrink from political power.

Wagner's female roles can be divided among the following types, some of which overlap:

1. The innocent victim: Ada *(Die Feen)*, Senta *(Der fliegende Holländer)*, Elisabeth *(Tannhäuser)*, Elsa *(Lohengrin)*, Brünnhilde *(Der Ring des Nibelungen)*, Isolde *(Tristan und Isolde)*
2. The self-sacrificing, loving woman: Senta (*Der fliegende Holländer*), Elisabeth (*Tannhäuser*)
3. The mistress: Venusberg women (*Tannhäuser*), Sieglinde and Gutrune (*Der Ring des Nibelungen*), Isolde (*Tristan und Isolde*), Eva (*Die Meistersinger von Nürnberg*)
4. The wife: Mariana (*Liebesverbot*), Ortrud (*Lohengrin*), Fricka (*Der Ring des Nibelungen*), the noblewomen of the chorus *(Tannhäuser)*
5. The evil, power-thirsty woman: Ortrud (*Lohengrin*)
6. The seductress who longs to be saved: Kundry (*Parsifal*)
7. The witch: Dilnovaz (*Die Feen*)
8. The sister: Lora (*Die Feen*), Isabella (*Liebesverbot*), Irene (*Rienzi*)
9. The loyal maidservant: Drolla (*Die Feen*), Dorella (*Liebesverbot*), Brangäne (*Tristan und Isolde*)
10. A woman dressed as a boy (Wagner's trouser roles): Adriano (*Rienzi*), a messenger of peace (*Rienzi*), four nobles and a young shepherd (*Tannhäuser*), and an esquire (*Parsifal*)
11. Mythological characters:
    a) Goddesses: Venus (*Tannhäuser*), Erda, Fricka, Freia (*Der Ring des Nibelungen*)

b) Demigoddesses: Brünnhilde, the Norns, Rhine maidens, other Valkyries
c) Fairies (Ada, Zemira, Farzana) and other embodiments of nature, such as birds in the forest and flower maidens[18]

Wagner almost invariably introduces love on the operatic stage through female characters. In *Der fliegende Holländer*, he describes Senta as "the woman of the future."[19] She sacrifices herself out of love to save a man. Here Wagner follows the motif of "redemption through the woman," of which Gretchen is the paradigm in the first part of Goethe's *Faust*. However, the endless sacrifices and love projects of Wagner's women are doomed to fail when they come up against men's actions and power. The same conflict between love and reality is found throughout Wagner's operas, including *Lohengrin*.

Lohengrin: Synopsis

Lohengrin is an opera in three acts that stylistically lies somewhere between a romantic opera and Wagner's later conception of a music drama. It is based on the medieval legend of a mysterious knight who arrives in a swan-drawn carriage to rescue a woman in distress. Overcoming the enemy, he takes her as his wife, but forbids her ever to ask him his name or origin. When she eventually does, he leaves her, never to return. The first German language version of the Lohengrin legend is *Parzival*, written around 1210 by Wolfram von Eschenbach, from which the characters in Wagner's opera are taken.

In Act I of *Lohengrin*, King Heinrich of Germany (bass) arrives in the rich Duchy of Brabant to levy a tax. He notes that disputes have arisen in the town since the death of the late Duke. The Duke's successor, Friedrich von Telramund (baritone), instead of giving the king an explanation, accuses Elsa von Brabant (soprano) of causing the disappearance of her younger brother, Gottfried (mute role). Telramund, in addition to being Elsa's and Gottfried's godfather, is also Elsa's rejected suitor. When the accusation is compounded by the possibility of fratricide, King Heinrich sees no alternative but to refer the matter to God's judgment. When no one appears to defend Elsa, she desperately prays that God may send her a champion in the person of a knight she saw in a dream. Miraculously, that knight (tenor) does appear, borne by a swan. He is ready to do combat for Elsa, but he requires of her that she never ask him his origin or name. Elsa gives her word. The knight confesses his love for her and she has no hesitation in agreeing to be his wife. The unknown knight then defeats Telramund in combat, but spares his life.

Telramund's wife, Ortrud (soprano/mezzo-soprano), is an ambitious woman and in Act II she works her manipulations on Telramund and Elsa. In Act III Elsa poses the forbidden question to her husband by asking him his name. Furious, he accuses her of betraying his trust. Now the knight must disclose his identity. He reveals that he is Lohengrin, the son of Parsifal, known to all from the story of the Holy Grail. After this announcement he must return to the Grail. Grieving, he bids farewell to the forlorn Elsa, leaving her his sword, a silver horn, and the ring of the Grail. Ortrud is overjoyed and convinced that she has now gained ascendancy in Brabant. At that moment Elsa's brother, Gottfried, reappears and is proclaimed the new ruler by Lohengrin.

The story of *Lohengrin* is a mixture of classical tragedy, Christian mythology, and nineteenth century melodrama. Following the latter's conventions, the characters represent polar opposites, such as good and evil or sin and innocence. Antagonists (Ortrud/Telramund) and protagonists (Elsa/Lohengrin) comprise the fundamental dramatic types. The drama begins with a moral conflict, the key theme of which involves sexual identity – particularly female virtue and purity. The virtuous woman suffers more deeply and sings with greater poignancy than all the rest.

Overture

The external story in *Lohengrin* is about combat and other characteristically masculine conflicts, whereas the internal story is about the unhappy love between Elsa, an earthly woman, and Lohengrin, a divine hero. The dramatic precision and consistency of the internal action rests on several elements: the prelude, Elsa's dream, the injunction against questioning, and its violation, and the climactic story of the Holy Grail in Act III.

The music in *Lohengrin* inhabits several worlds: the sphere of military conflict, Lohengrin's quest for the Grail, and, by contrast, the pagan world of black magic represented by Ortrud and Telramund. For the most part, Wagner keeps these worlds apart until the encounter between Elsa and Lohengrin. The pair's solemnity is the mood that pervades the opera.[20]

In an article on *Lohengrin*, Helga-Maria Palm finds the opera emotionally barren, since feelings are not openly expressed.[21] However, even if they cannot be seen, the emotions can be heard: the opera is permeated with longing and renunciation. The love of the Grail knight for the virgin Elsa remains unrequited. Pure love does exist between them, but a bodily union never takes place. The earthly and the heavenly cannot become one.

The internal action finds its finest expression in the prelude, built around the Grail theme as a symbol of sublime good. This symphonic poem establishes the emotional climate for the opera. It opens with a long crescendo played by the strings that seem to be holding their breath, accompanied by a few woodwinds alternating with the whispered pianissimo notes of a solo violin. The Grail theme is stated by the woodwinds together with the strings in a lower register, then by an English horn; and the climax is supported by trombones, trumpets, and a tuba.

The dramaturgy of the prelude tells the story of how the miraculous Grail was sent down to the earth, revealed to the people, and then taken up into the heavens again. As the goblet used in the Last Supper, the Grail is possessed of miraculous powers. According to legend, Joseph of Arimathea collected the blood of the Christ in it. Somehow the Grail has come into the possession of knights in distant Montsalvat in the Pyrenees. The sombre mood of the prelude suffuses the music of the internal action of the opera, the love between Elsa and Lohengrin. The Grail leitmotif, used sparingly in Act I, is heard in its entirety in the retelling of the story of the Grail that concludes the opera.

Elsa's dream (Act I, Scene 2)

Following the stately prelude, we are cast into the abrasive, masculine world of political conflict and warfare. A fanfare announces the royal presence, and a large male chorus backs the heavy voices of the two rulers, King Heinrich and Duke Telramund. When Elsa is called into the King's presence to defend herself from the accusations against her, the music shifts to the pale tones of the woodwinds. For Wagner, the oboe represents ingenuousness, innocence, and chastity, but he also associates it with lament, yearning, and pain.[22] Wagner increased the number of flutes, oboes, and bassoons in *Lohengrin*. The oboe is also used in conjunction with Elsa's counterparts, Senta in *Der fliegende Holländer*, and Elisabeth in *Tannhäuser*.

Elsa's dream state is signaled by a melody in the oboe that evokes her inner world. At her first appearance she approaches men timidly, but without fear. Charges are hurled at her, yet she remains abstracted and introspective. She stands alone, supported only by the female chorus that raises its voices when no one else is willing to defend her.

Elsa's dream is in three parts. The first, *Einsam in trüben Tagen* (Lonely, in troubled days) relates the hopelessness of her predicament. She then describes the knight who appears to her in her dream, *In lichter Waffen Scheine* (In splendid, shining armour), confident that he will come to her rescue. In the third part, she repeats the lines *des Ritters will ich wahren, er soll mein Streiter sein* (I will wait for the knight; he shall be my champion) as the time frame shifts to the future.

Elsa:	Elsa:
Einsam in trüben Tagen	Lonely, in troubled days
hab' ich zu Gott gefleht,	I prayed to the Lord,
des Herzens tiefstes Klagen	my most heartfelt grief
ergoss ich im Gebet.	I poured out in prayer.
Da drang aus meinem Stöhnen	And from my groans
ein Laut so klagevoll,	there issued a plaintive sound
der zu gewalt'gem Tönen	that grew into a mighteous roar
weit in die Lüfte schwoll:	as it echoed through the skies:
Ich hört' ihn fernhin hallen,	I listened as it receded into the distance
bis kaum mein Ohr er traf;	until my ear could scarce hear it;
mein Aug' ist zugefallen,	my eyes closed
ich sank in süssen Schlaf.	and I fell into a deep sleep.[23]

Elsa:	Elsa:
In lichter Waffen Scheine	In splendid, shining armour
ein Ritter nahte da,	a knight approached,
so tugendlicher Reine	a man of such pure virtue
ich keinen noch ersah:	as I had never seen before:
ein golden Horn zur Hüften,	a golden horn at his side,
gelehnet auf sein Schwert,	leaning on his sword –
so trat er aus den Lüften	thus he appeared to me
zu mir, der Recke wert;	from nowhere, this warrior true;
mit züchtigem Gebaren	with kindly gestures
gab Tröstung er mir ein;	he gave me comfort;
(mit erhobener Stimme)	*(in a louder voice)*
des Ritters will ich wahren,	I will wait for the knight,
(schwärmerisch)	*(dreamily)*
er soll mein Streiter sein!	he shall be my champion!

Elsa:	Elsa:
(hat Stellung und schwärmerische Miene nicht verlassen, alles blickt mit Gespanntheit auf sie; fest)	*(She still looks enraptured; everyone watches her in expectation)*
Des Ritters will ich wahren,	I will wait for the knight,
er soll mein Streiter sein!	he shall be my champion!
(ohne sich umzublicken)	*(without looking round)*
Hört, was dem Gottgesandten ich biete für Gewähr: –	Hear what reward I offer the one sent by God:
In meines Vaters Landen	in my father's lands
die Krone trage er;	he shall wear the crown.
mich glücklich soll ich preisen,	I shall consider myself happy
nimmt er mein Gut dahin –	if he takes my possessions –
will er Gemahl mich heissen,	if he wishes to call me spouse,
geb' ich ihm, was ich bin![24]	I shall give him all that I am!

In the dream story, the dramatic focus gradually moves away from Elsa's lamentation and increasingly onto the knight whom she is convinced will come to her aid. Elsa's situation is one of utter helplessness: no one is willing to fight for her. In the first part of the dream, this helplessness is expressed, but no male voices are heard. In the second and third parts, there are short interjections by King Heinrich and the male chorus, and the strings tacitly play the Grail leitmotif in anticipation of the knight's entrance.

Elsa is not the only character in Wagner to draw a man to her telepathically, as it were: in *Der fliegende Holländer* (Act II, Scene 3), Senta recounts a similar dream:

Senta:	Senta:
Versank ich jetzt in wunderbares Träumen,	Am I deep in a wonderful dream?
was ich erblicke, ist es Wahn?	What I see, is it mere fancy?
Weilt' ich bisher in trügerischen Räumen,	Have I been till now in some false world,
brach des Erwachens Tag heut an?	is my day of awakening dawning?
Er steht vor mir mit leidenvollen Zügen,	He stands before me, his face lined with suffering,
es spricht sein unerhörter Gram zu mir.	it reveals his terrible grief to me:
Kann tiefen Mitleids Stimme mich belügen?	can deep pity's voice lie to me?
Wie ich ihn oft gesehn, so steht er hier.	As I have often seen him, here he stands.
Die Schmerzen, die in meinem Busen brennen,	The pain that burns within my breast,
ach! dies Verlangen, wie soll ich es nennen?	ah, this longing, how shall I name it?
Wonach mit Sehnsucht es dich treibt – das Heil,	What you yearn for, salvation,
würd' es, du Ärmster, dir durch mich zuteil!²⁵	would it came true, poor man, through me!

Dramatic *Sprechgesang*, a kind of German *recitative*, is a particular way of treating language and dialogue. *Lohengrin* has his own, distinctive vocal melody, which, Palm suggests, together with the instrumentation, are the most important dramatic means of expression in the opera.²⁶ They both are used to advance the plot, whereas the purely orchestral passages only play a supportive and accompanying role.

Elsa's dream exemplifies vocal melody. The dream story is a coherent, systematically constructed verbal composition in which the evocation of a mood of lamentation is underscored by the choice of lyrics and the use of vowels. The mournful sound is created with vowels, especially the open *A* vowel:

> da drang aus meinem Stöhnen / ein L**a**ut so klagev**o**ll, der zu gewalt'gem Tönen / weit in die Lüfte schw**o**ll.

As Elsa falls asleep, Wagner brings the open *A* sound together with an alliterative phrase based on the *S* sound. The lament weakens and dissipates in sibilants: "Mein Aug' ist zugefallen, ich sank in süssen Schlaf."[27]

Then the miracle Elsa witnesses in the dream comes true, and a knight approaches in a boat drawn by a swan. Lohengrin's entrance is a choral epiphany in which the knight of the Holy Grail descends from the heavens to defend and save the innocent Elsa. In keeping with the structure of classical Aristotelian drama, many nineteenth-century operas and melodramas included a scene in which a revelation or an act of recognition gives a new, unexpected turn to events. Often the scene is built around the figure of a mysterious stranger. In *Lohengrin* this first takes place with the arrival of the knight, and it occurs once more in connection with the Grail story that brings the opera to a close. Lohengrin's magnificent entrance as the heavens part is a theatrical convention that satisfies the formulaic requirement of visual extravagance.

An important aspect of the emotional dramaturgy of the dream is that Elsa expects to receive not only help, but also gain a husband who will inherit her father's kingdom. In the libretto, her willing subjugation is explicit: *geb' ich ihm alles, was ich bin* (I shall give him all that I am). Elsa's submission is a token of her boundless gratitude for Lohengrin's heroic act and includes agreeing to his injunction against asking his name.

The Forbidden Question (*Frageverbot*) (Act 1, Scene 3)

The love that is kindled between Lohengrin and Elsa signifies the union of the heavenly and the earthly spheres, although it is conditional in Lohengrin's case:

Lohengrin: Elsa, soll ich dein Gatte heissen, soll Land und Leut' ich schirmen dir, soll nichts mich wieder vor dir reissen, musst eines du geloben mir: *(sehr langsam)* Nie sollst du mich befragen, noch Wissens Sorge tragen, woher ich kam der Fahrt, noch wie mein Nam' und Art! Lohengrin: *(gesteigert, sehr ernst)* Elsa! Hast du mich wohl vernommen? *(noch bestimmter)* Nie sollst du mich befragen, noch Wissens Sorge tragen, woher ich kam der Fahrt, noch wie mein Nam' und Art!²⁸	Lohengrin: Elsa, if I am to become your husband, if I am to protect country and people for you, if nothing is ever to take me from you, then you must promise me one thing: *(very slowly)* Never shall you ask me, nor trouble yourself to know, whence I journeyed, what my name is, or what my origin! Lohengrin: *(with passion, very earnestly)* Elsa! Do you understand what I am saying? *(even more forcefully)* Never shall you ask me nor trouble yourself to know whence I journeyed, what my name is, or what my origin!

This injunction, which also has a musical refrain related to Lohengrin's leitmotif, is the key to the fundamental conflict in *Lohengrin*. After it has been stated, the spectator watches the question begin to grow in Elsa's mind. It comes as a warning from somewhere between the world of the Grail and the realm of Ortrud's black magic, and acts to draw together and force apart. The divine cannot be joined with the human: to try is to commit an act of hubris that contains the seed of disaster.²⁹

The attempts of heroines in Wagner's operas to create a space for love are defeated by the deeds and power of men. In Elsa's case, Telramund, the rejected suitor, conspires with Ortrud to raise a false accusation of fratricide. Although King Heinrich is a benign patriarch, he must judge the matter according to the prevailing norms.

Elsa's unhappy fate is not due to the malicious scheming of

Telramund and Ortrud, but to Lohengrin's severe demand. We know that as a knight of the Grail he must not disclose his true identity, but he can also not reveal to Elsa that, were she only to wait one year, he would be relieved of his obligations toward the Grail and would be able to remain with her forever.

From Elsa's perspective, her beloved's withholding knowledge of his identity is cruel. Since naming is knowledge, and knowledge is power, she is rendered powerless by being excluded from that knowledge. Lohengrin's primary responsibility had been to discharge his duties as knight, and only secondarily, if at all, to become involved with a woman. From a feminist perspective, the story may be turned inside out so that the fairness and justification of Elsa's question to Lohengrin can be made visible.

Elsa's question matures (Act II, Scene 5; Act III, Scene 2)

The light and joy at the end of Act I is soon contrasted with the perfidious nighttime conversation between Ortrud and Telramund that opens Act II. Now the dominant mood is one of darkness, vengeance, and evil. As we enter into the world of Ortrud, we see that she is the dark force of the internal story. While Elsa's temptation does not originate with Ortrud, the latter makes every effort to incite Elsa. In Act II, Elsa makes preparations for her wedding as Ortrud keeps interrupting her. Telramund, disguised as a monk, also appears and insists that the people must know the knight's name, at which point Lohengrin defends himself:

Lohengrin:	Lohengrin:
Ja, selbst dem König darf ich wehren	Yes, I can resist even the King,
und aller Fürsten höchsten Rat!	and the highest counsel of princes!
Nicht darf sie Zweifels Last beschweren,	The burden of doubt will not trouble them;
sie sahen meine gute Tat!	they saw my good deed!
Nur eine ist's, der muss ich Antwort geben:	Only one person must I answer:
Elsa ...	Elsa ...

(Er hält betroffen an, als er, sich zu Elsa wendend, diese mit heftig wogender Brust in wildem inneren Kampfe vor sich hinstarren sieht.) Elsa! Wie seh' ich sie erbeben! In wildem Brüten muss ich sie gewahren! Hat sie betört des Hasses Lügenmund? O Himmel, schirm ihr Herz vor den Gefahren! Nie werde Zweifel dieser Reinen kund!³⁰	(Lohengrin stops in consternation as he turns to Elsa and notices that, with a heaving breast, she is staring in front of herself, torn by a violent inward struggle) Elsa! How she trembles! I must protect her from brooding wildly! Has the lying tongue of hatred beguiled her? O Heaven, protect her heart from danger! May this innocent one never be plagued with doubts!

In the finale of Act II, Lohengrin asks Elsa if she feels she must pose the forbidden question. "Elsa, arise! In your hand, in your devotion lies the pledge of all happiness! Does the force of doubt not leave you in peace? Do you wish to put the question to me?"³¹ Elsa replies:

(in heftiger innerer Aufregung und in schamvoller Verwirrung) Mein Retter, der mir Heil gebracht! Mein Held, in dem ich muss vergehn! (mit Bedeutung und Entschluss) Hoch über alles Zweifels Macht soll meine Liebe stehn! (Sie sinkt an seine Brust.)	(deeply agitated and in a state of confused embarrassment) My deliverer, who brought me salvation! My knight, in whom I must melt away! (with determination and clarity) High above the force of all doubt may my love stand! (She sinks upon his breast.)

Elsa and Lohengrin are married, but in Act II, Scene 2, the marriage is not consummated, for on the wedding night Elsa asks the forbidden question, and Lohengrin is ensnared in a political plot. The moment of the question is chosen with extreme care. Lohengrin looks at the nuptial bed and says that they are now alone for the first time. Elsa prepares the ground for her question by innocently asking whether Lohengrin's secret is truly such that he must continue to remain silent. Lohengrin, growing apprehensive, responds:

Lohengrin:	Lohengrin:
An meine Brust, du Süsse, Reine!	Come to me, O sweet, pure one!
Sei meines Herzens Glühen nah, dass mich dein Auge sanft bescheine, in dem ich all mein Glück ersah!	Be near my ardent heart, that the eyes in which I saw all my happiness may shine upon me softly!
(feurig)	*(passionately)*
Gönne mir, dass mit Entzücken ich deinen Atem sauge ein: lass fest, ach fest, an mich dich drücken, dass ich in dir mög' glücklich sein!	O, grant me that in sweet raptures I may breathe in your breath: O, let me clasp you to me so very firmly, that I may be happy in you!
Dein Lieben muss mir hoch entgelten für das, was ich um dich verliess; kein Los in Gottes weiten Welten wohl edler als das meine hiess.	Your love must be the highest recompense for that which I left behind for your sake; no destiny in all God's world could have been nobler than mine.
Bot' mir der König seine Krone, ich dürfte sie mit Recht verschmähn.	If the king offered me his crown, I should rightfully reject it.
Das einz'ge, was mein Opfer lohne, muss ich in deiner Lieb' ersehn!	The only reward for my sacrifice is your steadfast love!
Drum wolle stets den Zweifel meiden, dein Lieben sei mein stolz Gewähr!	Thus do I ask you to put doubt from your mind, may your love be my proud guarantee!
Denn nicht komm' ich aus Nacht und Leiden, aus Glanz und Wonne komm' ich her!³²	For I come not from darkness and suffering, I come from splendour and delight!

Lohengrin imposes a great demand on Elsa: "Your love must be the highest recompense for that which I left behind for your sake." Just as in stating the injunction about his name, Lohengrin here speaks mostly about himself – and Elsa's debt of gratitude keeps growing. It is not enough that she was placed in a position of total submission in Act I. Lohengrin invokes the splendor and honor he has relinquished on her behalf so she must feel obliged to concede to his terms.

The emotional tragedy is constructed upon Elsa's uncertainty and desire for knowledge, which contrasts with the Wagnerian paradigm that the woman must love at any cost and redeem the man through her love. With the emotional dissonance of the question growing in Elsa's mind, the audience is riveted, secretly hoping that Elsa will refrain from asking the fateful question.

But in the end she does: "Nothing can bring me peace, nothing can tear me from my madness, save – even if it should cost me my life – knowing who you are!" Lohengrin cries in reply: "Elsa, what are you saying?" But she persists: "Ill-fatedly noble man! Hear the question I must ask you! Tell me your name!"[33] Posing the question makes inevitable the tragic parting – not only because Elsa has proven incapable of keeping her promise, but because, above all, the knight of the Holy Grail cannot satisfy the conditions of humanity. For Elsa's part, she is compelled to know the identity of her beloved in order for their love to become a shared project; she wants to be initiated into whatever it is that governs his life.

The forbidden question has grave consequences, not only for Elsa but for Lohengrin as well. Although he has told Elsa that he has come from a region of splendor and delight and abandoned all measure of wonderful things for her, Elsa's challenge to his identity causes him to abandon her and return to the realm of the Grail. Confronted by human demands, his divine power appears to fail him.

The story of the Grail (Act III, Scene 3)

With the troops summoned for an early morning assembly, and as trumpets sound and the woodwinds play a stirring march, a heartbroken Elsa and an anguished Lohengrin step before the king. The opera reaches its climax in Lohengrin's story of the Grail, beginning *In fernem Land* (In a far-off land). Lohengrin, who until this moment has only been addressed as a knight or protector, now discloses his true identity, marking the end of the internal action.

Lohengrin:	Lohengrin:
(in feierlicher Verklärung vor sich hinblickend)	*(gazing forward, solemnly transfigured)*
In fernem Land, unnahbar euren Schritten,	In a far-off land, inaccessible to your steps,
liegt eine Burg, die Montsalvat genannt;	there is a castle by the name of Montsalvat;
ein lichter Tempel stehet dort inmitten,	a light-filled temple stands within it,
so kostbar als auf Erden nichts bekannt;	more precious than anything on earth;
drin ein Gefäss von wundertät'gem Segen wird dort als höchstes Heiligtum bewacht:	therein is a vessel of wonderous blessing that is watched over as a sacred relic:
es ward, dass sein der Menschen reinste pflegen,	that the purest of men might guard it,
herab von einer Engelschar gebracht;	it was brought down by a host of angels;
alljährlich naht vom Himmel eine Taube,	every year a dove descends from Heaven
um neu zu stärken seine Wunderkraft:	to fortify its wonderous power:
es heisst der Gral, und selig reinster Glaube erteilt durch ihn sich seiner Ritterschaft.	it is called the Grail, and the purest, most blessed faith is imparted through it to the Brotherhood of Knights.
Wer nun dem Gral zu dienen ist erkoren,	Whosoever is chosen to serve the Grail
den rüstet er mit überirdischer Macht;	is armed by it with heavenly power;

an dem ist jedes Bösen Trug verloren,	every evil deceit is powerless against him,
wenn ihn er sieht, weicht dem des Todes Nacht.	once he has seen it, the shadow of death flees him.
Selbst wer von ihm in ferne Land' entsendet,	Even he who is sent by it to a distant land,
zum Streiter für der Tugend Recht ernannt,	appointed as a champion of virtue,
dem wird nicht seine heilige Kraft entwendet,	will not be robbed of its holy power,
bleibt als sein Ritter dort er unerkannt;	provided that he, as its knight, remains unrecognised there.
so hehrer Art doch ist des Grales Segen,	For so wondrous is the blessing of the Grail
enthüllt muss er des Laien Auge fliehn;	that when it is revealed it shuns the eye of the uninitiated;
des Ritters drum sollt Zweifel ihr nicht hegen,	thus no man should doubt the knight,
erkennt ihr ihn - dann muss er von euch ziehn.	for if he is recognised, he must leave you.
Nun hört, wie ich verbot'ner Frage lohne!	Hear how I reward the forbidden question!
Vom Gral ward ich zu euch daher gesandt:	I was sent to you by the Grail:
mein Vater Parzival trägt seine Krone,	my father Parzival wears its crown,
sein Ritter ich – bin Lohengrin genannt.[34]	I, its knight – am called Lohengrin.

The final scene is heartrending. The knight of the Holy Grail, who laid down the conditions of his love with a stern divine injction and then angrily accused Elsa of betrayal, is now shown to be a deeply suffering man, gathering the last of his strength to depart forever. Elsa had occasioned an opportunity for him to flee from the emotionally alienated, semi-divine life he led as a knight and enter the world of men. However, her posing the forbidden question has made all that impossible. The foundation of trust broken, Lohengrin must withdraw from the human sphere to resume his life in service of the Grail. In the final scene a forlorn Elsa looks on as her equally forlorn husband slowly recedes, never to return.

Musical seduction: Spiritual missionary position

Lohengrin is a cruel drama. How can it then seduce the spectator? In *Angel's Cry: Beyond the Pleasure Principle in Opera*, Michel Poizat uses Lacanian psychoanalysis to explore why opera arouses such powerful emotions in an audience. He concludes that operagoers are in search of *jouissance* – eroticized, orgasmic pleasure. A musical-dramatic trajectory from a seductive introduction to a wrenching climax seems to be fundamental to opera, but this may be said of other musical genres as well. From the organ fugues of J.S. Bach to the symphonies of Johannes Brahms, music can call forth enormous libidinal energy, which is then either allowed to well up or is controlled to some degree. This view is supported by Wayne Koestenbaum in *The Queen's Throat: Opera, Homosexuality and the Mystery of Desire*, and by Sam Abel in *Opera in the Flesh: Sexuality in Operatic Performance*.[35]

As stated in Chapter 1, the term "body genre" used by Linda Williams to describe the type of film that elicits ecstatic feelings (from *ex-* "out of" and *stasis* "state of being") seems almost tailored for opera.[36] The word *melo(s)* in melodrama refers to an excess of music, while *drama* stands for the action that is performed. Emotion – so powerful that ordinary speech is incapable of expressing it – bursts forth in opera in the form of song, modulated through the intermediary of trained voices. Williams describes the effects of body genre as follows:

> A pertinent feature shared by these body genres is the focus on what could probably best be called a form of ecstasy. Contemporary meanings suggest components of direct or indirect sexual excitement and rapture, a rapture which informs even the pathos of melodrama.
>
> Visually ecstatic excesses could be said to share a quality of uncontrollable convulsion or spasm – of the body "beside itself" with sexual pleasure. Aurally excess is marked by recourse not to the coded articulations of language but to inarticulate cries.[37]

Ecstasy in operatic art is often associated with the union of love, sexuality, and death. The ideal love scene for Wagner is *Liebestod*, a mystical union of two lovers in death. Tristan and Isolde sing as one: "Now banish dread, sweet death – yearned for, longed for death-in-love! In your arms, consecrated to you, sacred elemental quickening force, free from the peril of waking!"[38] Isolde dies at the moment of her musical climax. The ecstatic nature of the death is underscored in both the music and the libretto, and the scene ends with the words *höchste Lust* (utmost rapture). The stage directions for the end of the same opera read: "Isolde sinks gently, as if transfigured, in Brangäne's arms, onto Tristan's body. Those looking on are awed and deeply moved. Mark blesses the bodies. The curtain falls slowly."[39] We are reminded of Hélène Cixous's funeral metaphor that links women, opera, sexuality, love, and death.

Many popular operas end with a dying tenor who embraces a lifeless, passive soprano or collapses onto her. Such a final gesture is emblematic of despair; it communicates to the audience a combined visual symbol of death/intercourse in a classic missionary position with the man on top and the passive, receiving woman under him. Examples include *Tannhäuser, Luisa Miller, Rigoletto* (with father and daughter), *La Traviata, Aida, Otello, Romeo and Juliet, Carmen, Lakmé, La Gioconda, Pagliacci* (two men, one alive, one dead, on top of a woman's body), *Manon, Manon Lescaut, La Bohème, Madama Butterfly,* and potentially all three acts of *Les Contes d'Hoffmann*. Abel wryly adds that Richard Strauss pours an entire regiment of soldiers on top of Salome for good measure.[40]

In some cases, the difference between this symbolic union in death and straightforward rape is very subtle. However, what is relevant about the final gesture is not sexuality, but its function as an expression of the woman's submissiveness. According to Susan McClary, the operatic orgasm makes the audience thirst for Carmen's death, to give just one example. The desire is not satisfied until Don José has stabbed Carmen, thereby symbolically raping and vanquishing the rebellious woman.[41]

Wagner develops a very systematic emotional drama in *Lohengrin*, making it logical for Elsa to ask the forbidden question, which simultaneously is the worst possible form of betrayal. The dream lays bare the starting point of the love story; the taboo inquiry reveals the underlying conditions of the relationship; and the disaster triggered by Elsa in the wedding chamber culminates in the story of the Holy Grail. The audience breathes in time to the ineluctable question swelling in Elsa's mind. Although asking the question may be reasonable from a human standpoint, it clashes with the moral dramaturgy of the opera, which requires that at least one head must fall. We need a betrayal and someone who is both victim and scapegoat, or else the operatic orgasm will not be achieved.

Lohengrin links the issue of knowing to Elsa's position as an innocent victim who blames herself for asking the most natural of questions: who are you, my love? A moment before Elsa begins to tell us her dream, the leitmotif of the Grail resounds with a rising interval that in Wagner's music is termed the "defiant fourth." It represents pure faith in which "eyes are fixed on Heaven," whose blue and silver are the colors of the knights of the Holy Grail.[42] The audience is reminded of the sublime goal of love: the highest good that admits no doubt.

Wagner even denies Elsa a *Liebestod*. Her humiliation is complete. The conclusion of Lohengrin marks Elsa's sole destruction, as Lohengrin frees the swan from Ortrud's spell, and Elsa's brother Gottfried is returned to the people. Although Lohengrin does not fall dead over Elsa, she swoons into the arms of her brother as Lohengrin slowly withdraws. Amid the grief over Lohengrin's farewell, the Grail leitmotif sounds a note of consolation and hope. Gottfried becomes the new ruler of Brabant and the triumph of masculine homosociality is complete.

While the opera is named after Lohengrin, its thematic heroine is Elsa. We follow her development and tragedy more closely than anyone else's. Yet all power remains concentrated in Lohengrin, confirming once more, as Teresa de Lauretis has written, "The hero, the mythical subject, is constructed as human being and as male; he is the active principle of culture."[43]

From a feminist perspective, the emotional dramaturgy of *Lohengrin* promulgates a moral universe in which standards and values are patriarchally defined through the forbidden question and the story of the Grail. A woman's fidelity and loyalty are crucial for the consummation of the love project. However, in keeping with this ideology, the opera makes no mention of the gendered system upon which its characters are based. It is up to the feminist beholder to use counter-reading to make visible what the opera chooses to ignore.

Notes

1. Walsh, *Keine Angst*, 157.

2. McClary *Feminine Endings*, 36.

3. Nieder, *Von der Zauberflöte zum Lohengrin*," 12. See also Honolka, *Kulturgeschichte des Librettos*; Scherle, *Das deutsche Opernlibretto*; Smith, *The Tenth Muse*.

4. Austin, *Feminist*, 1–2.

5. Weigel, *Der Schielende Blick*.

6. Fetterley, *The Resisting Reader*.

7. Kaplan, "Is the Gaze Male?", 231.

8. Melberg, Aristotle's *Poetics*.

9. Case, *Feminism and Theatre*, 11–12.

10. Ibid., 5–27.

11. Cixous, "Aller à la mer," 133–136: "Comment, femme, peut-on aller au théâtre? Sauf à s'y trouver en complicité avec le sadisme dont les femmes y sont l'objet. A se voir invité à prendre, dans la structure familiale-patriarcale, que le théâtre reproduit à l'infini, la place de la victime. Qui est elle? Toujours la fille-du-père, son objet à sacrifier, gardienne du phallus et support du fantasme narcissique à l'aide duquel de père pare à la menace de castration."

12. Clément's book, *L'opéra ou la défaite des femmes* (1979), did not attract attention until the publication of its English translation, *Opera or the Undoing of Women*, in 1988.

13. Abbate, "Opera" and "In search of Opera." See also Koestenbaum, *The Queen's Throat*.

14. Barthes, "Le grain de la voix." For an introduction to Barthes's later writing, see Kolesch, *Roland Barthes*.

15. This pair of semiotic concepts refers to two levels of the sign and can be also regarded as denoting expression/content.

16. Wagner, *Dichtungen und Schriften*, 238.

17. Ibid., 114–115.

18. The categories are based on a lecture entitled *The Woman of the Future: Women and Women's Voices in Wagner's Oeuvre* given by German musicologist Susanne Vill at the University of Stockholm in November 1996. See Vill, "Das Weib der Zukunft"; Parly, *Vocal Victories*; Riegel, *Richard Wagner's Women*.

19. Wagner, *Dichtungen und Schriften*, 238.

20. Ralf, *Comments on Lohengrin*, 35

21. Palm, *Wagners Lohengrin*, 51.

22. Voss, *Instrumentation Richard Wagners Lohengrin*, 127.

23. English translations of the librettos are taken from http://www.rwagner.net.

24. Wagner, *Lohengrin*, 3–4.

25. Wagner, *Der fliegende Holländer*, 14 (II 2–3).

26. Palm, *Wagners Lohengrin*, 261.

27. Ibid.

28. Wagner, *Lohengrin*, 8.

29. Tchaikovsky, a great admirer of *Lohengrin*, based the main theme of *Swan Lake* on the *Frageverbot*.

30. Wagner, *Lohengrin*, p. 23

31. Ibid., 24.

32. Ibid., 28.

33. Ibid., 29.

34. Ibid., 29–30.

35. Poizat, *Angel's Cry*; Koestenbaum, *The Queen's Throat*; Abel, *Opera in the Flesh*.

36. Williams, "Film Bodies," 3.

37. Ibid., 4.

38. Wagner, *Tristan und Isolde*, 27.

39. Ibid., 42–43.

40. Abel, *Opera in the Flesh*, 94.

41. McClary, *Feminine Endings*, 22.

42. Ralf, *Comments on Lohengrin*, 36.

43. de Lauretis, *Alice Doesn't*, 118–119.

Works Cited

Abbate, Carolyn. "Opera; or, the Envoicing of Women." In *Musicology and Difference: Gender and Sexuality in Music Scholarship*, edited by Ruth A. Solie, 225–258. Berkeley: University of California Press, 1993.

———. *In Search of Opera*. Princeton: Princeton University Press, 2001.

Abel, Sam. *Opera in the Flesh: Sexuality in Operatic Performance*. Boulder, CO: Westview Press, 1996.

Austin, Gayle. *Feminist Theories for Dramatic Criticism*. Ann Arbor: University of Michigan Press, 1990.

Barthes, Roland. "Le grain de la voix." In *L'oblivie et l'obtus. Essais critiques III*, 236–245. Paris: Éditions de Seuil, 1982.

Case, Sue-Ellen. *Feminism and Theatre*. New York: Routledge, 1988.

Cixous, Hélène. "Aller à la mer." In *Twentieth Century Theatre: A Sourcebook*, edited by Richard Drain, 133–135. London: Routledge, 1995. Originally published in *Le Monde*, 28 April, 1977. English translation in *Modern Drama* 27, no. 4 (1984): 546–548.

Clément, Catherine. *Opera, or the Undoing of Women*. London: Tauris, 1997.

de Lauretis, Teresa. *Alice Doesn't: Feminism, Semiotics, Cinema*. Bloomington: Indiana University Press, 1984.

Drain, Richard, ed. *Twentieth Century Theatre: A Sourcebook*. London: Routledge, 1995.

Fetterley, Judith. *The Resisting Reader: A Feminist Approach to American Fiction.* Bloomington: Indiana University Press, 1978.

Honolka, Kurt. *Kulturgeschichte des Librettos: Opern, Dichter, Operndichter.* Wilhelmshaven: Heinrichshofen, 1979.

Kaplan, E. Ann. "Is the Gaze Male?" In *Women and Values: Readings in Recent Feminist Philosophy*, edited by Marilyn Pearsall, 289–302. Belmont, CA: Wadsworth, 1986.

Koestenbaum, Wayne. *The Queen's Throat: Opera, Homosexuality, and the Mystery of Desire.* London: Penguin, 1993.

Kolesch, Doris. *Roland Barthes.* Frankfurt: Campus Verlag, 1997.

McClary, Susan. *Feminine Endings: Music, Gender, and Sexuality.* Minneapolis: University of Minnesota Press, 1991.

Melberg, Arne. "Introduktion." In *Om diktkonsten*. Swedish translation of Aristotle's *Poetics* by Jan Stolpe. Göteborg: Anamma, 1996.

Nieder, Christoph. *Von der "Zauberflöte" zum "Lohengrin." Das deutsche Opernlibretto in der ersten Hälfte des 19. Jahrhunderts.* Stuttgart: Metzler, 1989.

Palm, Helga-Maria. *Richard Wagners Lohengrin. Studien zur Sprachbehandlung.* München: Wilhelm Fink Verlag, 1987.

Parly, Nila. *Vocal Victories. Wagner's Female Characters from Senta to Kundry.* Chiccago: Chicago University Press, 2011.

Poizat, Michel. *Angel's Cry: Beyond the Pleasure Principle in Opera.* Ithaca: Cornell University Press, 1992.

Ralf, Klas. *Comments on Lohengrin, A Romantic Opera in Three Acts.* Stockholm: Royal Opera, 1974.

Rieger, Eva. *Richard Wagner's Women.* New York: Boydell Press, 2011.

Scherle, Arthur. *Das deutsche Opernlibretto von Opitz bis Hoffmansthal.* Dissertation. München: Ludwig-Maximilians-Universität München, 1954.

Smith, Patrick J. *The Tenth Muse: A Historical Study of the Opera Libretto.* London: Gollantz, 1971.

Vill, Susanne, ed. *Das Weib der Zukunft. Frauengestalten und Frauenstimmen bei Richard Wagner.* Stuttgart: Metzler, 2000.

Voss, Egon. *Studien zur Instrumentation Richard Wagners.* Regensburg: Bosse Verlag, 1970.

Wagner, Richard. *Lohengrin, A Romantic Opera in Three Acts.* Libretto in German and Swedish, sheet music excerpts, and annotations. Stockholm: Royal Opera, 1974.

———. *Tristan und Isolde.* Libretto in German and Swedish, presentation of leitmotifs with sheet attachment. Stockholm: Royal Opera, 1974.

———. *Der fliegende Holländer, A Romantic Opera in Three Acts.* Libretto in German and Swedish, sheet music excerpts, and annotations. Stockholm: Royal Opera, 1977.

———. *Dichtungen und Schriften, Jubiläumsausgabe in 10 Bänden.* Vol. VI. Frankfurt: Insel Verlag, 1983.

Walsh, Michael. *Keine Angst vor der Oper.* München: Piper Verlag, 1997.

Weigel, Sigrid. *Der Schielende Blick: Thesen zur Geschichte weiblicher Schreibpraxis. Die verborgene Frau.* Berlin: Argument Verlag, 1983.

Williams, Linda. "Film Bodies: Gender, Genre, and Excess." *Film Quarterly* 44 (1991): 2–13.

Madama Butterfly (Giacomo Puccini). Asmik Grigorian (Butterfly), Royal Opera, Stockholm, 2014. Photographer: Marcus Gårder. Copyright CC-BY-NC-ND, Royal Opera, Stockholm.

3. Who's Who Underneath the Kimono? Queer Mysteries of *M. Butterfly*

> For the myths of the East, the myths of the West,
> the myths of men, and the myths of women –
> these have so saturated our consciousness that truthful contact
> between nations and lovers can only be the result of heroic effort.
> Those who prefer to bypass the work involved
> will remain in a world of surfaces, misperceptions running rampant.
> This is, to me, the convenient world in which
> the French diplomat and the Chinese spy lived.
> This is why, after twenty years, he had learned nothing
> about his lover, not even the truth of his sex.
>
> David Henry Hwang, *M. Butterfly*[1]

On 11 May 1986, *The New York Times* published a short article on how a French diplomat and a Jīngjù performer with the Beijing opera had been sentenced to six years in prison on spying charges by the People's Republic of China. The curious thing about the incident was that it was surrounded by a secret, forbidden love affair, based on sexual misconception. French diplomat Bernard Boursicot, who was accused of revealing classified information while stationed in Beijing, had fallen in love with Chinese actress, Shi Pei Pu. For twenty years he had labored under the impression that Pu was a woman.

Such misconceptions regarding gender offer a prime opportunity for voyeurism and for stirring up scandal, as was the case here. Playwright Henry Hwang saw in this story the potential for a deconstructed version of Giacomo Puccini's *Madama Butterfly* with a libretto by Luigi Illica and Giuseppe Giacosa. The libretto

---

How to cite this book chapter:
Rosenberg, Tiina 2016. Who's Who Underneath the Kimono? Queer Mysteries of *M. Butterfly*. In: Rosenberg, Tiina *Don't Be Quiet, Start a Riot! Essays on Feminism and Performance*. Pp. 52–79. Stockholm: Stockholm University Press. DOI: http://dx.doi.org/10.16993/baf.c. License: CC-BY 4.0

presents an excellent metaphor for a French diplomat who mistakes a Jíngjù performer for a woman. The Frenchman is unaware that all Jíngjù parts are played by men. Hwang also depicts cultural blindness, which he finds entirely predictable: the ignorant "masculine" West dominates and manipulates the submissive "feminine" East. The West is portrayed as a man who never questions his own cultural standing. In turn, Asia is viewed as a woman who adapts to circumstances at any price.

> The West thinks of itself as masculine – big guns, big industry, big money – so the East is feminine – weak, delicate, poor ... but good at art, and full of inscrutable wisdom – the feminine mystique. Her mouth says no, but her eyes say yes. The West believes the East, deep down, wants to be dominated – because a woman can't think for herself.[2]

It is instructive to examine Hwang's *M. Butterfly* against the background of post-colonial concepts and queer theory. The play expands its theme so that it pertains to questions of ethnicity as well as gender and sexuality. Hwang questions clichéd Western attitudes toward such matters and toward what has been called the "Orient." Like notions regarding femininity and masculinity, the Orient is a concept of Western perceptions that offers people an opportunity to exempt themselves from their own contradictions.

PINKERTON'S RACIAL OBLIGATION

Puccini's *Madama Butterfly* is the cruel tale of a 15-year-old Japanese geisha named Cio-Cio-San, who is also known as Butterfly. She falls in love and marries a US Marine Lieutenant, Benjamin Franklin Pinkerton. It is the turn of the twentieth century and Pinkerton's boat is anchored in Nagasaki Bay for a few months. To while away the time, Pinkerton decides to marry Butterfly "in the Japanese style," and so a 999-year marriage contract that the man is allowed to renounce every month is drawn up. Pinkerton has no strong feelings about the duration of the marriage. An American consul named Sharpless warns Pinkerton not to toy with Butterfly's emotions. However, Pinkerton brushes him off and proposes a toast to the day when he will have a "genuine" marriage to an American.

Thus Butterfly and Pinkerton are wed, and soon after the wedding Pinkerton rejoins his company and his ship departs. In Act II, a distraught but faithful Butterfly endures three long years waiting for Pinkerton to return. One day Sharpless visits Butterfly in order to inform her that Pinkerton has remarried in America and is now coming back to Japan. However, Sharpless keeps getting interrupted and is unable to tell Butterfly the whole story. At that moment a wealthy prince named Yamadori arrives and proposes to Butterfly, but she refuses him. When Sharpless advises Butterfly to accept the prince's proposal, she becomes angry and asks him to leave. Soon, however, she relents and surprises Sharpless by introducing her son to him. Sharpless, unaware of the child's existence until now, promises to tell Pinkerton at once. When guns are heard in the harbor saluting the arrival of a ship, Butterfly decorates her home with flowers and, together with her son and her maid, Suzuki, waits through the night for Pinkerton's arrival.

As the curtain rises on Act III, a male choir in Nagasaki is singing. This will be Butterfly's last day. Suzuki and Butterfly stand motionless, waiting for Pinkerton. When he fails to appear, Butterfly goes indoors with her son. Shortly afterward, Sharpless, Pinkerton, and Pinkerton's wife, Kate, arrive at the house. They plan to coax Butterfly into giving up her son to Kate, and they ask Suzuki to help them. Pinkerton, finally grasping the magnitude of his betrayal, leaves the house so that he does not have to face Butterfly. However, Butterfly insists that the boy's father come himself if he wishes to claim his son.

When she was a hopeful, happy bride arriving at her (sham) wedding, Butterfly had wrapped a few keepsakes in the sleeve of her kimono and brought them to the house. One of them was a slim case containing a dagger. The Mikado had once sent this dagger to Butterfly's father, urging him to commit suicide because his family had fallen into ruin. In the wrenching final scene, Butterfly sees no alternative other than to take her life with this same dagger:

> Butterfly: Go, Go, and obey my order.
> *(Makes Suzuki, who is weeping bitterly, rise, and pushes her outside the exit on the left. Suzuki's sobs are heard. Butterfly lights the lamp in front of the Buddha. She bows down. Butterfly remains motionless, lost in sorrowful*

thought. Suzuki's sobs are still heard; they die away by degrees. Butterfly has a convulsive movement. Butterfly goes towards the shrine and lifts the white veil from it, throws this across the screen, then takes the dagger, which, enclosed in a waxen case, is leaning against the wall near the image of the Buddha. Butterfly piously kisses the blade, holding it by the point and the handle with both hands.)

Butterfly: Death with honour is better than life with dishonour.
(Points the knife sideways at her throat.)

(The door on the left opens, showing Suzuki's arm pushing in the child towards his mother: he runs in with outstretched hands. Butterfly lets the dagger fall, darts toward the child, and hugs and kisses him almost to suffocation.)

You? you? you? you? you? you? you?
Beloved Idol!
Adored, adored being,
Fairest flower of beauty.
(Taking the child's head in her hands, she draws it to her)
Though you ne'er must know it
This for you, my love, for you I'm dying,
Poor Butterfly
That you may go away
Beyond the ocean,
Never to feel the torment when you are older,
That your mother forsook you!
(Exaltedly)
My son, sent to me from Heaven,
Straight from the throne of glory,
Take one last and careful look
at your poor mother's face!
That its memory may linger,
one last look!
Farewell, beloved! Farewell, my dearest heart!
Go, play, play.

(Butterfly takes the child, seats him on a stool with his face turned to the left, gives him the American flag and a doll and urges him to play with them, while she gently

bandages his eyes. Then she seizes the dagger, and with her eyes still fixed on the child, goes behind the screen. The knife is heard falling to the ground, and the large white veil disappears behind the screen. Butterfly is seen emerging from behind the screen; tottering, she gropes her way towards the child. The large white veil is round her neck; smiling feebly, she greets the child with her hand and drags herself up to him. She has just enough strength left to embrace him, then falls to the ground beside him.)

Pinkerton *(within, calling)*: Butterfly! Butterfly! Butterfly!

(The door on the right opens violently – Pinkerton and Sharpless rush into the room and up to Butterfly, who with a feeble gesture points to the child and dies. Pinkerton falls on his knees, whilst Sharpless takes the child and kisses him, sobbing.)[3]

"Con onor muore, chi non può serbar vita con onore," those who cannot live with honour, must die with honour – this is the summation of Puccinis's tragic opera, but it is also the theme of Hwang's play *M. Butterfly*. Watching Puccini's opera one does not make one want to burst into applause and shout one's admiration aloud. We feel that we are witnessing a ritual in which a woman must be sacrificed. A culturally unacceptable love affair, the opera seems to tell us, can only end with Butterfly's death.

Butterfly's final words call to mind Edward Said's definition of orientalism. Said reprimands Westerners for injecting their own images into a concept they themselves have created and called the "Orient" – an exotic, strange place that becomes known as the Other. According to Said, orientalism is a Western mind-set for "dominating, restructuring and having authority over the Orient."[4] He claims that Western culture, by which he means European culture for the most part, "gained in strength and identity by setting itself off against the Orient as a sort of surrogate and even underground self."[5]

In *Madama Butterfly* Puccini appropriated concepts of the East prevalent in his time. By combining exoticism, sexism, and racism in *Madama Butterfly*, he was able to reinforce imperialism in general. Said shows that at the turn of the twentieth century, the years during which Puccini's opera is set, Orientalists constructed a deeply-rooted form of racism that still characterizes many people's attitudes toward Arabs and Jews. The prejudices and values contained in Puccini's opera legitimize Pinkerton's racist views that a "Japanese-style" marriage has no validity and a true marriage can only be entered into with a cultural equal, a white American.

Hwang confronts this subject by thrusting his protagonist, René Gallimard, into a *M. Butterfly* fantasy sequence between Sharpless and Pinkerton:

> Sharpless: Are you serious about this girl?
> Pinkerton: I'm marrying her, aren't I?
> Sharpless: Yes – with generous trade-in-terms.
> Pinkerton: When I leave, she'll know what it's like to have loved a real man. And I'll even buy her a few nylons.
> Sharpless: You aren't planning to take her with you?
> Pinkerton: Huh? Where?
> Sharpless: Home!
> Pinkerton: You mean America? Are you crazy? Can you see her trying to buy rice in St. Louis?[6]

The raw tone of the scene suits Pinkerton's character, as presented in Puccini's opera. A more fitting conclusion to *Madama Butterfly* might have been to have the dagger thrust into Pinkerton. However, that would not have suited the opera's orientalist aesthetics, just as academic orientalism is also founded on Western perceptions of hegemony in the Orient. These notions try to emphasize Western superiority over Eastern regression. As Said writes, "Orientalism depends for its strategy on this flexible *positional* superiority, which puts the Westerner in a whole series of possible relationships with the Orient without him ever losing the relative upper hand."[7] Said continues:

> The imaginative examination of things Oriental was based more or less exclusively upon a sovereign Western consciousness out of whose unchallenged centrality an Oriental world emerged, first according to general ideas about who or what was an Oriental, then according to a detailed logic governed not simply by empirical reality, but by a battery of desires, repressions, investments and projections.[8]

Madama Butterfly is filled with notions of Western sovereignty that a little Butterfly-geisha must not challenge or even dream of challenging. Her death itself is orientalist and a kind of "feminine" solution: better suicide than overt rebellion.

A vision of the perfect woman

The dramaturgy of Hwang's *M. Butterfly* is built around René Gallimard's last days in a Paris jail. He speaks directly to the audience of his life, and his story is punctuated with dream and fantasy sequences in which his Chinese lover, Song Liling, appears among other characters. Scenes from past and present supplement Gallimard's story. Hwang's time frame extends from the Vietnam War and China's Cultural Revolution to the present day. In Act I Gallimard is in 1960s Beijing. There his diplomatic career is on the rise and he meets Song Liling. Their relationship develops in Act II. Then in Act III comes Song Liling's revelation and Gallimard reaction as he copes with the truth.

Gallimard had fallen in love with an Eastern stereotype derived from a fantasy: "I, René Gallimard, you see, I have known, and been loved by the perfect Woman."[9] Gallimard's favorite opera is Puccini's *Madama Butterfly* and he fancies himself a kind of Pinkerton, with Butterfly as his lover. However, at the end of the play he reveals *himself*, to be, in fact, Butterfly: his feelings of love have been taken advantage of by a Chinese spy, who is revealed to be the true Pinkerton of the scenario.

In the setup Gallimard describes Puccini's Eastern heroine, Butterfly, as a kind of feminine ideal who is both beautiful and brave. Conversely, the presumptive Western hero, Pinkerton, is no more than a mediocre charlatan. Racism and sexism are seamlessly incorporated into Gallimard's outlook on life. In one scene he presents an imagined meeting between Pinkerton and Sharpless:

> Pinkerton: Cio-Cio-San. Her friends call her Butterfly.
> Sharpless: She eats out of my hand!
> Sharpless: She's probably very hungry.
> Pinkerton: Not like the American girls. It's true what they say about Oriental girls. They want to be treated bad.[10]

It is not enough that a woman will eat out of the palm of a man's hand; she must also crave to be abused. Upon her first meeting with Gallimard around 1960 at the home of the German Ambassador to Beijing, the beautiful Song Liling immediately defies this Orientalist notion. She performs the final scene from *Madama Butterfly* for the invited guests, and is afterward drawn into a conversation with Gallimard. When he praises her convincing performance, she answers:

> Song: Convincing? As a Japanese woman? The Japanese used hundreds of our people for medical experiments during the war, you know. But I gather such an irony is lost on you.
> Gallimard: It's a very beautiful story.
> Song: Well, yes, to a Westerner.
> Gallimard: Excuse me?
> Song: It's one of your favorite fantasies, isn't it? The submissive Oriental woman and the cruel white man.
> Gallimard: Well, I didn't quite mean . . .
> Song: Consider it this way: what would you say if a blonde homecoming queen fell in love with a short Japanese businessman? He treats her cruelly, and then goes home for three years, during which time she prays to his picture and turns down marriage from a young Kennedy. Then, when she learns he has remarried, she kills herself. Now, I believe you would consider this girl to be a deranged idiot, correct? But it's because an Oriental who kills herself for a Westerner – ah! You find it beautiful.[11]

Some time later Song becomes flirtatious and parades before Gallimard all the characteristics of Orientalist femininity: shyness, perturbation, and clemency. This conventionality allows her to manipulate Gallimard, who is starting to enjoy his conquest and begins to feel the first intimations of the absolute power of manhood.[12]

The euphoria that Gallimard describes is very similar to Toni Morrison's finding of an "American" phenomenon in literature whose traits are "new, male, and white." In her long essay "Playing in the Dark," Morrison analyzes how life in a racially segregated society has influenced the work of American authors. Contrary to Said's concept of orientalism, she defines a black individual's present alienation in the US as Africanist. An example Morrison gives that may be equated with the power euphoria Gallimard feels is Bernard Bailyn's study of European migrant farmers who become increasingly Americanized. Bailyn describes Scottish scientist and author William Dunbar as overwhelmed by the previously unthinkable power he possesses when, through the slave trade, he finds himself in complete control of another human being's life. Dunbar felt "a sense of authority and autonomy he had not known before, a force that flowed from his absolute control over the lives of others; he emerged a distinctive new man, a borderland gentleman, a man of property in a raw, half-savage world."[13]

We may wonder what was going through Gallimard's mind when he met Song Liling. He had received a good education, lived in the sophisticated city of Paris, and enjoyed the privileged status of a diplomat. But none of this seemed to bestow on him the sense of authority or self-determination that only came when he was able to control Song Liling, a feeling the playwright describes as "a rush of power – the absolute power of a man." According to Morrison:

> This force is not a willed domination, a thought-out, calculated choice, but rather a kind of natural resource, a Niagara Falls waiting to drench Dunbar [or Gallimard – T.R.] as soon as he is in a position to assume absolute control. Once he has moved into that position, he is resurrected as a new man, a distinctive man – a different man. And whatever his social status in London [or Paris – T.R.], in the New World [or in the Orient – T.R.] he is a gentleman. More gentle, more man. The site of his transformation is within rawness: he is backgrounded by savagery.[14]

When a beautiful woman is finally under Gallimard's control, he cruelly abuses this power, as he readily admits.[15] Act I ends with the initial love scene, whose associations and staging are realized through butterfly symbolism:

> Gallimard: Are you my Butterfly?
> Song: What are you saying?
> Gallimard: I've come tonight for an answer: are you my Butterfly?
> --------------------------

> Song: I don't want to!
> Gallimard: Are you my Butterfly?
> *(Silence; he crosses the room and begins to touch her hair.)*
> I want from you honesty. There should be nothing false between us. No false pride.
> *Pause.*
> Song: Yes, I am. I am your Butterfly.
> Gallimard: Then let me be honest with you. It is because of you that I was promoted tonight. You have changed my life forever. My little Butterfly, there should be no more secrets: I love you.
> *(He starts to kiss her roughly. She resists slightly.)*[16]

The seduction scene contains direct quotations from Puccini, thus reinforcing Gallimard's position as the dominant Pinkerton, and Song Liling as the submissive Butterfly. When Song accepts the part of Butterfly, Gallimard carries her to the bed. Song remains standing in the dark, fully clothed, reluctant to get undressed, as she is told to do. A chaste Chinese woman does not undress, not even in front of her lover. Gallimard is drunk with power. It fuels his enamorment and sexual pleasure so much that he does not question Song's "Chinese" disposition. Song plays her ideologically orientalist role with mastery. She knows Gallimard has no self-awareness and is so confident in his own cultural standing that he has formed a relationship with her based solely on his personal needs. He enjoys his conquest and smugly states that although "we men may all want to kick Pinkerton, very few of us would pass up the opportunity to be Pinkerton."[17]

The idea of possessing a perfect woman allows Gallimard to consider himself the perfect man. In reality, he only loves himself. The relationship with Song offers him a chance to obtain power, but also an opportunity for sexual exploration without revenge or counter-demands. It is part of Gallimard's hierarchical, heterosexual self-image that he be the one to plunge inside and attain satisfaction. However, at no point does he arouse his submissive partner, regardless of whether he thinks that partner to be a woman or a man. In postcolonial terms, when the "masculine" West controls and manipulates the submissive "feminine" East, the Asian ultimately plays the role of the adaptive "female."[18]

Song Liling and Gallimard's relationship becomes serious and their courtship begins. In Act II Gallimard describes the life that he and Song Liling shared in 1960s Beijing:

> Gallimard: And so, over the years 1961, 1962, 1963, we settled into our routine, Butterfly and I. She would have prepared a light snack and then, ever so delicately, and only if I agreed, she would start to pleasure me. With her hands, her mouth, too many ways to explain, and too sad, given my present situation. But mostly we would talk. About my life. Perhaps there is nothing more rare to find than a woman who passionately listens.[19]

He enjoys being taken care of. Song plays her part with sovereignty and she listens to Gallimard. In order to tighten her grip on him, she asks, "What would I love most of all? To feel something inside me – something I know is yours."[20] Then Gallimard takes up a simultaneous relationship with an European woman called Renée, his namesake. Western kinship is underscored with the matching first names. René and Renée are cultural siblings, although the European female is direct, confident, and sexually demanding. René Gallimard wonders if a woman can be so unabashedly sexual that it seems almost masculine.[21] However, despite not really caring very much for Renée, he does not end the affair:

> Gallimard: But I kept up our affair, wildly, for several months. Why? I believe because of Butterfly. She knew the secret I was trying to hide. But, unlike a Western woman, she didn't confront me, threaten, even pout. I remembered the words of Puccini's Butterfly:
> Song: "Noi siamo gente avvezza / alle piccole cose / umili e silenziose."
> Gallimard: "I come from a people / who are accustomed to little / humble and silent." I saw Pinkerton and Butterfly, and what she would say if he were unfaithful. . . . Nothing. She would cry, alone, into those wildly soft sleeves, once full of possessions, now empty to collect her tears. It was her tears and her silence that excited me, every time I visited Renée.[22]

Song continues to play the part of the perfect Orientalist woman. She knows that the secret Gallimard is trying to keep is that the perfect woman is actually a man because only another man can know what a man truly wants. Gallimard and Renée's relationship is about pleasure, which Gallimard feels when he is in control of Song/Butterfly, who remains faithful regardless of what Gallimard/Pinkerton does. An Eastern woman's complete submission sexually arouses Gallimard. That he should give up anything for the sake of a mutual relationship does not even cross his mind. He takes what he wants.

Travesti and theatre

René Gallimard sees himself as having loved the perfect woman. It is revealed, however, that this woman is actually a man – or is she? As in the case of Gallimard, the male protagonist in Balzac's novella "Sarrasine" is deeply in love with an opera singer named La Zambinella. But La Zambinella is not a woman; he is a castrato. This comes to Sarrasine as a surprise, as he was unaware of the practice of cross-dressing in theatre.[23]

Cross-dressing is a long-standing practice in Asian and Western theatre traditions. Men in ancient Greece and to some extent in Rome performed women's roles. From castratos in opera, and trouser roles in drama, opera, and ballet, to female impersonators in drag shows, contemporary performance, and cinema, cross-dressing characters have appeared both conventionally and experimentally.[24] The same is true of classical Chinese and Japanese theatre. Seen in historical perspective, the performing arts have never concerned themselves much about mimetic correlation between off-stage gender and the onstage voice and body.

However, cross-dressing and transvestism are not synonymous. Transvestism is used in modern psychology to express the need to dress in the attire conventionally associated with the opposite sex. The word was first used in 1910 by German sexologist Magnus Hirschfeld.[25] In theatre the term for disguise is *travesti, travesty,* or *en travesti*. The origin of the word is unclear and is sometimes given as Italian, sometimes French. Traditionally, the concept of travesti in theatre and literature refers to concealing one's identity under some sort of a *disguise*. Its secondary meaning is to ridicule, distort, twist, or parody. Only its tertiary sense signifies to dress as a member of the opposite sex.[26] Both the French en travesti and the Italian travestire mean to cross-dress, and derive from the Latin *trans* (to cross) + *vestis* (clothes). Thus, the English term cross-dressing is the equivalent of the Latin and is generally applied to either men dressing in women's clothing or women dressing in men's clothing.

Gallimard is what we would least expect: a culturally ignorant diplomat. He is unaware that the travesti tradition in classical Western and Asian theatre is the norm, not the exception. To this day, classical Asian theatre uses full travesti: an actor painstakingly dresses as a character of the opposite sex, such as in South India's *kathakali*, and is experienced as such by both cast and audience. Marjorie Garber refers to the eighteenth century Japanese actor Yoshizawa Ayames's statement that only a male actor can create the ideal woman.[27] Ayame himself was an *onnagata*, a male actor in Kabuki theatre who specialized in female roles. His claim leads one to believe that if a biological woman had sought a female role in Kabuki, she would have had to learn how to "play a woman" from an onnagata. Biologically speaking, an onnagata is non-female, but cannot categorically be said to be male either. The focal point of the travesti role is that an actor is perceived to be a woman. This practice is what Hwang appropriates with irony in *M. Butterfly*:

> Song: I'm an artist, René. You were my greatest . . . acting challenge.
> *(She laughs)*
> It doesn't matter how rotten I answer, does it? You still adore me. That's why I love you, René.[28]

The objective of male-to-female travesty in Asian theatre is an ideal and the ultimate femininity – a sexualized abstraction that only men are capable of embodying and fully understanding. From a feminist perspective, this "perfect woman" is a suspect character who has been constructed for a man's man. Hwang does not question this issue.

As engaging as *M. Butterfly* may be dramatically, it is not a very feminist text. The play focuses on male self-pity more than anything else. It offers Gallimard a "dual woman" as the object of his affection: the "masculine" European Renée, and the "feminine" Asian Song, who is ultimately revealed to be a cross-dressed man.

The play's biologically sound women – Gallimard's wife Helga, his Danish lover and namesake Renée, and his Chinese Communist comrade Chin – are more caricatures than real people. Garber notes that Hwang allows male cross-dressers to symbolize category crisis between sex and gender and East and West. The biological women in the play are examples of "failed" femininity, without their being entitled to the same universality as men.[29]

One can find in Western literature, theatre, and more recently cinema a tendency to internalize travesti roles as a part of the storyline: cross-dressing is not aimed at conjuring up a picture of the opposite gender in the mind of the audience, but the same gender that the actor/singer/dancer otherwise represents. These types of travesti roles are explained and defended by possibilities that the dramaturgy unfolds. Instances of cross-dressing, whatever their intention was, are often followed by misunderstandings, conflicts, or complications brought about by the actions of the actor in disguise.

Very commonly the disguise fools a character of the opposite sex, who takes the other person to be of the gender she or he portrays. Central to the cross-dressing dramaturgy are ensuing difficulties that point toward the "impossible" (read: homosexual) relationship. A central aspect of the irony of drama is that the audience knows more than the characters.[30] While cross-dressing has most commonly been utilized in comedies, it has also allowed taboos regarding homosexuality to be sidestepped more easily.

The taboos of homosexuality

Homosexuality is first mentioned at the beginning of Gallimard and Song's relationship in Act I of *M. Butterfly*. Gallimard stands with Song's letter in his hand and announces that he disapproves of her calling him a "friend": "When a woman calls a man her 'friend,' she's calling him a eunuch or a homosexual."[31] René does not like the emasculating tone the word carries. His whole attraction to Song is based on masculine Western superiority, hence the term "friend" displeases him.

According to the rules of René and Song's courtship, Song must never appear nude. Whether satisfying Gallimard orally or anally, she is always fully dressed. In his mind, Gallimard wants to interpret their anal intercourse as vaginal, but he never confronts the issue directly. Why this avoidance, although their relationship spans two decades? There is no simple answer. It may be because his relationship with Song is a complicated mix of cultural and gender domination and submission, wishful thinking, homophobia, and love for a projection of his perfect woman in the person of Song.

Gallimard does not initially accept Song's disguise. In Act II he insists that Song undress, resulting in a tense moment. What would Song do if she were to be exposed? And what would Gallimard do if the truth were to come out? However, Song realizes that Gallimard does not necessarily wish to see her naked. What he wants is her submission. She cleverly eases her way out of a particularly tight spot:

> Song: No, René. Don't couch your request in sweet words. Be yourself – a cad – and know that my love is enough, that I submit – submit to the worst you can give me. *(Pause)* Well, come. Strip me. Whatever happens, know that you have willed it. Our love is in your hands. I'm helpless before my man. *(Gallimard starts to cross the room.)*
>
> Gallimard: Did I not undress her because I knew, somewhere deep down, what I would find? Perhaps. Happiness is so rare that our mind can turn somersaults to protect it. At the time I only knew that I was seeing Pinkerton stalking towards his Butterfly, ready to reward her love with his lecherous hands. The image sickened me, pulled me to my knees, so I was crawling towards her like a worm. By the time I reached her, Pinkerton had vanished from my heart. To be replaced by something new, something unnatural that flew in the face of all I'd learned in the world – something very close to love.[32]

With this exchange Hwang connects the Pinkerton subject to Gallimard's proper recognition of his own homosexuality. Now for the first time Gallimard, who is reluctant to discuss the subject of homosexuality, deals with lust, the elusiveness of gender, homosexuality, and love. Gallimard realizes inside himself that everything would fall apart if Song were to disrobe. As for Song, she knows how much Gallimard fears what he dares not verbalize: he is in love with a man.[33]

By the time Gallimard makes it to the other side of the room, he has shed his inner Pinkerton entirely, and in its place is filled with something that changes his disposition toward everything he has ever learned. Gallimard pairs this new sensation with the idea of the unnatural, and it reminds him that homosexuality is against nature and therefore morally reprehensible.

If Song has used Gallimard, the political system of China subsequently abuses and despises Song. "Don't forget: there is no homosexuality in China!" says Comrade Chin to Song.[34] Later in the same Act, when Song states that s/he too has served the revolution, Comrade Chin retorts that such a statement is "bullshit," and that all Song did was wear dresses. She harshly tells Song to "shut up" and to stop "stinking up China" with his "pervert stuff."

Whereas the first half of *M. Butterfly* deals with Gallimard as the controlling Pinkerton, in the second half Gallimard loses the position of power he has attained during his years in Beijing. His premonitions regarding the political situation in Indochina do not come to pass, and he is recalled to France. In the spirit of the Chinese Cultural Revolution, Song is also sent to France, but as a spy. Thus, s/he is now situated at the source all human pollutants, including homosexuality, come from: the West.[35]

By linking homosexuality and the West, Hwang refers to the typical accusations that are directed at homosexuals. Gay people are said to have learned their sexual inclinations from the perversions and decadence of the West. But same sex relationships are not the only thing that attracts this kind of thinking. In many respects, human rights and the democratic governance model are seen as Western inventions and therefore undesirable.[36] In China, homosexuality was declared a threat to socialist culture. Despite his work to bring about the political utopia of the People's Republic, Song is declared an enemy of the state and banished to an isolated labor camp. He is also humiliated at his trial and forced to confess his greatest crime of all: homosexuality.

In Paris, stepping once again into the role of Butterfly, Song acts more openly as a spy and manages to recruit René as his courier. René photographs confidential documents that Song then forwards to the Chinese Embassy. Song's "true" identity is dramatically revealed in a way typical of the genre. Travesti roles must culminate in a dénouement. In *M. Butterfly*, the revelation takes place during the trial, when the French police expose the duo. Removing his wig and kimono, the Chinese lover, wearing a Western suit by Armani, stands in front of René. It is the judge who then asks the question that has been on everyone's mind, namely, has Gallimard been aware the whole time that Song is, in fact, a man? Refusing to answer Song articulates two rules instead. Rule One is that men always believe what they want to hear. Rule Two is that the West has some kind of international rape mentality toward the East: "Her mouth says no, but her eyes say yes."[37]

Rather than submit in an open political confrontation or make the admission the judge desires, Song finally relinquishes his status as the Oriental Butterfly. Someone in a position of power seldom has to answer direct questions. On the other hand, those in the minority must often justify themselves. Despite his minority status, Song rejects the judge's question because her/his relationship with René Gallimard is too complex to do justice to in a simple answer.

Queer positions

Is homosexuality the central theme of *M. Butterfly*? Hwang had intended calling his play *Monsieur Butterfly*, but ultimately preferred the ambiguity of *M. Butterfly*.[38] Just as the letter "M" encompasses both Madame and Monsieur, the line between Madame and Monsieur Butterfly is repeatedly crossed in the drama. The clearest instances are when Song shifts his role from the submissive Oriental Butterfly to the severe Pinkerton. Gallimard's initial status as the superior Western Pinkerton also changes, and he becomes the play's true Butterfly.

However, an unequivocal response to the Madame-Monsieur Butterfly relationship is not given, even at the end of the play when Song Liling becomes "the man" and René Gallimard "the woman." Thus, the problematics of *M. Butterfly* not only pertain to René and Song's relationship, but to the meaning and relation of gender and sexuality.

The central aspect of *M. Butterfly* is the travesti. If we were to focus purely on hetero- or homosexuality and the sadomasochistic interplay between dominant and submissive, we would fail to recognize the more adaptive category that travesti enables. Garber states that the easiest thing to do is declare that Gallimard is in love with a man, but that Gallimard does not want to see or recognize his own homosexuality.[39] Another simplistic plot summary might be that the calculating Chinese Communist spy deceived Gallimard, but this leaves out the attraction and the love that is central to the story.

The relationship between Song and René, however strange it may seem, is nevertheless mutual. The most provocative aspect of *M. Butterfly* is probably the idea of the "wrong" sex eliciting genuine feelings of love. This can be ignored if one chooses to interpret Song's gender illusion as a fraud. However, Song and René's ever-growing attraction reveals the reciprocity that underlies it:

> Song: We always held a certain fascination for you Caucasian men, have we not?
> Gallimard: But that fascination is imperialist, or so you tell me.
> Song: Do you believe everything I tell you? Yes. It is always imperialist. But sometimes it is also mutual.[40]

A great deal has been written on the subject of cross-dressing across a wide spectrum of discourse. Such investigations are part of queer studies, where the focus is on gender, sexuality, and fluctuations in defining identity. Just as queer can mean odd or strange (in addition to its use as a derogatory term for homosexuality), it can also refer to radical sexual political attitudes that question standardized categories of gender and sexual identification.

"Queer" and "homosexual" are, however, not synonymous. Many argue that "anti-normal" is a more fitting synonym for queer. Judith Butler has urged gender scholars to be "critically queer," in other words, to take upon themselves a systematic disobedience towards traditional identities. The term "queer" is associated with a theoretical and activist attitude that fits the dissonant informal usage of queer as a verb "to ruin," "to destroy."

For Butler the concept of queer is not to be defined. She feels that the moment its meaning becomes official it will cease to exist. The term is usually construed as meaning non-heterosexual dissonance that did not form a single harmonious whole but suggested instead a mass of tension.[41] AnnaMarie Jagose summarizes and defines the concept of queer studies as follows:

> While there is no critical consensus on the definitional limits of queer – indeterminacy being one of its widely promoted charms – its general outlines are frequently sketched and debated. Broadly speaking, queer describes those gestures or analytical models which dramatize incoherencies in the allegedly stable relations between chromosomal sex, gender and sexual desire. Resisting the model of stability – which claims heterosexuality as its origin, when it is more properly its effect, queer has been associated most prominently with lesbian and gay subjects, but its analytic framework also includes such topics as cross-dressing, hermaphroditism, gender ambiguity and gender-corrective surgery. Whether as transvestite performance or academic deconstruction, queer locates and exploits the incoherencies in the impossibility of a 'natural' sexuality; it calls into question even such apparently unproblematic terms as 'man' and 'woman.'[42]

Song Liling's travesti figure makes it clear that, as a matter of practicality, it is difficult to situate oneself outside of the female/male divide. Every human is categorized as either a man or a woman. Gender binary logic does not have a term for a human body that is not on one side or another of this dichotomy. Homosexuality confounds the idea that desire must automatically be directed toward members of the opposite sex because desire is an urge that falls outside of the standard heterosexual matrix and is, therefore, considered taboo.

According to Butler, gender and sexuality are neither internal qualities, metaphysical substances, nor straightforward identities. They are discursive, defined by discrimination, and reinforced by the act of stylized repetition.[43] The heterosexual matrix formalizes what is considered socially acceptable or unacceptable. This matrix calls for a gender system with two clearly defined sexes. Gender is not a form of being, but active imitative doing. Its social stability is founded on repetition and therefore embodies the capacity for change. Since reproducing or mimicing anything exactly the same way every time is impossible, each repetition is a challenge to avoid greater or smaller changes. Gender can both consciously and unconsciously be "right" or "wrong." Most people abide by given gender norms, which in turn ensure maintaining and reinforcing their own identities. Gender parodies radicalize the idea that there is only one alternative. "In imitating gender," Butler writes, "drag implicitly reveals the imitative structure of gender itself – as well as its contingency."[44]

Butler considers that both gender and the heterosexuality, that has now become an institution in itself, are social constructions, not natural but political quantities. Gender is constructed performatively through gestures that have generally been construed as consequential and reflective. Performativity does not primarily aim for a result (*being*), but is directed instead at action (*doing*), which leads to gender development. Gender recalls *Gestus*, of which Bertolt Brecht speaks. Gestus manifests itself in social situations, where it acts as a gesture that is representative of ideology or attitude. In other words, gender is mainly an implementation, a kind of performance.

The representation of troubled genders is the driving force behind *M. Butterfly*. The play does not culminate in the dramatic revelation of Song's "true" identity, but with the incongruity of his male body and feminine gender.

> Gallimard: Please. This is unnecessary. I know what you are.
> Song: Do you? What am I?
> Gallimard: A – a man.
> Song: You don't really believe that.
>
> ---------
>
> Gallimard: Look at you. You're a man!
> *(He bursts into laughter again)*
> Song: I fail to see what's so funny!
> Gallimard: "You fail to see!" I mean, you never did have much of a sense of humor, did you?
> I think it's ridiculously funny that I've wasted so much time on just a man!
> Song: Wait. I'm not "just a man."
>
> -----------

Song: I'm not just any man!
Gallimard: Then, what exactly are you?

Song: I'm your Butterfly. Under the robes, beneath everything, it was always me. Now open your eyes and admit it – you adore me.
(*He removes his hand from Gallimard's eyes*)
Gallimard: You, who knew every inch of my desires – how could you, of all people, have made such a mistake?
Song: What?
Gallimard: You showed me your true self. When all I loved was a lie. A perfect lie, which you let fall to the ground and now it's old and soiled.
Song: So – you never really loved me? Only when I was playing a part?[45]

The issue comes to a head in this exchange. Did Gallimard love a person named Song Liling, or just the image of a person who bore that name? Did he love the gender, or the actual person, who may not be so easily categorized as female or male? Butler warns against interpreting gender as a simple case of roleplay. It is a role that cannot express or conceal its inner "self," regardless of whether the "self" is manifested as a gender or not. Gender is acted out in performance and creates a social fiction by putting forth its psychological content.[46]

Song's question, whether René only loved "her" as a character and not a person, is justified. Travesti places Song outside binary gender logic. A person who embodies a two-fold gender identity does not fit within the "normal" social categories, and is therefore seen as untrustworthy. Garber states that untrustworthiness is traditionally associated with those who disguise themselves for various reasons: actors, diplomats, transvestites, and spies.[47] In *M. Butterfly* all of these categories are juxtaposed. The term "spy" is associated with espionage, but also voyeurism.

Ultimately, René chooses the "fantasy" over the "reality." If his Butterfly is not the woman of his dreams, then *he* will turn into this woman. At the end of *M. Butterfly*, Song appears as a Chinese Pinkerton, whereas Gallimard, wearing the same wig and kimono that Song has discarded, is dressed as the Oriental Butterfly. He applies his make-up, then takes dagger in hand and performs ritual suicide as Puccini's music resounds from the speakers. The concluding scene mirrors the opening one. Song, dressed in male attire, stares at the "woman" in Oriental dress and calls out, "Butterfly? Butterfly?"

Was French diplomat Bernard Boursicot mistaken when he took Shi Pei Pu for a woman and fell in love with her? Was René Gallimard mistaken when he believed Song Liling was a woman and loved her? The play leaves us with a sense of lost happiness. The encounter of Gallimard and Song may have led them to experience things they had never known before, for which neither was prepared. The character of Song offered Gallimard a fantasy that made his world complete. In sustaining that delusion, Gallimard speaks a language that blurs the line between dream and reality. Only in this way can his words hold back the world that closes in on him. Song Liling echoes this sentiment:

> One, because when he finally met his fantasy woman,
> he wanted more than anything to believe that she was,
> in fact, a woman.
> And second, I am an Oriental.
> And being an Oriental, I could never be completely a man.[48]

Notes

1. Hwang, *M. Butterfly*, "Afterword," 100.

2. Ibid., III, 1, 83.

3. Puccini, *Madama Butterfly*, conclusion of Act III.

4. Said, *Orientalism*, 3. He defines orientalism as follows: "Anyone who teaches, writes about, or researches the Orient – and this applies whether the person is an anthropologist, sociologist, historian, or philologist – either in its specific or its general aspects, is an Orientalist, and what he or she does is Orientalism."

5. Ibid., 3. Said claims that "to speak of Orientalism is to speak mainly of a British and French cultural enterprise. . . . Orientalism derives from a particular closeness experienced between Britain and France

and the Orient, which until the early nineteenth century had really meant only India and the Bible lands. From the beginning of the nineteenth century until the end of World War II France and Britain dominated the Orient and Orientalism; since World War II America has dominated the Orient, and approaches it as France and Britain once did."

6. Hwang, M. Butterfly, I, 4, 6–7.

7. Said, Orientalism, 7.

8. Ibid., 7–8.

9. Hwang, M. Butterfly, I, 3–4.

10. Ibid., I, 6, 6.

11. Ibid., I, 6, 17.

12. Ibid.

13. Morrison, Playing in the Dark. Her source is Bernard Bailyn, Voyagers to the West: A Passage in the Peopling of America on the Eve of the Revolution (New York: Knopf, 1986).

14. Ibid., 61.

15. Hwang, M. Butterfly I, 11, 36.

16. Ibid., I, 13, 3–40.

17. Ibid., II, 1, 42.

18. Kondo, "M. Butterfly," 17; see also Spivak, Other Asias. During the last fifteen years scholarship on postcolonial theory and queer theory has been increasingly published. See Hawley, Postcolonial Queer: Theoretical Intersections; Puar, Terrorist Assemblages.

19. Hwang, M. Butterfly, II, 5, 49.

20. Ibid., II, 6, 51.

21. Ibid., II, 6, 54.

22. Ibid., II, 6, 56.

23. Roland Barthes is referring to Balzac's "Sarrasine" in S/Z.

24. See Baker, Drag: Bullough & Bullough, Cross Dressing; Garber, Vested Interests; Ferris, Crossing the Stage; Gilbert & Gubar,

Sexchanges; Senelick, *The Changing Room*. See also Abbate, *In search of Opera*; André, *Voicing Gender: Castrati, Travesti, and the Second Woman in Early Nineteenth-Century Italian Opera*; Blackmer & Smith, *En Travesti*.

25. Magnus Hirschfeld, *Die Transvestiten. Eine Untersuchung über den erotischen Verkleidungstrieb* (Berlin: Pulvermacher, 1910). See also the same author's *Sexuelle Zwischenstufen. Das männliche Weib und der weibliche Mann* (Bonn: Marcus & Weber, 1918). For a transvestite, female clothing has a fetishistic function. It is an implication of a heterosexual or homosexual man's "female identity." Transsexualism, on the other hand, is when a man feels himself to be a woman or when a woman feels herself to be a man. D. O. Cauldwell first began using this term, and Harry Benjamin popularized it in the 1960s.

26. "Travesti," *Enciclopedia dello Spettacolo*, Roma: Casa Editrice Le Maschere, 1954-1962. For a discussion of how the concept of travesti originally referred only to disguising oneself, see André, *Voicing Gender*; Hov, *Kvinnerollene*, 11–12; Rosenberg, *Byxbegär*.

27. Garber, *Vested Interests*, 245. See also Leonard Cabell Pronko, *Theater East and West* (Berkeley: University of California Press, 1967).

28. Hwang, *M. Butterfly*, II, 7, 63.

29. Garber, *Vested Interests*, 249.

30. In the Howard Hawks classic comedy *Bringing Up Baby* (1938), Aunt Elizabeth (Mary Robson) asks Dexter (Cary Grant), who is clad in a women's dressing robe adorned with feathers, if he customarily dresses in such attire. Grant spreads his arms and yells: "No! I've just gone *gay* . . . all of a sudden!" The scene reflects two stereotypes of a man in women's clothes: on the one hand, all the associations of gay culture tied to cross-dressing, drag, *voguing* performances, and pop icons such as David Bowie, Boy George, and The New York Dolls; and on the other, the comedic cross-dressed characters on stage, television, and in the movies. Charley's Aunt, Tootsie, Mrs. Doubtfire, Dame Edna, and Lily Savage are only a few examples of cross-dressing in modern cinema.

31. Hwang, *M. Butterfly*, I, 11, 35.

32. Ibid., II, 7, 60.

33. From this point on in the text, Song Liling shall be referred to as "he."

34. Hwang, *M. Butterfly*, II, 4, 48.

35. Ibid., II, 11, 72.

36. See Blackwood & Wieringa, *Female Desires*; Bullough & Bullough, *Cross Dressing*.

37. Hwang, *M. Butterfly*, III, 1, 83.

38. Ibid., "Afterword," 95.

39. Garber, *Vested Interests*, 236.

40. Hwang, *M. Butterfly*, I, 8, 22.

41. Rosenberg, *Byxbegär*.

42. Jagose, *Queer Theory*.

43. Butler, *Gender Trouble*, 124.

44. Ibid., 137.

45. Hwang, *M. Butterfly*, III, 2, 87–88.

46. Butler, "Performative Acts," 279.

47. Garber, *Vested Interests*, 256.

48. Hwang, *M. Butterfly*, III, 1, 83.

Works Cited

Abbate, Carolyn. *In Search of Opera*. Princeton: Princeton University Press, 2001.

André, Naomi. *Voicing Gender: Castrati, Travesti, and the Second Woman in Early Nineteenth-Century Italian Opera*. Bloomington: Indiana University Press, 2006.

Baker, Roger. *Drag: A History of Female Impersonation in the Performing Arts*. London: Cassell, 1994.

Barthes, Roland. *S/Z*. Translated by Richard Miller. New York: Hill & Wang, 1974.

Blackmer, Corinne E., and Patricia Juliana Smith, eds. *En Travesti: Women, Gender Subversion, Opera*. New York: Columbia University Press, 1995.

Blackwood, Evelyn, and Saskia E. Wieringa, eds. *Female Desires: Same-Sex Relations and Transgender Practices Across Cultures.* New York: Columbia University Press, 1999.

Bullough, Vern, and Bonnie Bullough. *Cross Dressing: Sex, and Gender.* Philadelphia: University of Pennsylvania Press, 1993.

Butler, Judith. *Gender Trouble: Feminism and the Subversion of Identity.* New York: Routledge, 1990.

———. "Performative Acts and Gender Constitution: An Essay in Phenomenology and Feminist Theory." In *Performing Feminisms: Feminist Critical Theory and Theatre*, edited by Sue-Ellen Case, 270–281. Baltimore: Johns Hopkins University Press, 1990.

Ferris, Leslie, ed. *Crossing the Stage: Controversies on Cross-Dressing.* London: Routledge, 1993.

Garber, Marjorie. *Vested Interests: Cross-Dressing and Cultural Anxiety.* New York: Routledge, 1992.

Gilbert, Sandra M. and Susan Gubar. *No Man's Land: The Place of Woman Writer in the Twentieth Century.* New Haven: Yale University Press, 1989.

Hawley, John C., ed. *Postcolonial Queer: Theoretical Intersections.* New York: State University of New York, 2001.

Hov, Liv. *Kvinnerollene i antikkens teater – skrevet, spilt og sett av men* (Women's Roles in Ancient Theatre - Written, Played, and Viewed by Men). Dissertation. University of Oslo, 1998.

Hwang, David Henry. *M. Butterfly, with an Afterword by the Playwright.* New York: Plume, 1988.

Jagose, Annamarie. *Queer Theory: An Introduction.* New York: New York University Press, 1996.

Kondo, Dorinne K. "M. Butterfly: Orientalism, Gender, and a Critique of Essentialist Identity." *Cultural Critique*, Fall 1990: 5–29.

Morrison, Toni. *Playing in the Dark: Whiteness and the Literary Imagination.* Cambridge, MA: Harvard University Press, 1992.

Puar, Jasbir K. *Terrorist Assemblages. Homonationalism in Queer Times.* Durham: Duke University Press, 2007.

Puccini, Giacomo, *Madama Butterfly*. 1904. Original Italian text by Luigi Illica and Giuseppe Giacosa. English translation taken from R.H. Elkin, *Libretto for Madama Butterfly: An Opera in Three Acts (English and Italian Edition)*. Translated by Ruth and Thomas Martin. New York: Metropolitan Opera Record Club, 1957.

Rosenberg, Tiina. *Byxbegär* (Desiring Pants). Göteborg: Anamma Böcker, 2000.

Said, Edward. *Orientalism*. London: Penguin, 1995 [1978].

Senelick, Laurence. *The Changing Room: Sex, Drag, and Theatre*. London: Routledge, 2000.

Spivak, Gayatri Chakravorty. *Other Asias*. New Jersey: Wiley-Blackwell, 2007.

Zarah Leander after a concert at Waldbühne in Berlin, July 1957. Archiv Paul Seiler Berlin, http://www.zarah-leander.de. Photographer: Georg Ebert. Copyright CC-BY-NC-ND: Paul Seiler, Sammlung Seiler Berlin. www.zarah-leander.de

4. Queer Feelings: Zarah Leander, Sentimentality, and the Gay Diva Worship

The Swedish actress and singer Zarah Leander (1907–1981) may have been the most complex star in Nazi German cinema. She never offered any excuses or explanations for what she did during the years she was active in Nazi Germany, calling herself "a political idiot" who just wanted to work and make money, no matter where and under what circumstances. Three celebrated female stars, Kristina Söderbaum, Zarah Leander, and Lilian Harvey, political idiots or not, played a crucial role in Joseph Goebbels's entertainment industry.[1] The money the Nazi regime made through them was immediately allocated to the German war effort.

The official start of Leander's stage career took place in 1929 in the popular theatre of Ernst Rolf. She then performed in a variety of films and theatrical productions. From 1936 until 1943 she was based in Berlin and starred in Nazi cinema. In 1943 Leander moved back to Sweden and as a result fell out of favor with the Nazi propagandists. She was banned from appearing in Sweden, Austria, and Germany until 1948, but her legendary comeback concerts in Malmö, Stockholm, and Berlin in 1949 returned her to the public's favor. Leander's *schlager* repertoire, dark voice, and performance style made her a celebrated entertainer in the 1950s and 1960s. Even to this day she remains an icon in the gay community.[2]

The political shame of being an ex-Nazi star never left Leander. The argument that what she did was "only entertainment" was not sufficient to explain away all her years working in the Nazi film industry. But, as Antje Ascheid points out, female movie stars are in many ways the antithesis of the prototypical Nazi female, and so Leander appears as one of Nazi cinema's most contradictory

---

How to cite this book chapter:
Rosenberg, Tiina 2016. Queer Feelings: Zarah Leander, Sentimentality, and the Gay Diva Worship. In: Rosenberg, Tiina *Don't Be Quiet, Start a Riot! Essays on Feminism and Performance.* Pp. 80–98. Stockholm: Stockholm University Press. DOI: http://dx.doi.org/10.16993/baf.d. License: CC-BY 4.0

figures.³ Ascheid claims that Leander's star persona has always been a pleasurable negotiation of antagonistic positions and spectatorship issues, strikingly articulated through her immense popularity in the post-war gay community.⁴

Queer feelings have been linked to diva worship with regard to the "phenomenon Leander" in the post-war period in Sweden, Germany, and internationally. The queer quality of Leander is to be found in the transgressive erotic representation of her vocal gender ambiguity, recast through gay male diva worship as counter-political resistance to "normalcy," although she also had a lesbian following.⁵

The queer diva

The diva has a special place in gay male aesthetics. The extraordinary, tragic, comic, angry, nasty, glamorous, provocative, sentimental, and intelligent diva is generally a straight, but not necessary heteronormative, woman. Gay divas like Maria Callas, Joan Crawford, Bette Davis, Marlene Dietrich, Greta Garbo, Judy Garland, Zarah Leander, Madonna, Bette Midler, Asta Nielsen, Birgit Nilsson, Edith Piaf, and Barbra Streisand, to a name a few in the West, are all artists who have challenged both social norms and heteronormative femininity.

The diva sometimes has a lesbian address, or at least a strong lesbian subtext, as do Asta Nielsen, Greta Garbo, Marlene Dietrich, and Zarah Leander. This subtext is expressed through a specific gender appearance, female bonding, and the "sapphonic" voice, a term coined by musicologist Elizabeth Wood.⁶ Diva worship is not merely about a traumatic shame community; it is also a form of queer cultural resistance. One of the aesthetic products of closet culture, a *Verfremdung* of heteronormativity, is camp, an old, community-based communication system mainly found in gay male culture. Divas and a specific musical repertoire are its cornerstones.⁷ In the 1970s the Swedish gay men's magazine *Revolt* wrote: "Zarah Leander was so popular that many gay men publicly stated that they disliked her because they did not want to be branded as gay."⁸ Diva worship can have many reasons, and the adoration of gender ambiguity connected to sexual ambivalence is one of them. Leander's greatest fan, Paul Seiler in Berlin, states: "We were addicted to Zarah for her pathos-filled style, for her larger-than-life emotional outbursts, for her *Valkyrie* appearances, dark, almost masculine voice. For many of us she was both father and mother; she was also the surrogate drug for all our closeted emotions."[9] Seiler has explained the specifics of his Leander adoration at length:

> She was the great star and acted so perfectly at live performances. She did not enter the stage; she took up the whole space. She had an aura of loftiness about her. The statuesque body emphasized her charisma, and only the wide gestures of her arms and hands brought some movement into her performances. She raised her arms towards the end of the song as if she wanted to say "This is me and that's it!"[10]

Richard Dyer, who has written about the worship of Judy Garland at mid-century, says that when Garland was fired by MGM in 1950 and tried to commit suicide, "It constituted for the public a sudden break with Garland's uncomplicated and ordinary MGM image, made possible a reading of Garland as having a special relationship to suffering, ordinariness, normality, and it is this relationship that structures much of the gay reading of Garland."[11] In 1952 she abandoned her film career and started making concert appearances, beginning at the London Palladium. Dyer claims that post-1950 readings of Garland were anachronistically shifted back into her earlier films, recordings, and biography in the light of her subsequent history.[12] Television and repertory cinemas that specialized in nostalgic revivals facilitated both Garland and Leander's careers as entertainers.[13]

The diva of shame

Sweden both profited from World War II and emerged from it with an intact infrastructure. As the ex-star of Nazi German cinema Leander was one of the few public figures in Sweden to be accused of Nazi sympathies at the time. "What shall we do with shame?" the queer scholar Michael Warner once asked rhetorically, and answered: "Put it on somebody else!"[14] The individual experience of shame might feel like a personal and private emotion, but it is also a public phenomenon. The stigmatized individual is observed; she/he is highly visible and cannot hide from the gaze of fellow citizens. Shame as a negative self-image is linked to social or political repercussions, or both, that turn it into a social act. The visibility of shame is the outcome of violating social norms.

Same-sex desires and sexualities are one form of social norm violation that bears a special relationship to gender. While the specificity of Leander's shame and its public impact are linked to her past in Nazi Germany, she also *embodied* Swedish catharsis as a visible scapegoat after the war. She was covered in shame. With the rest of the nation pointing to her, she could feel free of collective guilt for any Nazi sympathy shown during the war. The idea of Sweden as a small, innocent nation surrounded by large and powerful enemies has only occasionally been questioned.[15] Therefore, the national narrative of innocence is illuminating in the catharsis that the instance of Leander provided. That narrative demanded a scapegoat, and by appointing one the Swedish nation was symbolically purified through her shame. As the feminist scholar Sara Ahmed points out, "By witnessing what is shameful about the past, the nation can 'live up to' the ideals that secure its identity or being in the present."[16]

However, the social norms Leander violated concerned not only her dubious past. Her persona was also provocative in itself. The Leander performances of *Kann denn Liebe Sünde sein?; Nur nicht aus Liebe weinen; Ich weiß, es wird einmal ein Wunder gescheh'n; Jede Nacht ein neues Glück; Waldemar; Yes Sir;* and *Merci, mon ami, es war wunderschön,* to mention only a few of the songs that made her the gay icon of the 1950s and 1960s, together with her ambiguous gender, enabled a gay identification and desire across heteronormative gender boundaries. Gay men have historically had difficulties identifying with hegemonic forms of masculinity. In Leander's case the diva, "the fallen woman," emerges from certain forms of closet culture – and later also openly gay culture – as a stand-in for the gay male. In her songs and in her habitus Leander broke various taboos. Her frankness in confronting social, sexual, and gender norms resonated with many in the Swedish and international gay communities. Guido Knopp comments that the mixture of *Übermutter* and vamp guaranteed her the love and adoration of her gay audience.[17]

Queer scholars J. Jack Halberstam, Eve Kosofsky Sedgwick, and others who have written extensively about gay shame, posit an early childhood experience of sexual shame that has to be reclaimed, reinterpreted, and resituated by a queer adult who, if armed with theoretical language about her or his sexuality, can transform past experiences of abjection, isolation, and rejection into legibility, community, and love.[18] Halberstam writes:

> Gay shame, in this scenario, becomes the deep emotional reservoir upon which an adult queer sexuality draws, for better or for worse. And the sexual and emotional scripts which queer life draws upon, and which oppose the scripts of normativity, are indebted oddly to this early experience with shame, denial, and misrecognition. When we seek to reclaim gay shame and we oppose the normativity of 'gay pride' agenda, we embrace these awkward, undignified, and graceless childhoods and we choose to make them part of our political future.[19]

As Brett Farmer observes, "Much of the breathtaking success with which mainstream culture is able to install and mandate a heteronormative economy depends directly on its ability to foster a correlative economy of queer shame through which to disgrace and thus delegitimize all that falls outside the narrow purview of straight sexualities."[20]

Diva worship as a reparative position

According to the testimony of gay contemporaries, Leander's intense, almost male contralto was at its best when it expressed troubled love, fear of isolation, and persecution. In a review of her 1937 film *Zu neuen Ufern* (To New Shores), *Der Berliner Lokalanzeiger* wrote: "What dominates the film is the shimmer of Leander's voice: a voice as intoxicating as heavy, dark wine . . . as powerful as the sound of an organ . . . as transparent . . . as glass, as deep as metal. Everything is in this voice: jubilation, happiness, the drunken melody, and the wild pain of life."[21] Erica Carter finds that what is noteworthy in this reviewer's representation of the effects that Leander's voice had on film spectators was the mention of qualities that bourgeois aesthetics attribute not to the beautiful, but to the sublime.

> Accounts of the sublime since Kant have emphasized both its dynamism (the Kantian sublime 'moves', whereas the beautiful produces 'quiet contemplation'), and its ambivalence (hence the Kantian *Abgrund*, or abyss). Leander's voice operates, this review suggests, in a similar mode, stirring the very body of a spectator in whom it produces 'jubilation', certainly, but also jubilation's darker aspects: 'drunken melody', 'wild pain'.[22]

Farmer takes this notion even further, with the concept of "queer sublimity." Gay historian Daniel Harris finds that at the heart of gay diva worship is the almost universal homosexual experience of ostracism and insecurity, and the desire to elevate oneself above one's antagonistic surroundings.[23] Wayne Koestenbaum similarly claims that "gay culture has perfected the art of mimicking a diva – of pretending, inside, to be divine – to help the stigmatized self imagine that it is received, believed and adored."[24]

Farmer writes in similar terms that "tuned to the chord of reparative amelioration, diva worship emerges here as a practice of resistance, queer utopianism, or what might be more suggestively termed *queer sublimity*: the transcendence of a limiting heteronormative materiality and the sublime reconstruction, at least in fantasy, of a more capacious, kinder, queerer world."[25] Kosofsky Sedgwick calls these survivalist dynamics of queer culture "reparative" in the sense given to the term in object relation theory as an affirmative impulse to repair or make good the losses of subjective constitution. "Because there can be terrible surprises, however, there can also be good ones. Hope, often a fracturing, even traumatic thing to experience, is among the energies by which the reparatively positioned reader tries to organize the fragments and part-objects she encounters and creates."[26]

Diva with a voice

Carter notes that in a song dripping with the pathos of parting and loss, Leander's voice derives melodramatic intensity from the use of close sound and the absence of ambient noise. According to Carter, in her 1930s films the visual figuring of Leander as a singing body, and her various narrative positionings as a revue or opera diva, recording artist, or music-hall star, serve to reproduce an "image of corporeal unity" between body and voice as a key source of the "auditory pleasure."[27] The harmonious integration of spectator and film text through the fixing of voice to body image is also reinforced by Leander's vocal capacity for depth and resonance – qualities that embrace her cinema audience within a "sonorous envelope."[28]

Carter claims that Leander's singing voice breaks the link between body and voice, both by a spatial treatment that ruptures their unity, and by a textual structure that situates the musical number, rather than the narrative, as the fulcrum of dramatic development.[29] She writes that the genre shift from *Musikfilm* to *Schlagerfilm* was evident in Leander's Ufa productions on several occasions and became her specialty in the 1950s and 1960s.

> In these slippages it becomes evident how Leander's voice begins to detach itself from the diegetic and visual spaces of the film text, and to assume the identity it possesses within the public space of mass culture as a disembodied acoustic presence. For if the first apparatus of representation that displaces Leander's voice from its location in the individual film text is genre, then the second is the culture of Schlager, or hit song itself as it developed within the popular music industry in tandem with sound film.[30]

Leander's particular transgender appeal resided in her distinctive voice. Described as baritone, sometimes as bass, it entered an "unnatural," inadmissible range that could signal an erotic dissonance or queerness.[31] Elizabeth Wood's characterization of what she calls the "sapphonic voice" – the voice that signifies lesbian difference and desire – can equally apply to Leander's flexible negotiation and integration of an exceptional range of registers. Leander crosses boundaries among different voice types and their representations to challenge polarities of both gender and sexuality as these are socially – and vocally – constructed. [32]

Alice A. Kuzniar writes that Leander's "phantasmatic voice indeed recreates, by transgendering, the body, particularly to have it imitate her model, only in reverse, now male-to-female. Indeed, the two Zarah-impersonators that I have heard perform live, Christina and Tom Fisher, are so remarkable because their haunting and haunted voices possess the phantasmatic capacity of evoking Zarah's presence: in this gender-bending reincarnation, a woman's masculine voice thrillingly issues from a man's body."[33]

Schlager and the perverse sentimentalist

The shift from cinema to the culture of schlager was presaged by Leander's vocal performance in her films. She moved in the postwar period from cinema to live performance with songs and schlager. The latter is a popular genre that has never been expected to generate highbrow interest. It represents sentimentality with the decaying fragrance of the dancehall and shattered dreams. Schlager is both banality and magnificence rolled into one, with the two often intimately connected: "I love you, I miss you, I can't live without you!" All this is easier to express when someone sings these words that can be so hard to say. Like many other genres, schlager is an emotional messenger.

Schlager has a special, highly ambiguous relationship to modernity and modernism. On the one hand, schlager music is dependent on modern media and technology such as radio, microphones, recordings, and cinema. On the other hand, it is often characterized as anti-modern in its appeal to old-fashioned feelings and its dependency on obsolete conventions. Schlager originated in nineteenth-century Viennese operetta and chapbooks. The latter were often dramatic and gory, with violent death perpetually lurking on the next page, unlike what would eventually constitute genuine schlager, which was mainly about longing and being (unhappily) in love.

Schlager is sentimental popular music, if one defines sentimentality as exaggerated emotionality, insincerity, and something generally of low aesthetic standing. Modernism initiated a shift in values, which Rita Felski has characterized as a "cultural remasculinization."[34] The emotionality that had previously been common to both sexes was not feminized until the emergence of modern Western culture, at which time a detached, non-emotional approach attained a higher status than emotionality, which was increasingly associated with pretense and sexuality. Terms such as sentimental, melodramatic, theatrical, and romantic were increasingly given negative connotations and thought of as referring solely to beautiful illusions or exaggerated emotional expression, as opposed to critical analysis.

Deborah Knight has analyzed the categorical negation of sentimentality in philosophy of art.[35] Sentimentality is often associated with soft, comforting, tender feelings such as care, sympathy, affection, and empathy. While these feelings may not immediately arouse protests from aestheticians, the direction these affects take in sentimental pleasure does. Anti-sentimental critics claim that sentimentality is a case of boundless and uninhibited delight that is simply tasteless. According to Knight, standard anti-sentimental philosophic opinion condemns sentimentality as immoral and unworthy.

The critics of sentimentality, Joseph Kupfer among them, primarily object to sentimental *pleasures*, which they describe as perverse, excessive, and repetitive.[36] The consumer of sentimental art repeatedly watches the same sentimental films, listens to the same sentimental music (including melodramatic bel canto arias and bombastic Wagner overtures), and indulges in sentimental pastimes. Kupfer claims that sentimentality is a character fault, rather than an aesthetic expression.[37] He views the sentimentalist with repulsion as a perverse, self-centered person who wallows in a sentimental flood of emotions. For Kupfer the object of sentimentality is the sentimentalist her or himself.

Sentimentality and kitsch

Schlager has a bad reputation because of its kitsch aesthetics. Those scholars and theorists who associate sentimentality with kitsch, and especially the ones who do so with a political agenda, position sentimentality in a cultural and political context that goes beyond loving and tender feelings. Although there is no consensus regarding the definition of kitsch, the term has had a negative connotation ever since it was coined in Germany around the middle of the nineteenth century. Kitsch has been synonymous with worthless, commercial, mediocre, or simply bad art. But not all substandard art qualifies as kitsch, nor should kitsch be seen unconditionally as artistic failure, something in which everything went wrong.[38]

Both schlager and kitsch are often defined as "bad taste," although it has been hard to identify exactly what constitutes this bad taste. Kitsch forms an aesthetic category of its own. It shares with queer the status of being culturally undesirable. Like queer, kitsch has been banished into the shadows of negative cultural history, the domain of the invisible and inaudible. Similar to the way in which sentimentality is denied and described as perverse, the disdain for kitsch appears to create a special form of cultural and artistic "unpresence" that constantly calls attention to itself, but must be disregarded in order not to sully normative, great art and culture.

Although the aesthetic content of high culture consists of the fine arts, that content has occasionally been extended to include more popular expressions of art. Unsophisticated junk, however, the refuse of the art world, has a very special and unique allure. The philosophers and cultural theorists who gravitated around the Frankfurt School criticized mass culture and its devastating effects with reference to Nazism. Kitsch in this analysis was a fundamentally despised element. In a definitive essay on kitsch theory entitled "Einige Bemerkungen zum Problem des Kitsches" (Some Comments on the Problem of Kitsch), Hermann Broch designates kitsch as the evil element in the value system of art.[39] Aesthetically, kitsch is associated with subject matter such as weeping children and sunsets in cheap poster art. Common to all kitsch products is that they are variations on the theme of beauty and are often exceedingly charged with emotional, sentimental stereotypes that "spontaneously" arouse pre-programmed responses, such as tears. Typically, the subject is rendered in a way that makes it easy to identify as kitsch. Kitsch is a mirror that reflects the desires and fears of the person who stands before it. Kitsch is something that actively engages the beholder.[40]

With their shifting and heavy expressions of longing, Leander's emotive schlager performances belong to the category of escapism, imagination, melodrama, and sentimentality. Sentimentality is the distinguishing feature that sets kitsch apart from other expressions of popular culture. The Frankfurt School and subsequent critics of kitsch have disparaged it and sentimentality on the grounds that they both are an opiate of the people in the Marxist sense. A kitsch-oriented person's way of relating to the world, unlike that of the discerning consumer of culture, is conditioned by "lascivious absorption and merging."[41] If the aesthetics of schlager belong to the world of kitsch, it is nevertheless enjoyed in gay culture as camp, one of the most visual expressions and resistance strategies of gay culture. It has served as a haven for gays by being a refuge from heteronormativity.[42]

The shameless stickiness of pleasure

Leander's comeback and golden era were in the 1950s and 1960s, but by 1958 she wrote that the diva was dead:

> There are no divas today. Not the divas we read about in our childhood, whom we worshipped on stage and screen. Not the divas buried in flowers who proffered their bejeweled hands to hand-kissing gentlemen, not the divas who sauntered along the boulevards escorted by infatuated adorers and a brace of hounds. How did the celebrated diva die? Well, it happened so fast. One fateful day, the diva went down to the store to buy some bread for breakfast – and on that day she died, never to live again.[43]

In the 1970s, the gay movement discovered its own political songs. In a more open political context, many people experienced Leander worship as stale and outmoded, a remnant of the closet culture. Yet the diva cult has survived in male gay culture to this day. The link to the 1950s Leander worship has been sustained in the works of Rainer Werner Fassbinder. Two of Leander's most famous films, *Zu neuen Ufern* and *La Habanera*, were also among Fassbinder's favorites. They were both directed by Detlef Sierck, later known as Douglas Sirk. Kuzniar writes that "As is well-known, Sirk's melodramas were Fassbinder's most influential models, and the latter's essay on the master's 1950s Hollywood films demonstrates how he (ir)reverently read them as camp."[44] Kuzniar claims that Leander's transvestetic performance of femininity is echoed in several of Fassbinder's characters. "Queer German cinema follows a circuitous route indeed from Nazi melodrama to Fassbinder's transgendered fantasies."[45] In Sweden the Leander tradition has been continued by the drag group After Dark, which has recreated acclaimed Leander acts in its shows since the late 1970s.

Ludwig Giesz has characterized the self-centered and uninhibitedly pleasure-oriented sentimentalist experience as a perversion aimed at self-gratification (*Selbstgenuss*).[46] Some art scholars and philosophers, such as Kathleen Higgins and Robert C. Solomon, speak of "sweet kitsch" and want to shift the focus from the objects of pleasure to what they consider to be the essential aspects of kitsch, namely, the response and the experience.[47] Higgins claims that kitsch and non-kitsch objects arouse the same kinds of feelings. What sets the two categories apart is not the experience itself but that some are drawn to kitsch, while others shy away from its unsophisticated and blatant sentimentality. Solomon also places value on the tender feelings that the sentimental experience evokes, rather than sentimentality itself.[48]

A key to understanding the resistance that sentimentalism arouses may lie in the "stickiness" (*Klebrigkeit*) of schlager and the sentimental genres. All music is penetrating, but kitsch sentimentalism has an appeal that wields an astonishing, compelling force. It bypasses reason and goes straight for the feelings. This ability pierces us whether we try to resist it or not. In "Der Fall Wagner" Nietzsche writes that Wagner's music not only attacks the listener but persuades the nerves (*die Nerven überredet*).[49] Such overwhelming compositions operate bodily-physically in approximately the same way as drugs or ecstatic sex.

Schlager merges the worlds of sexuality and sentimentality: tears, body, and sensuality form a unity that does not loosen its grip, which is why it is said that schlager is sticky and cannot be shaken off. Sticky things, like bodily effluents, are soft, flowing, and flexible. They shape themselves according to movement. In the same way that they mix the positions of subject and object, they are on the one hand passively receptive, and on the other actively penetrating. In short, stickiness symbolizes the sensual and sexual being and the concrete experience of this sensuality.

The sentimental schlager experience includes an embracing of stickiness as an essential element. Alongside the concrete sensual participation – especially sing-alongs binding others together in the same subculture – there is also the revelation of the sticky boundary that "the kitsch person" (*der Kitschmensch*) transcends by singing schlager. The resulting experience transcends detached observation and penetrates the skin, entering every bodily pore.

Modern Western masculinity is intimately associated with self-control. Claes Ekenstam writes that, "Men should be strong, upright, and guided by common sense. Chest out, stomach in, and teeth firmly clenched, men should walk straight ahead with a steady gaze, whether they are marching as soldiers for their country or navigating the pitfalls of their career. Under no circumstance must they fall!"[50] In the eyes of heteronormativity, gay men who relish schlager and may occasionally lapse into tears appear to challenge contemporary masculinity. According to Ekenstam, they are, in fact, resurrecting an older tradition in Western cultural history, when men's tears flowed freely. In the Bible as well as in the Odyssey men shed tears. The renaissance poet Petrarch believed in the cathartic power of tears. Goethe's pre-romantic Sturm-und-Drang hero Werther was forever resorting to tears and in fact suffered from sudden fits of swooning. However, a growing emphasis on male self-control has created a negative attitude toward male tears, until they have come to be seen as a sign of weakness that reveals an underlying lack of masculinity.[51]

The gay male schlager and diva culture can be interpreted as a defense of sentimental culture, which it embraces as a source of power and joy. Leander's concerts were one of the few places where gay men could meet and socialize openly in the 1950s and 1960s in Sweden and Germany. The ageing, abject, and monumental Leander, with her jewelry, wigs, and makeup, was received with open arms by the gay community.[52] In Paul Seiler's words of homage: "I turn to the immortal Zarah and I can see her with her majestic head high and with a proud, but sad look in her eyes; and I hear the dark, raw timbre of her voluminous organ voice with its capacity to raise trivial entertainment to nobleness."[53]

Notes

1. Ascheid, *Hitler's Heroines*, 8.
2. Ibid., 155.

3. Ibid., 217.

4. Ibid., 9.

5. Kuzniar, *Queer German Cinema*, 62.

6. Wood, "Sapphonics."

7. Heteronormativity as a concept is used to analyze the structural privileges associated with heterosexuality. For the concept of camp, see Cleto, *Camp: Queer Aesthetics*.

8. Holm, "Bögarnas Zarah," 16.

9. Seiler, *Zarah Leander*, 8; Rosenkranz & Lorenz, *Hamburg*, 132.

10. Seiler, *Zarah Leander*, 109.

11. Dyer, "Judy Garland," 138.

12. Ibid., 139.

13. Ibid.

14. Warner, *Normal*, 3.

15. Boëthius, *Heder och samvete*.

16. Ahmed, *Cultural Politics*, 109.

17. Knopp, *Hitlers Frauen*, 30.

18. Halberstam, "Queer Studies," 63.

19. Ibid. The attachment of shame to queer has been a large part of several influential projects in Queer Studies, including Michael Warner's critiques of "normal," Eve Kosofsky Sedgwick's theory of shame, Leo Bersani's work on "homos," and Douglas Crimp's on queer before gay. Crimp shows very explicitly that the queer is the pre-history of gay – a history that should not be left behind in the rush to embrace gay pride, but must be excavated in all its contradictions, disorder, and eroticism.

20. Farmer, "Fabulous Sublimity," 167.

21. Knopp, *Hitlers Frauen*, 296.

22. Carter, *Dietrich's Ghosts*, 183–184.

23. Harris, *Rise and Fall of Gay Culture*, 10.

24. Koestenbaum, *The Queen's Throat*, 133.
25. Farmer, "Fabulous Sublimity," 170.
26. Kosofsky Sedgwick, "Paranoid Reading," 146.
27. Carter, *Dietrich's Ghosts*, 192.
28. Ibid., 193.
29. Ibid.
30. Ibid., 195.
31. Kuzniar, *Queer German Cinema*, 63.
32. Wood, "Sapphonics," 33; Rosenberg, "Touch of Opera," 31.
33. Kuzniar, *Queer German Cinema*, 63.
34. Felski, *Gender of Modernity*.
35. Knight, "Sentimentality."
36. Kupfer, "Sentimental Self."
37. Ibid.
38. Broch, "Zum Problem des Kitsches."
39. Ibid.
40. Kulka, "Kitsch," 252; Kraus, *I love Dick*, 21.
41. Felski, *Gender of Modernity*, 118.
42. Cleto, *Camp*.
43. Leander, *Vill ni se en diva?* 7.
44. Kuzniar, *Queer German Cinema*, 2.
45. Ibid.
46. Giesz, *Phänomenologie des Kitsches*.
47. Higgins, "Sweet Kitsch."
48. Solomon, "In Defense of Sentimentality."
49. Nietzsche, "Der Fall Wagner."
50. Ekenstam, "Rädd att falla," 45.
51. Ibid., 55.

52. Kuzniar, *Queer German Cinema*, 276.

53. Seiler, *Zarah Leander*, 183–184.

Works Cited

Ahmed, Sara. *The Cultural Politics of Emotion*. New York: Routledge, 2004.

Ascheid, Antje. *Hitler's Heroines: Stardom and Womanhood in Nazi Cinema*. Philadelphia: Temple University Press, 2003.

Boëthius, Maria-Pia. *Heder och samvete: Sverige och andra världskriget* (Honor and conscience: Sweden and WWII). Stockholm: Ordfront, 1991.

Broch, Hermann. "Einige Bemerkungen zum Problem des Kitsches." In *Dichten und Erkennen: Gesammelte Werke. Essays*, Band 1. Zurich: Rhein Verlag, 1955.

Carter, Erica. *Dietrich's Ghosts: The Sublime and the Beautiful in Third Reich Film*. London: British Film Institute, 2004.

Cleto, Fabio. *Camp: Queer Aesthetics and the Performing Subject. A Reader*. Ann Arbor: University of Michigan Press, 1999.

Dyer, Richard. "Judy Garland and Gay Men." In *Heavenly Bodies: Film Stars and Society*. 2nd edition, 137–191. London: Routledge, 2004.

Ekenstam, Claes. *Rädd att falla: Studier i manlighet* (Afraid to Fall: Studies of Masculinity). Stockholm: Gidlunds, 1998.

Farmer, Brett. "The Fabulous Sublimity of Gay Diva Worship." *Camera Obscura* 20 (2005): 165–195.

Felski, Rita. *The Gender of Modernity*. Cambridge, MA: Harvard University Press, 1999.

Giesz, Ludwig. *Phänomenologie des Kitsches*. Munich: Wilhelm Fink Verlag, 1971.

Halberstam, J. Jack. "Queer Studies." In *A Companion to Gender Studies*, edited by Philomena Essed, David Theo Goldberg, and Audrey Lynn Kobayashi, 62–72. Malsen, MA: Blackwell, 2005.

Harris, Daniel. *The Rise and Fall of Gay Culture*. New York: Ballantine, 1999.

Higgins, Kathleen. "Sweet Kitsch." In *The Philosophy of Visual Arts*, edited by Philip Alperson, 568–581. New York: Oxford University Press, 1990.

Holm, Michael. "Bögarnas Zarah." *Revolt* 11 (1981): 18.

Knight, Deborah. "Why We Enjoy Condemning Sentimentality: A Meta-Aesthetic Perspective." In *Journal of Aesthetics and Art Criticism* 57 (1999): 411–420.

Knopp, Guido. *Hitlers Frauen und Marlene*. Munich: Bertelsmann, 2001.

Koestenbaum, Wayne. *The Queen's Throat: Opera, Homosexuality and the Mystery of Desire*. London: Penguin, 1993.

Kosofsky Sedgwick, Eve. "Paranoid Reading and Reparative Reading, or, You're So Paranoid, You Probably Think This Essay Is About You." In *Touching Feeling: Affect, Pedagogy, Performativity*. Durham: Duke University Press, 2003.

Kraus, Chris. *I love Dick*. Cambridge, MA: MIT Press, 2006.

Kulka, Tomas. "Kitsch." *British Journal of Aesthetics* 28 (1988): 18–27.

Kupfer, Joseph. "The Sentimental Self." *Canadian Journal of Philosophy* (1996): 543–550.

Kuzniar, Alice A. *The Queer German Cinema*. Stanford, CA: Stanford University Press, 2000.

Leander, Zarah. *Vill ni se en diva?* (Would you like to see a diva?). Stockholm: Wahlström & Widstrand, 1958.

Nietzsche, Friedrich. "Der Fall Wagner." *Sämtliche Werke, Band 6*. Munich: DTV, 1988.

Rosenberg, Tiina. "Schlager, känslor och svensk homokultur" (Schlager, Emotions, and Swedish Gay Culture). In *Queersverige*, edited by Don Kulick, 336–363. Stockholm: Natur och Kultur, 2005.

———. "The Touch of Opera: Or, Can a Feminist Forgive Anything for a Good Tune?" *Journal of Theatre and Drama* 4 (1998): 23–36. Reprinted in this volume.

Rosenkranz, Bernhard, and Gottfried Lorenz. *Hamburg auf anderen Wegen. Die Geschichte des schwulen Lebens in der Hansestadt.* Hamburg: Lambda, 2005.

Seiler, Paul. *Zarah Leander. Ein Kultbuch.* Hamburg: Rowohlt, 1985.

Solomon, Robert C. "In Defense of Sentimentality." *Philosophy and Literature* 14 (1990): 304–323.

Warner, Michael. *The Trouble with the Normal: Sex, Politics and the Ethics of Queer Life.* Cambridge, MA: Harvard University Press, 1999.

Wood, Elizabeth. "Sapphonics." In *Queering the Pitch: The New Gay and Lesbian Musicology,* edited by Philipp Brett, Elizabeth Wood, and Gary C. Thomas, 27–66. New York: Routledge, 1994.

Guerrillero Heroico. Ernesto Che Guevara at the funeral for victims of the La Coubre explosion, 1960. Photographer: Alberto Diaz Gutierrez (Alberto Korda). Public domain / Museo Che Guevara (Centro de Estudios Che Guevara en La Habana, Cuba). https://en.wikipedia.org/wiki/Guerrillero_Heroico#/media/File:Heroico1.jpg

5. The Soundtrack of Revolution: Memory, Affect, and the Power of Protest Songs

Overture

We have all been there: Suddenly a melody comes into our heads without our knowing how it got there. On a recent trip to Cuba I heard the refrain of a long forgotten song: "Aquí se queda la clara / la entrañable transparencia / de tu querida presencia / Comandante Che Guevara" (Your beloved and luminous presence / became clear here / Comandante Che Guevara). With tears in my eyes I tried to explain to my partner that they were playing *the* song. "Which song?" she asked, but I was already heading for the bandstand, drawn by the music of *Hasta Siempre* (Forever), the popular song about Ernesto Guevara, better known to the world as Che or "Comandante."

It was my emotional and melodramatic soundtrack talking back to me. Many cultural representations in the form of songs, photographs, literature, theatre, film, television, and other media are so deeply ideologically engraved in our hearts that they are often difficult to define or analyze. Whether we like it or not, emotions are embedded as a cultural and social soundtrack of memories. Feminist scholarship over the past decade has emphasized that affects and emotions are the foundation of human interaction. The cognitive understanding of the world has given way to a gender analysis in which questions about the relationship between "our" and the "other's" feelings and how we relate to the world as human beings are central.[1] The world is an affective place and life supplies us with melodies to accompany us on our journey.

What made me wonder was how the memory of a forgotten song transformed itself into a haunting melody? *Hasta siempre* is

---

How to cite this book chapter:
Rosenberg, Tiina 2016. The Soundtrack of Revolution: Memory, Affect, and the Power of Protest Songs. In: Rosenberg, Tiina *Don't Be Quiet, Start a Riot! Essays on Feminism and Performance.* Pp. 100–116. Stockholm: Stockholm University Press. DOI: http://dx.doi.org/10.16993/baf.e. License: CC-BY 4.0

performed everywhere in Cuba, but it was not the performance I recalled; it was the melody that persisted, clinging to me, and refusing to let go. It welcomed me and my memories back to Cuba.

The haunting melody

The interaction between melody and memory is complex. In *The Haunting Melody*, psychoanalyst Theodor Reik discusses his experiences in life and music. He asks what it means when a melody intrudes in the middle of unrelated thoughts, while your mind is occupied with rational and purposive considerations.[2] Musical memory is linked to the process of retention, recall, and recognition, a notion that Sigmund Freud mentions in passing in his *Psychopathology of Everyday Life* but does not develop further. Freud's general aversion to music is his well-known, although late in life he developed a fondness for Mozart, especially *Don Giovanni* and *Le nozze di Figaro*. Brisk walks used to stimulate the flow of Freud's thoughts, rather than music. One of the reasons he disliked music has been identified as musicogenic epilepsy, a strong physical and memory-based epileptic reaction to music that Freud also observed in his patients.[3] It is, of course, difficult to say why someone as culturally well-rounded as Freud was not found of music. He simply described himself as being "ganz unmusikalisch," totally unmusical.[4]

Other psychoanalysts have taken an interest in music, Reik among them. His curiosity in this area was awakened when a melody from Mahler's *Symphony No. 2, The Resurrection,* lodged in his mind during a walk in the Alps, an experience that he said took him a lifetime to understand.[5] Reik describes how he was beset by Mahler's music, which refused to leave him. This experience made him want to write a book about melodies that haunt people. Reik hoped that an analysis of this phenomenon in general, and his own attraction to Mahler's symphony in particular, would help him understand the message of his unconscious. The outcome was a unique and fascinating self-analysis of what Reik heard in Mahler's music: it was the fundamental conflict that guided Reik's whole life, namely, the struggle between shameful feelings of worthlessness and grandiose overcompensation.

Reik discovered that melodies give voice to the unconscious: the unknown self begins to sing because music is so close to our emotions. He also found that the triumph of Mahler's symphony was not that it consoled him for the loss of a beloved friend, Karl Abraham; rather, it expressed his forbidden joy in Abraham's death. Reik had secretly longed to supplant Abraham in 1925 as the world's leading psychoanalyst. He now concluded that the haunting melody that would not leave him was his unconscious trying to tell him something about his own self that had been forgotten or become constricted, something that was once important to him.

Protests in public places

It is midnight in Chicago's Grant Park on November 4, 2008. Barack Obama has just been elected the first African-American president of the United States. He stands on a platform in the chill night air and tells 100,000 cheering supporters, "It's been a long time coming, but tonight, because of what we did on this day, in this election, at this defining moment, change has come to America."[6] The line has a familiar ring. It is a paraphrase of words written by soul singer Sam Cooke some forty-five years earlier: "It's been a long, a long time coming, but I know a change gon' come. . ." At this historic moment, the president-elect borrowed the most memorable line of his acceptance speech from an old protest song.

Most cities have a public space in the form of a central square. Recent demonstrations in the Middle East, at Syntagma Square in Athens, the Occupy Wall Street movement in the US, Los Indignados in Spain, and the student revolts in Chile are just a few examples of the return to the *agora*, Athens' classic square in which free citizens (women and slaves excluded) could participate in their city's democratic processes. Although today new social media are effective in spreading information, demonstrations still require the bodily presence of individuals in order to instill power into political slogans. There are many examples of the organization of public space in the history of demonstrations. The large trans-local Vietnam demonstrations of the late 1960s, the demonstrations of the anti-globalization movement that began in Seattle in 1999, the anti-war demonstrations over the invasion of Iraq in the early 2000s, and the massive demonstrations in different parts of the world in 2010 and 2011 (so numerous and intense that

Time magazine chose The Protester as the 2011 personality of the year) all showed how to occupy and use public space.

Public protests are a significant part of activist culture. The post 9/11 period has greatly restricted protests and the use of public space in the West. At the beginning of the twentieth century it was still possible to shut down factories, and sometimes even whole cities, through strikes. Protest occupations and sit-ins were a tool the labor movement used to challenge the capitalist political economy. Trade unions were linked in solidarity to form a larger social movement. "It created an awareness of the importance of 'taking' physical locations," observed historian Rosemary Feuer in an interview.[7] New social media are important, but there is no revolt possible without a physical presence and the collective corporeality of specific locations. What remains of this tradition today, according to Feuer, are solidarity rallies that last for a day or two. She believes that the Arab Spring and its spin-off in the Occupy Wall Street movement have reminded people of the need to have *physical* social spaces in order to build protest movements and communities.[8]

Protest songs

Demonstrations, however, require more than physical locations in which to gather; the atmosphere is equally important. As a result, demonstration movements depend on certain vital aesthetic elements such as music. During the Arab Spring of 2011, several songs were performed and recorded in Tahrir Square. The singer known as El General (Hamada Ben Amor) challenged the Tunisian president (now ex-president) Zine El Abedine Ben Ali with the song *Mr. President, Your People are Dying*, a protest refrain that quickly spread via the Internet. Hip-hop and rap have emerged as the genres of the younger generation's protest music because they are simply and cheaply produced, and because of their immediacy. In place of a band of musicians, all a rapper needs is a beat and something to say. It has become the undisputed contemporary genre for advancing social criticism.[9]

Protest and battle songs date back millennia. During the French Revolution people were marching to the tune of *La Marsellaise*, which was later to become the country's national anthem: "Aux armes, citoyens / formez vos bataillons / marchons, marchons! / Qu'un sang impur / Abreuve nos sillons!" (To arms, citizens / form your battalions! / March, march! / Let impure blood water our furrows!) *The Internationale*, the song of the labor movement that dates back to the early 1900s, is still sung on squares around the world on May Day in celebration of the movement's birth. In the 1960s, the music of Bob Dylan and Joan Baez attracted thousands of people to outdoor concerts, while the London riots of 2011 were accompanied by dance music that created a completely different atmosphere, reminiscent of some of the sounds of The Clash's classic *London Calling*.[10]

The commitment and mood of political gatherings are what drew people to such demonstrations. Baez, who rose to prominence at the Newport Festival in 1960, fought against racism with Martin Luther King Jr., traveled to Vietnam, and was imprisoned, has stated that "politics would be very unrealistic in the streets unless it involves music. The music pours forth from the soul, especially in times of crisis."[11] She sees rock and pop music as having coincided in a fruitful union in the American protest movements of 1960s and 1970s: "I call it 'the perfect storm': the music, politics, the civil rights movement, the war in Vietnam."[12] Dorian Lynskey writes that in order for a protest song to take hold it must be part of a larger political movement. He concludes that while the past fifteen years may have seen many protest songs, no larger social movement has emerged to unite them. However, music can act as a mediator and cohesive element, as has happened to the Internet-based music culture of the Arab Spring.[13]

Lynskey treats protest songs as a form of pop music that arises out of concern, anger, doubt, and, in almost every case, sincere emotion. However, film scholar Linda Williams points to melodrama, horror, and pornographic films as "body genres" that use tears, fear, and sexual arousal to elicit visceral reactions among viewers.[14] Her idea recalls Aristotle's theory of catharsis and can also be applied to a certain kind of music that requires immense exertion from performers and, in turn, provokes strong corporeal responses among members of the audience. Protest song is such a genre.

An emotion is usually the immediate physiological reaction to a stimulus. Characteristic of emotions is that they are bodily expressions, and bodily responses are more immediate than conscious emotional awareness. Human beings become aware of their reactions only after the fact. Affects are inscribed on our emotional and memory-based soundtracks early in life. These memories are archived and may appear when least expected. Bodily-based affects are the total sum of the events one has experienced. Thus, how people relate to their emotions is not only determined by the individual, but by one's life history and the culture of which we are all a part as well. My trip to Cuba brought something vital from the past to life again. In my own case it took the form of tears.

The refrain of a song

Hasta siempre exists in a number of versions: the Cuban revolutionary original, a rock tune, Latino pop, jazz, salsa, bolero, reggae, and hip-hop/rap. The Cuban composer Carlos Pueblo wrote it in 1965 in response to Che Guevara's farewell letter to the Cuban people. *Hasta siempre* expresses the gratitude of the Cuban people to their beloved Che.

> Aprendimos a quererte / desde la histórica altura donde el sol de tu bravura / le puso cerco a la muerte. *Chrous:* Aquí se queda la clara / la entrañable transparencia / de tu querida presencia / Comandante Che Guevara. Tu mano gloriosa y fuerte /sobre la historia dispara / cuando todo Santa Clara / se despierta para verte. *Chorus:* Aquí se queda la clara / la entrañable transparencia / de tu querida presencia / Comandante Che Guevara. Vienes quemando la brisa / con soles de primavera/ para plantar la bandera / con la luz de tu sonrisa. *Chorus:* Aquí se queda la clara / la entrañable transparencia / de tu querida presencia / Comandante Che Guevara. Tu amor revolucionario / te conduce a nueva empresa / donde esperan la firmeza / de tu brazo libertario. *Chrous:* Aquí se queda la clara / la entrañable transparencia / de tu querida presencia / Comandante Che Guevara. Seguiremos adelante/ como junto a ti seguimos / y con Fidel te decimos: Hasta siempre, Comandante! *Chrous:* Aquí se queda la clara / la entrañable transparencia / de tu querida presencia / Comandante Che Guevara.

In English translation, the song goes something like this:

We learned to love you / from the heights of history / with the radiance of your bravery / you laid siege to death. *Chorus:* Your beloved and luminous presence / became clear here / Comandante Che Guevara. Your glorious and strong hand / fires at history / when all of Santa Clara / awakens to see you. *Chorus:* Your beloved and luminous presence / became clear here / Comandante Che Guevara. You come burning the winds / with spring suns to plant the flag / with the light of your smile. *Chorus:* Your beloved and luminous presence / became clear here / Comandante Che Guevara. Your revolutionary love / leads you to a new undertaking / where they are awaiting the firmness/ of your liberating arm. *Chorus:* Your beloved and luminous presence / became clear here / Comandante Che Guevara. We will carry on / as we did together with you / and with Fidel we say to you / You will always be with us, Comandante! *Chorus:* Your beloved and luminous presence/ became clear here / Comandante Che Guevara.

Hasta siempre has clear religious overtones that it associates with a male revolutionary hero. It is not difficult to recognize the worship of another stereotypical altruistic male revolutionary, Jesus Christ, as the paradigm of *Hasta siempre*. It may, therefore, be relevant to ask whether I, as a queer feminist, can forgive anything for a good tune. Why am I crying as I listen to *Hasta siempre,* although I can understand all the problems connected with this sort of worship? I have elsewhere dealt with affect, voice, gender, and sexuality: the mezzo soprano in trouser roles ("the Sapphonics"); women in Wagner's operas (voice and power); Zarah Leander and queer diva culture; and, most recently, anger, hope, and solidarity.[15] The emotional connections are complex and we are not always in control of how our internal soundboard resonates when played upon by certain melodies. In Reik's psychoanalytical terms it is the unknown or forgotten self that sings in our heads.

As described in earlier essays in Chapters 1 and 2, Roland Barthes proposes the rebirth of the author "inside" of the artwork. He eliminates a specifically male position (i.e., the author, logos) by supplanting it with its overtly female, musical force: the voice. What we experience, Barthes writes, is the voice, not the musical notation, and it transcends its "masculinity."[16] In Barthes's thought, as in French poststructuralist theory in general, the feminine is a utopic space – the Promised Land we have not yet experienced. The voice is characterized by a certain instability that a prescriptive narrative has difficulty controlling. Thus, the person who gives voice to a haunting melody in a performance does not merely convey a given piece of music. She unlocks something forgotten that was once important to the listener, whose reaction need not be one of Freudian musicogenic epilepsy, although it is a physical occurrence nonetheless.

For Barthes, listening is a space where body and language meet, yet without completely merging into one another.[17] In this combination of the abstract and the corporeal he sees an art form devoid of a system of signifier and signified. The grain of the voice is the materiality of the body speaking its mother tongue. In my own case *Hasta siempre* carried me back to my personal entrance into leftist politics. The military takeover by Augusto Pinochet in Chile in 1973 awakened me politically when I was fifteen years old. This early political engagement was accompanied by a musical repertory of protest songs that I have carried in my memory to this day. *Hasta siempre*, in Barthes's terms, was my memory speaking in its mother tongue.

Sentimentality and revolutionary kitsch

I understand, of course, that I am the perfect target for the Cuban tourist industry in branding revolutionary nostalgia as kitsch and selling it to middle-aged leftist visitors from the West. My tears over unfinished revolutions of all kinds are an illustration of political sentimentality (but also frustration) over the state of leftist politics today.

Sentimentality has gotten a bad reputation because of its tawdry aesthetics. The scholars and theorists who associate sentimentality with kitsch, especially those who do so with political aspirations, are not only attentive analysts of loving and tender feelings: they also position sentimentality in a broader cultural and political context. There is no consensus as to what constitutes kitsch, but ever since the term was coined in Germany around 1870, it has enjoyed a certain notoriety as an epithet that denotes worthless, commercial art, or simply any kind of poor, mass-produced art with direct access to the emotions.[18] Emotions have long been viewed with suspicion, although some philosophers such as Hume have praised the value of emotions in relation to reason, rationality, and morality. Research increasingly shows that emotions cannot only be seen as a threat to rationality, but may be a prerequisite to it.[19] Theorists have emphasized how affects have assumed a central role in society, especially as elements of social networks and new social media.

Feminist theorist Sara Ahmed explores how emotions work to shape the "surfaces" of individual and collective bodies, so that bodies take the shape of the contact they have with objects and others.[20]

> One way of reflecting on this history of thinking about emotion is to consider the debate about the relation between emotion, bodily sensation and cognition.
> Emotion is the feeling of bodily change. The immediacy of the 'is' suggests that emotions do not involve processes of attribution or evaluation: we feel fear, for example, because our heart is racing, our skin is sweating. A cognitivist view would be represented by Aristotle, and by a number of thinkers who follow him.[21]

Approaching emotions as a form of cultural politics or world-making, Ahmed finds that the cultural politics of emotions

> developed not only as a critique of the psychologizing and privatization of emotions, but also as a critique of a model of social structure that neglects the emotional intensities, which allow such structures to be reified as forms of being. Attention to emotions allows us to address the question of how subjects become *invested* in particular structures such that their demise is felt as a kind of living death.[22]

The early critique of kitsch and sentimentality in the 1950s and 1960s was based on an analysis of Nazism and its use of emotionality for political propaganda. Queer theorists interested in camp as a special cultural sensibility have reevaluated this notion for queer culture. Susan Sontag was the first to do so in her groundbreaking essay "Notes on Camp," followed by a number of queer scholars writing on aesthetic theory.[23] David Bergman has formulated a general definition of camp as follows:

First, everyone agrees that camp is a style (whether of objects or of the way objects are perceived is debated) that favors 'exaggeration', 'artifice' and 'extremity'. Second, camp exists in tension with popular culture, commercial culture, or consumerist culture. Third, the person who can recognize camp, who sees things as campy, or who can camp is a person outside of the cultural mainstream. Fourth, camp is affiliated with homosexual culture, or at least with a self-conscious eroticism that throws into question the naturalization of desire.[24]

In this reinterpretation of kitsch as an element of camp, it forms its own aesthetic category, a status it shares with queer as culturally undesirable. Also, like queer, kitsch has been banished to the nether realms of cultural history, to oblivion, the domain of the invisible and inaudible. As stated in the previous chapter, much like the way sentimentality is denied or described as perverse, the disdain for kitsch appears to have created for itself a special place of cultural and artistic non-existence that constantly demands vigilance to keep contained, but at the same time has to be disregarded so as not to sully normative 'great' art and culture. Nevertheless, unsophisticated junk – artistic detritus – has a unique allure.[25] There is a reason why Flaubert's Emma Bovary wallows in a sentimental flood of emotions. It is about pleasure, shameful and guilty as it may be, but still pleasurable in opposition to the dreariness of work and everyday routines. Richard Dyer writes that the dream of being at one with one's body and in harmony with other bodies (united in and through differences) is the feeling of socialism. However, socialism does not emanate from us naturally: it is the harmony we create together.[26]

Last movement

I enjoyed my revolutionary kitsch because it reminded me of many things I still believe in.[27] While a great deal of music is compelling, kitschy sentimentalism seems to possess overwhelming power that circumvents common sense and goes straight for the emotions. As in the case of Zarah Leander in Chapter 4, revolutionary kitsch merges tears, body, and sensuality to form a unity that does not slacken its grip.

The complex emotions *Hasta siempre* aroused in me after so many years are a tribute to the emotional power of music. Music as a mediator of the emotions is more potent than words because melody is closer to our feelings than logos. By the time a melody resurfaces and takes possession of our minds, we may wonder how it came there. The haunting Cuban melody also reminded me that one never gets the revolution one wants. Human life and social justice require solidarity, but solidarity cannot be their sole element. New social movements and their accompanying coalition politics often refuse to let themselves be guided by political parties or parliamentary systems. While they may make room for novel social forces that may emerge, they often fail to achieve a durable, comprehensive political solution without falling into totalitarianism.

If political empathy makes us share the feelings and experiences of others, solidarity, which affirms our humanity, becomes an attribute with principles. Empathy can foster individualization or a group-specific collectivization of emotion, but it may not necessarily extend to broader social issues. It is in the recognition of the other's needs that politics begin, a process that also plays a vital role in art.

Feminists cannot focus exclusively on gender, just as socialists cannot concern themselves only with class relations. Contemporary leftist movements that deal with commonalities do not require uniformity in their political ranks, but they must stress multi-solidarity. Being a member of the anti-racist struggle should make it easier to have a feminist perspective on racism, tie the fists against homophobia, and believe that a clear boundary will always exist between rich and poor. Multi-solidarity means that although a person may feel most at home in one social movement, other perspectives should not be rejected. Even Marxist theorist Antonio Gramsci realized that the Left needs to incorporate new social movements, regardless of their transient ideological status.[28] The price for not doing so is reaction and ultimately fascism, as the dominant classes and their representatives come to fear that such movements may threaten their interests.

Multi-solidarity is inspiring, not divisive. It forces us to cooperate with one another across borders, but not at each other's expense. The decision to give priority to class struggle was used by the early labor movement as an argument against addressing women's demands for action. Not until the 1970s did socialist feminists dare to question such a dichotomy and unite under a new slogan: "No class struggle without women's struggle, no women's struggle without class struggle." Multi-solidarity encourages parallel perspectives. One form of discrimination recognizes the other, and so both are addressed by a larger social movement where political questions are voiced and negotiated. Freedom requires interpersonal solidarity, ethical action, meaningful work, cultural awareness, and shared prosperity. People can only be free together, not in isolation.

The Cubans have had considerable success in developing a musical culture to accompany the Revolution. The iconic power of the Cuban Revolution has inspired the kind of solidarity and devotion that Wayne Koestenbaum has characterized in his works on Maria Callas and Jackie Kennedy.[29] The worship of these two icons can be puzzling, but seems to release a yearning for a different kind of life among their devoted fans. Emotional experiences are amplified and have legitimacy when others share them, enabling the many to do things they could not have accomplished on their own. One way to bring this about is by rallying people around common symbols. Dyer points out that entertainment "presents, head-on as it were, what utopia would feel like, rather than how it would be organized. It thus works at the level of sensibility, by which I mean an affective code that is characteristic of, and largely specific to, a given mode of cultural production."[30] In a word, *Hasta siempre* makes me *feel* the revolution.

There are certainly many important things I have forgotten over my life's course – memories that need to be acknowledged and reflected upon. These memories are no coincidences, Freud would say; they are my forgotten self singing to me. Embarrassing, perhaps. But Reik's recollection of two lines from a childhood song that came back to him while writing *The Haunting Melody* is comforting. It was a refrain that seemed to echo the final scene in Odysseus' wanderings when, with an oar on his shoulder, he sets forth once more from his cherished home to seek an abode of peace. His quest seems to mirror Reik's own thought: "Wo man singt, da lass dich ruhig nieder, böse Menschen haben keine

Lieder" (Where people are singing, that's where you should settle down. Evil men don't have songs.)[31]

Notes

1. Ahmed, *Cultural Politics*, 5–12.
2. Reik, *Haunting Melody*, vii.
3. Roth, "Freud's Dislike of Music."
4. Ibid., 759.
5. Reik, *Haunting Melody*, 220.
6. Lynskey, *Thirty-three Revolutions*, xiii.
7. Quoted in Hellquist, *Mästare i protester*, 6.
8. Ibid.
9. Eyerman & Jamison, *Music and Social Movements*; Hebdige, *Subculture*; Lynskey, *Thirty-three Revolutions*; Rose, *Hip Hop Wars*; Sernhede & Söderman, *Hip Hop in Sweden*.
10. Lynskey, *Thirty-three Revolutions*; xiii.
11. Ibid.
12. Quoted in Hellquist, *Mästare i protester*.
13. Lynskey, *Thirty-three Revolutions*, xiii-xvi.
14. Williams, *Film Bodies*.
15. Rosenberg, *Byxbegär*; "Touch of Opera"; "Elsa!"; *Bögarnas Zarah*; *Ilska, hopp och solidaritet*.
16. Barthes, *Le grain de las voix*.
17. Ibid.
18. Broch, "Einige Bemerkungen."
19. Ahmed, *Cultural Politics*; Berlant, *Compassion*; Cvetkovich, *Archive of Feelings*; Nussbaum, *Upheavals of Thought*.
20. Ahmed, *Cultural Politics*, 1.
21. Ibid., 2.
22. Ibid., 12.

23. Sontag, "Notes on 'Camp'"; Cleto, *Camp*; Dyer, "Entertainment and Utopia"; Koestenbaum, *The Queen's Throat*.

24. Quoted in Cleto, *Camp*, 4.

25. Rosenberg, *Bögarnas Zarah*.

26. Dyer, "A Bit of Uplift," 13.

27. Higgins, "Sweet Kitsch."

28. Gramsci, *Prison Notebooks*.

29. Koestenbaum, *The Queen's Throat*; *Jackie Under My Skin*; *Cleavage*.

30. Dyer, "Entertainment and Utopia," 20.

31. Reik, *Haunting Melody*, 145

Works Cited

Ahmed, Sara. *The Cultural Politics of Emotion*. New York: Routledge, 2004.

Barthes, Roland. *Le grain de la voix: Entretiens 1962–1980*, Paris: Editions de Seuil, 1981.

Berlant, Lauren, ed. *Compassion: The Culture and Politics of an Emotion*. New York: Routledge, 2004.

Broch, Hermann. "Einige Bemerkungen zum Problem des Kitsches." In *Dichten und Erkennen, Essays – Band 1 (Gesammelte Werke [6])*, 295–309. Zurich: Rhein Verlag, 1955.

Cleto, Fabio. *Camp: Queer Aesthetics and the Performing Subject. A Reader*. Ann Arbor: University of Michigan Press, 1999.

Cvetkovich, Ann. *An Archive of Feelings: Trauma, Sexuality, and Lesbian Public Cultures*. Durham: Duke University Press, 2003.

Deutschmann, David, and Deborah Shnookal. *Fidel Castro Reader*. Melbourne: Ocean Press, 2007.

Dyer, Richard. "Entertainment and Utopia." In *Only Entertainment*, 19–36. London: Routledge, 2002 [1992].

———."A Bit of Uplift." In *Only Entertainment*, 10–13. London: Routledge, 2002 [1992].

Eyerman, Ron, and Andrew Jamison. *Music and Social Movements: Mobilizing Traditions in the Twentieth Century*. Cambridge, UK: Cambridge University Press, 1998.

Felski, Rita. *The Gender of Modernity*. Cambridge, MA: Harvard University Press, 1995.

Giesz, Ludwig. *Phänomenologie des Kitsches*. Munich: Wilhelm Fink Verlag, 1971.

Gramsci, Antonio. *Selections from the Prison Notebooks*. London: Lawrence & Wishart, 1971.

Hebdige, Dick. *Subculture: The Meaning of Style*. London: Methuen, 1979.

Hellquist, Annie. "Mästare i protester" (Masters of Protests). *Arbetaren* 51–52 (2011): 6.

Higgins, Kathleen. "Sweet Kitsch." In *The Philosophy of the Visual Arts*, edited by Philip Alperson, 568–582. New York: Oxford University Press, 1990.

Knight, Deborah. "Why We Enjoy Condemning Sentimentality: A Meta-Aesthetic Perspective." *Journal of Aesthetics and Art Criticism* 57 (1999): 411–420.

Koestenbaum, Wayne. *The Queen's Throat: Opera, Homosexuality and the Mystery of Desire*. London: Penguin, 1993.

———. *Jackie Under My Skin: Interpreting an Icon*. London: Penguin, 1996.

———. *Cleavage: Essays on Sex, Stars, and Aesthetics*. New York: Ballantine, 2000.

Kulka, Thomas. "Kitsch." *British Journal of Aesthetics* 28 (1988): 18–27.

Kupfer Joseph. "The Sentimental Self." *Canadian Journal of Philosophy* 20 (1996): 543–550.

Lynskey, Dorian. *33 Revolutions Per Minute: A History of Protest Songs from Billie Holiday to Green Day*. London: Harper Collins, 2011.

Nietzsche, Friedrich. *Der Fall Wagner: Schriften und Aufzeichnungen über Richard Wagner*. Frankfurt: Insel Verlag, 1983 [1888].

Nussbaum, Martha. *Upheavals of Thought: The Intelligence of Emotions.* Cambridge, UK: Cambridge University Press, 2003.

Reik, Theodor. *The Haunting Melody: Psychoanalytic Experiences in Life and Music.* New York: Farrar, 1953.

Rose, Tricia. *Black Noise: Rap Music and Black Culture in Contemporary America.* Liverpool: Wesleyan University Press, 1994.

———. *The Hip Hop Wars: What We Talk About When We Talk About Hip Hop and Why It Matters.* New York: Basic Books, 2008.

Rosenberg, Tiina. "The Touch of Opera: Or, Can a Feminist Forgive Anything for a Good Tune?" *Journal of Theatre and Drama* 4 (1998): 23–36.

———. *Byxbegär* (Desiring Pants). Gothenburg: Anamma, 2000.

———. "Elsa! Har du väl förstått mig? Feministiska reflexioner kring Wagners *Lohengrin* ("Elsa! Do You Understand What I Am Saying? Feminist Reflections on Wagner's *Lohengrin*"). In *Operavärldar,* edited by Torsten Pettersson, 191–218. Stockholm: Atlantis, 2006.

———. *Bögarnas Zarah: Diva, ikon, kult* (Queer Zarah: Diva, Icon, Cult). Stockholm: Normal Förlag, 2009.

———. *Ilska, hopp och solidaritet. Med feministisk scenkonst in i framtiden* (Anger, Hope, and Solidarity. Carrying Feminist Performance into the Future). Stockholm: Atlas, 2012.

Roth, Nathan. "Sigmund Freud's Dislike of Music: A Piece of Epileptology." *Bulletin of the New York Academy of Medicine* 62 (1986): 759–765.

Sernhede, Ove, and Johan Söderman. *Hip Hop in Sweden: A Voice for Marginalized Youth.* New York: Peter Lang, 2012.

Sontag, Susan. "Notes on 'Camp.'" In *Against Interpretation, and Other Essays,* 275–292. New York: Farrar, 1964.

Williams, Linda. "Film Bodies: Gender, Genre, and Excess." *Film Quarterly* 44 (1991): 2–13.

PART 2:
SCANDINAVIAN CLASSICS

The Queen's Diadem (Carl Jonas Love Almqvist). Elin Klinga (Tintomara) and Anja Lundquist (Adolfine). Royal Dramatic Theatre, Stockholm, 2008. Photographer: Roger Stenberg. Copyright CC-BY-NC-ND, Royal Dramatic Theatre, Stockholm.

6. Queer Tintomara: Ephemeral and Elusive Gender(s) in *The Queen's Diadem*

> No one will find me,
> I will find no one.
> I smile at each one,
> they all smile at me.
>
> Tintomara's Song (QD, 134)[1]

Transcending borders has been one of the key terms of queer theory. The prefix "trans" indicates the possibility of moving between different gender roles and sexual categories. This type of kinesis interests queer theorists, who aim at creating more flexible options for the heteronormative definitions of gender and sexuality. Ideas and practices that cross borders, however, are not limited to recent contemporary theorists; they also apply to a novelist of the Romantic period who delights in transformations and unforeseen encounters. One work in particular, *The Queen's Diadem* (*Drottningens juvelsmycke*), is considered a true gender classic of Swedish literature. The novel was written by Carl Jonas Love Almqvist (1793–1866) in 1834 as the fourth installment in a series entitled *Törnrosens bok* (The Book of the Thorn Rose). Almqvist creates a theatrical fantasy world where boundaries are transcended. *The Queen's Diadem* also presents the intriguing figure of Azouras Lazuli Tintomara, an androgynous character loved by women and men alike, but who in fact does not love anyone apart from her mother.[2]

The Queen's Diadem forms an important bridge between the Romantic and the Postmodern eras as a work of literature, and for its gender thematics. Objects of desire shift according to the

---

How to cite this book chapter:
Rosenberg, Tiina 2016. Queer Tintomara: Ephemeral and Elusive Gender(s) in *The Queen's Diadem*. In: Rosenberg, Tiina *Don't Be Quiet, Start a Riot! Essays on Feminism and Performance*. Pp. 118–149. Stockholm: Stockholm University Press. DOI: http://dx.doi.org/10.16993/baf.f. License: CC-BY 4.0

ever-changing gender status of Tintomara. Examining aspects of Tintomara's androgyny, that is, her sexuality or asexuality, will show how the variability of her gender kindles a passion in others, and allows desire to blossom into a realm of possibilities.

A queer interpretation

A contemporary reading of *The Queen's Diadem* cannot help drawing attention to its queer potential. The foundation of the queer perspective is that the predominant culture is heteronormative, but not necessarily heterosexual. In the Western world a certain tension or ambiguity, perhaps also an uncertainty, exists between homophobia and homoerotics, and the issue of whether same-sex desire may only be limited to homosexuals. If such longing applies to everyone, heterosexual culture and its manifestations are hardly as clear-cut as one may assume: fragments of queer may be embedded.[3]

Queer has acquired multiple meanings over the past few decades. It is most commonly perceived as a synonym for lesbian, gay, bisexual, transgender, or queer (LGBTQ) identities, or as an umbrella term for a variety of non-heterosexual and non-normative gender statuses. However, queer has occasionally been applied to non-heterosexual phenomena that cannot be clearly labeled as LGBTQ. In these cases queer appears to internalize or allude to one or more of the above categories, sometimes in a confusing or incongruous manner. Queer has also been used to indicate forms of spectator perspectives, interpretations, works of art, cultural phenomena, and textual coding systems that fall outside the gender and sexual conceptions related to heterosexual or LGBTQ identities. Thus, the term queer may apply to anything beyond the traditional categories of gender and sexuality.[4]

Queer reading has its roots in the approach to literature that allows alternative interpretation. It leans toward the feminist tradition and is informed by lesbian and gay studies in the humanities. Nevertheless, queer interpretation is not entirely synonymous with classic feminist methodology, which does not hesitate to go against the grain in order to highlight inherent sexism – or, conversely, hidden feminist traits.

Queer interpretation goes a step further by juxtaposing itself to non-queer. However, its intention is not only to produce analyses of literary or other artistic works by non-straight authors and artists. Its theoretical starting point is that queer is at the nexus of culture, just as non-queer has been. Queer interpretation, therefore, must assume that queer has the potential to be present in all works of art. Queer readings may be applied to any text, film, theatrical performance, artwork, or product of popular culture, without the interpreter needing to cite queer as a prominent element in such work.

Tintomara: The androgyne in literary study

The Queen's Diadem takes place in Sweden in 1792. An opera masquerade ball coincides with the assassination of "Theatre King" Gustav III of Sweden. The novel centers around the theft of a priceless royal gem. The curious and remarkably beautiful Tintomara, a dancer, is the protagonist who has stolen the jewel – a diadem. However, unbeknownst to Tintomara, she also serves as Gustav III's decoy at the fatal opera masquerade. Tintomara is the half-sister of the heir apparent; Equerry Munck is supposedly her father. She is soon to be swept up in a political power struggle that erupts as a backlash to the king's murder. A pawn in the cunning scheme, Tintomara is ultimately shot by an assassin.

Desired by women and men alike, Tintomara comes between two sisters, Amanda and Adolfine, and their suitors, Captain Ferdinand and Major Clas Henrik. The recurrence in the novel of the five of spades and the five of hearts symbolizes the conflict. A case of mistaken identities entangles the two couples in a drama of jealousy enacted in a dream-like forest in northern Stockholm. The story has clear parallels to Mozart's operas *Così fan tutte* and *Le nozze di Figaro*. It culminates in a duel between Ferdinand and Clas Henrik.

The prominence of androgyny in *The Queen's Diadem* was noticed soon after the novel first appeared. The role gender plays is so apparent that omitting it from an analysis would almost be impossible. Nevertheless, the first person to study gender and sexuality in Almqvist's works to any extent was Karin Westman Berg, a women's studies pioneer, whose work established the foundation for gender-based Almqvist research in Sweden.[5]

The issue of androgyny is discussed early on in Johan Mortensen's 1905 essay on the background of the Tintomara character. Mortensen sees French fairy tales and Matthew Lewis's classic Gothic novel *The Monk* (1796) as possible models for Tintomara. In the expanded 1917 version of his study, Mortensen deals with the erotic and demonic features of *The Queen's Diadem*, drawing comparisons to another androgynous figure, Goethe's Mignon. Hans Hagedorn Thomsen continues this line of thought in a 1970 analysis that aligns Tintomara with other androgynous literary characters. Thomsen emphasizes Tintomara's metaphysical nature: on the one hand she represents human striving toward an "ultimate goal," and on the other she embodies the creative process. Hagedorn Thomsen interprets Tintomara as a fiction within a fictitious world that is devoid of any socially significant incongruities with regard to gender. He highlights the central symbolism surrounding Tintomara: the ruby, the hermaphrodite, and the square room, which he construes as totality symbols. However, Olle Holmberg, who republished Almqvist's novel in 1922, saw no meaningful link between the character of Tintomara and the androgynous musings of the German Romantics. Rather than having two genders, Tintomara, according to Holmberg, was genderless. He describes her as a "painted arabesque," a beautiful but hollow helix who loves no one and lives by no rules.[6]

A work that more clearly assesses the gender issue in *The Queen's Diadem* is Eva Adolfsson's article "Det androgyna skapandet: en Almqvistläsning" (The androgynous creation: An Almqvist reading), which considers alternate understandings of the text. Initially, the androgynous character may be seen as a metaphor for the masquerades played by society. However, such an interpretation, Adolfsson cautions, takes one nowhere. She then deals with the polarities of freedom and isolation, describing Tintomara as a hero/heroine of neither sex, but rather an amalgam of both female and male characteristics. Tintomara lives outside the laws of god and man; her home is a peaceful, non-verbal maternal sanctuary.[7]

Anna Cavallin has brought the interpretation of Almqvist a step closer to the gender studies of today. She examines the mercurial nature of Tintomara's make-up as an illustration of the social construction of gender. By polemicizing earlier research, Cavallin weighs questions of gender, body, and power, concluding that Tintomara's acting constitutes resistance. Tintomara refuses to take on a submissive status, and in the end she perishes.[8]

A queer interpretation of *The Queen's Diadem* have also been made by Laura Margaret Desertain in a 1982 dissertation that emphasizes the novel's same-sex desire and sums up Tintomara as a natural lesbian. A 1999 article by Eva Borgström cites desire and queer erotics as the main themes of the novel. For her, the singing voices of the four young members of the nobility constitute a symbolic scale that encompasses both female and male voices. She draws comparisons to Plato's *Symposium* as one of the foremost intertexts of *The Queen's Diadem*, and also compares Almqvist's novel to Diderot's *Les bijoux indiscrets* (1748).[9]

Plato's *Symposium* and the myth of the androgyne

When Tintomara is first mentioned in *The Queen's Diadem*, surgeons are have been ordered by the police to inspect her body in order to determine her "true" sex.

> But certainly there must be something odd about this creature. The throat and the beginning of the chest, which I saw, were of a very pleasing, but strange structure, which seems to allow the former to be raised sometimes in conjunction with the contraction or hardening of the latter; on the contrary, at other times, the latter might be expanded, in conjunction with the diminution of the whole figure. (QD, 40-41).[10]

Tintomara is said to try have sometimes tried to escape "with the caressing, appealing expression of a suffering siren," but "at other times the same person would assume, suddenly and with fiery pride, a note of resistance which might almost seem masculine" (QD, 41).[11] The surgeon's remarks are directed solely at Tintomara's chest, voice, and temperament; the reader is therefore not privy to any observations regarding her genitalia (QD, 40-41).[12]

Tintomara, referred to with Almqvist by the Swedish feminine personal pronoun *hon* (she) despite the character's androgyny, is in police custody for questioning when at least six socialites (women and men) commit suicide after falling hopelessly in love with her. Why, we wonder, should the police even care? Unable to arrive at any conclusion, the surgeons wonder how to classify Tintomara, or why she needs to be categorized in the first place.

One of them offers the resigned comment, "The police don't seem to be able to tolerate one and the same individual being loved by all kinds of persons" (QD, 40).[13] Here Almqvist's narrative shows its indebtedness to a conversation on love that took place almost 2,500 years ago.

Plato's *Symposium* is generally acknowledged to be the background to *The Queen's Diadem*. Same-sex eroticism was on a higher plane in the *Symposium* than heterosexual eroticism. For Plato, the love (*eros*) between two men was above the love of a woman and a man. The *Symposium* is a conversation that Plato is supposed to have heard about and recorded. In it, seven men, including Socrates, attend a banquet where they take turns discussing the principles of love.

In pursuit of its origins, Socrates presents as Plato's voice a myth about androgynies. In the beginning, the human body was not singular but dual. It had two faces, four arms, four legs, and two sets of genitals. "Man" was self-absorbed, closed off, harmonious, a perfect entity, a whole unto himself. However, he was so content enjoying his own company that he neglected his responsibilities towards the gods. This angered the gods, so they decided to reconfigure the human body and split it into two parts. Since that moment, each half has been searching the world, longing to reunite with its counterpart.[14]

According to this myth, which Socrates ascribes to a priestess named Diotima, the human being originally represented three genders simultaneously: male-male, female-female, and the third gender, androgyny, in which female and male were amalgamated. When this whole was divided in two, the genders we recognize were formed as female and male. Three genders thus became two. Or was it four, as Eva Borgström proposes? According to her, the answer depends on how one interprets the *Symposium*.[15]

The halves with male genitalia, whose former halves also had male genitalia, began searching for their lost male counterparts. Today, such individuals are referred to as gay males, a term with which neither Plato nor Aristotle were familiar. Individuals with female parts who had previously been one with another female half were the predecessors of lesbians. While Plato did not seem to think of women roaming the earth in search of their lost female half, he nevertheless referred to women loving other women as a familiar practice.

The third gender, the androgyne that was both female and male, was split into two types of heterosexual halves. The myth describes heterosexual love as we generally know it today as having its roots in the original androgynous (*andros* "man" and *gyne* "woman") human body, which for Plato, speaking through Socrates, represented a kind of gender deviation. Fully female and fully male humans thus searched for same-sex love upon being cloven in two. According to this interpretation, today's norms derive from the androgynous beings of a previous time, and the Platonic Socrates' same-sex beings also provide the template for deviations from those norms.[16]

Almqvist's surgeons attempted to discover why both women and men fell in love with Tintomara, although personally the surgeons seemed to have nothing against the idea in itself. The surgeon who supports the myth of the androgyne does not consider it a clear explanation (*logos*), but only a story (*mythos*) that provides some form of hesitant account for lack of a better explanation: "This thing about androgynies is something people have made up to find an explanation for what they don't understand" (QD, 43).[17] The myth of the androgyne and the birth of love are presented in *The Queen's Diadem* as follows:

> An androgyne was understood to be something strange, something mystical in fact. You see, the belief was – there are several reasons for believing this – that humans were originally created simply as *human beings*. Not man, not woman, but simply *human being*; do you understand, my friend? Still, I don't know whether "androgyne" should refer to a creature who is *neither* sex or *both*. The former seems extremely sad; the ancients have thought much about the latter. For in the latter case, my friend, there would be a whole, uniting the nature of both sexes in itself . . . . The ancients, who imagined the androgyne to be such a complete, self-sufficient, and, according to their ideas, blessed creature, added that it was precisely the *fall* of man, or at least an integral part of the fall, that the human being was *cloven* in two, fell apart into two sexes, whose destiny it would be to chase each other forever, to fortune or to misfortune. Through the division of the originally united human

being, there developed two hemispheres instead of one sphere: two kinds of beings, man and woman; through this, my friend, the possibility of love (Eros) occurred, but also of discord (Eris). (QD, 42)[18]

The passage above encompasses numerous themes from *The Queen's Diadem*. They are admittedly all based on Almqvist's interpretation of Plato. One example is the kinship between Eros and Eris. The novel is filled with love, jealousy, aggression, and dissonance. The themes of eroticism and violence go hand in hand, although this does not correspond to Plato's philosophy, as Borgström points out. She sees the myth of Eros depicted in a heterosexualized manner in Almqvist's novel. The narration only mentions the precursors of heterosexuals, but the bi-gendered body that spawned same-sex love is not named.

In Plato's thinking homoeroticism induces shifts in cultural values and political renewal because older men teach and inspire the younger male generation. Similarly, homoerotic desire acted as a driving force for youths seeking new information to foster their development and bring them closer to fulfilling their roles as purveyors of culture and pillars of society. Socrates only mentions female-to-female love on one occasion and as a matter of symmetry, as Page du Bois notes in *Sappho is Burning*.[19] Such love is not given any significance other than the satisfaction or fulfillment it brings to the lovers. Although the *Symposium* mentions women, the thought of love and eroticism between them is excluded completely.

In addition to his allusions to the *Symposium*, Almqvist indicates elsewhere in the novel that androgyny can be perceived as a kind of perfect human form. An androgynous person, according to him, is a closed entity in which femininity and masculinity come together to form a flawless creature who, in addition, does not experience human erotic desires that others suffer from. An androgyne is the object of its own desire, a complete being who feels no sexual urge, as it already embodies everything. Passions that spawn pleasure and suffering are not the drawback they may be to other people.

The androgyne of Almqvist's novel can be seen either as suffering from a relentless and insatiable desire, or as immune from any sense of deprivation or craving. Both options would suit Tintomara. While Tintomara mourns for those whose lives she has ruined, she has no wish to be loved. At the end, she even begs: "Promise me, Georg, that you, at least, don't love me. . . . All the others love me; they wither, die, perish, break. . ." (QD, 162).[20]

The surgeons' discussion suggests that androgyny is a form of gender melancholy, and they wonder whether androgyne is female, male, or perhaps neither one of them. Melancholia may be present in the *Symposium* through its intermediate tragic state of the human when it has been divided but has yet to assume the gender(s) we recognize today. According to myth of eros that Socrates offers, the hunger for one's other half was so consuming that humans made do with whomever they could find, regardless of whether they were "female" or "male", and clung to them so fiercely that one or the other perished from thirst or hunger. The surviving being then found someone new to cling to, but his or her desire was never satiated because the human genitals were situated in the wrong location. Finally, when humankind threatened to become extinct, the gods stepped in and decided to relocate the genitals to their current place. This then allowed women and men to fulfill their desires, curb their longing, and reproduce.[21]

Melancholia, from the Greek *melas* (black) and *khole* (bile), is interpreted in Hippocratic medicine as a malady. According to ancient theory regarding bodily liquids, bile in copious amounts caused a heavy heart; that is, melancholia, and filled one's soul with gloom, weighing it down. However, melancholic despondency did not imply desperation or death. Instead, it also provided the seed for rebirth. Judith Butler, connecting gender melancholy to a heterosexual matrix that culturally denies the mourning of a homosexual love lost, writes:

> What ensues is a culture of gender melancholy in which masculinity and femininity emerge as the traces of an ungrieved and ungrievable love; indeed, where masculinity and femininity within the heterosexual matrix are strengthened through the repudiations that they perform. In opposition to a conception of sexuality which is said to "express" a gender, gender itself is here understood to be composed of precisely what remains inarticulate in sexuality.[22]

Butler's notion of gender melancholy is based on the idea that heterosexuality naturalizes itself by insisting on the radical otherness of homosexuality. Heterosexual identities are purchased through a melancholic incorporation of the love that they disavow. For Butler, the man who insists upon the coherence of his heterosexuality will claim that he never loved another man, and hence never lost another man. The consequence is that the love attachment becomes subject to a double disavowal: a never having loved, and a never having lost. This "never–never" thus founds the heterosexual subject, as it were; it is an identity based upon the refusal to avow an attachment, hence, the refusal to grieve.[23]

Tintomara: Fostered by the theatre

Almqvist wrote several plays in the 1830s. *The Queen's Diadem*, although a novel, contains a great many theatre-esque and theatrical traits. Theatre is also one of its central themes, and its text is notably rich in dialogue. The plot also embodies a meta-theatrical structure (a play within a play), which is connected to the general concept of *theatrum mundi* – the world as a stage in which life is role-playing and where masquerading belongs to life.

Ulla-Britta Lagerroth has analyzed the ways which theatricality may be tied to the written text. A text can be 'themed' by a theatre context and deal with matters relating to theatre: performances, fictitious actors, directors, and the like. Theatrical traits can be brought into a text formally or structurally through standard ways of representing theatre: dialogue, tableaus, demarcated performance and audience situations, or theatrical language, including gestural rhetoric. Characters may be used as metaphors or symbols, their lives partaking of the dynamics of the stage. A text may include several of these mechanisms.[24]

Tintomara is represented as having grown up in the theatre. Her mother is an actress and her father, Equerry Munck, is rumored to be Gustav III's proxy for the heterosexual obligations of marriage. As an actress, dancer, and androgyne, Tintomara plays a liminal role. A permanent half-status in terms of gender does not result in positive reactions from those she meets. Tintomara is also viewed warily because individuals with a two-fold gender identity fall outside "normal" social categories. In *Vested Interests*, Marjorie Garber suggests that suspicion is traditionally expressed toward individuals who disguise themselves or dress as someone else as part of their lives: actors, diplomats, transvestites, and spies.[25]

Theatricality does not only appear in exceptional scenes in *The Queen's Diadem*. It is also present in the novel's outbursts of emotions and the feelings of exaltation contained in its grand gestures, and can be seen in those characters who are performers on the stage of everyday life. This is apparent in tableau-like scenes that include melodramatic gestures typical of the theatre at that time.

The Queen's Diadem creates a meta-stage consisting of the volatile Tintomara and an epic storyline. Tintomara's stage is a tableau, a *mise en abyme* or internal mirror. It is an element introduced into narrative by another art form to reflect the theme of an entire text. This strategy may also include Tintomara's gender turnovers. Such theatralization has been widely used in the nineteenth-century English novels of Jane Austen, Charlotte Brontë, George Eliot, Charles Dickens, and William Makepeace Thackeray.

The philosophy of enjoyment was important to Almqvist. He believed that art should bring people pleasure, and that an author should not teach readers without also entertaining them. He maintains the dramatic tension of *The Queen's Diadem* by incorporating into the novel a complex model based on curiosity and anticipation that he borrowed from melodrama. Theatricality also allows for the exploration of gender and sexuality without creating a general sense of taking things too far. Thus, Almqvist could write freely about eroticism, a subject that novels, books of etiquette, and the rules of the church and society were silent about at the time.[26]

Flight, volatility, and disguise

Tintomara is taken advantage of by Ferdinand and Clas Henrik in their conspiracy against Gustav III. They give her the task of luring the King into the main hall of the Royal Opera House, where he is shot. After the King's assassination, the protagonists flee Stockholm to the forests of Kolmården. Distraught by the part their fiancés played in the murder, Adolfine and Amanda remain at their family estates in Östergötland. Meanwhile, Clas Henrik and Ferdinand are hiding only a few miles away, near the shores of

Bråviken. Tintomara, using the name Lazuli, arrives in Kolmården cross-dressed as a man. The four young aristocrats all fall in love with this androgynous person and are slowly driven mad by their passion. During a key scene in the dark of night, the four youths advance toward Tintomara at a crossroads in Lindamot, each coming from a different direction.

> Tintomara's voice stopped abruptly and her head jerked to one side, for her sharp eyes seemed to see something actually approaching, and it was as if all those to whom she was saying goodbye in her singing imagination came to say goodbye to her as well. She saw movement on the four roads; she saw something approaching simultaneously along the long, black lanes. It approached deliberately, silently, but identical on all four roads. On all four of them, it approached so carefully as if each one on its road did not want to be noticed by anything else. (QD, 170)[27]

This X-pattern recurs several times in the novel. Tintomara is like a mysterious vertex, towards which all passion and yearning is directed.

Tintomara flees love, but Baron Reuterholm, the power-hungry villain of the piece, arrives at the Stavsjö estate in Östergötland and blocks her escape. In the company of Reuterholm, Tintomara returns to the political grand stage in Stockholm. But would-be suitors in the capital also plague her. This wild and free doe-like character is to be tamed by Duke Charles, taken as his lover, and inured to the lavish boudoirs of the castle.

Nerverthless, once again Tintomara flees. She enlists as a musician in the Royal Swedish Army Band, then misbehaves during a parade. While being pursued by Reuterholm's spies, she violates military regulations and is sentenced to death. Following a lengthy deliberation, a mock execution is performed with empty rounds fired. After the smoke has cleared, it is revealed that Ferdinand has returned to Stockholm from Kolmården. Now taking his place as a member of the firing squad, he fires live rounds and kills Tintomara. We learn that he had previously shot Clas Henrik, and later is himself executed. Adolfine and Amanda, although they remain alive, go mad.

The heroines of plays and novels often cross-dress for a brief period when an enemy appears or danger threatens. Flight is a typical literary device for cross-dressing female literary characters. Since searching for a wronged love is often their object, masquerading as a man becomes a practical option. Gertrud Lehnert has stated that women do not cross-dress because of a longing for freedom or independence, but to resolve a problem that they can more effectively pursue if they present themselves as men. In male attire, women are able to gain access to a man's world.[28]

In *The Queen's Diadem* the flight motive is tied to Tintomara's impulsiveness and peculiarity. Volatility, androgyny, and "animality" are all intertwined in the novel. One surgical consultant links androgyny to bestiality, whereas another speaks of an *animal coeleste*, a divine animal:

> The animal's way of being, instinctual life, demonstrates the harmonious, appealing picture of a creature totally in union with itself. You will be familiar with the theory of the mystics, about the *animal coeleste*? The aim of human beings, it is said, is in fact eventually to become nature once again, to become like an animal. (QD, 42-43)[29]

In medieval scholastic cosmology *animal coeleste* referred to immortal heavenly creatures. Almqvist has tailored its meaning to refer to the moral purity of animals and to emphasize the importance of instinct. Depending on one's interpretation, a "divine creature" may be understood as some kind of external or superior being apart from the existing gender dichotomy. Animalism is exhibited in how Tintomara becomes enchanted with the forests of Kolmården. There "with a smile, she regards the shape of her feet, often putting her two hands next to them to compare" (QD, 80).[30] Tintomara's transcendental quality is also emphasized by the fact that she has not been baptized. Not only is her gender undetermined; she exists outside the Christian community.

Tintomara represents a person in an instinctive, totally natural state. In a comprehensive study of the novel written in 1919, Henry Olsson underscores Tintomara's proximity to nature, exoticism, and innocence. He sees her as a combination of Rousseauian savage and provincial country girl. She also represents art and theatre in the emotional aspect of her being. Olle Holmberg examined Almqvist's version of *animal coeleste*, whose innocence is emotional rather than logical. Through their unreflective, spontaneous natures, divine creatures can live in harmony with themselves and their surroundings. Almqvist saw Tintomara as an ideal romantic persona – comparable to Schiller's notion of the play instinct as a human perfector – that combined spirituality and animality.[31]

From a queer perspective, the figure of Tintomara explains why other characters in the novel feel erotically and emotionally drawn to a person of their own sex. Amanda and Adolfine fall in love with Tintomara when they think – but are unsure – that she is a man. Ferdinand and Clas Henrik also fall in love, but apparently before they realize Tintomara is "actually" a woman. This is a classic example of a queer thought line. The androgyne sparks a great deal of desire all around. A cross-dressed woman seems to be an especially popular object of desire. Jonathan Dollimore refers to this as "the perverse dynamic." Homosexuality is both an intimidation and an enticement. This bipolar repulsion and fascination is not caused by homosexuality as such, but by the instability of heterosexuality. That the dominant culture defines itself as heterosexual is a basic queer point. Queer, however, is driven into obscurity, cut off, and discarded as a mere fragment of cultural history.[32]

Same-sex eroticism, particularly between two women, has always been characterized by a degree of sexual ambivalence. Martha Vicinus has identified four historical types that are paradigms for modern definitions of lesbian identity:

- A cross-dressing woman or a transvestite character
- A masculine woman who represents female masculinity
- A free and independent woman, in charge of her own sexuality, who engages in sexual relationships with both women and men
- Romantic friendships between women that take on the form of a Sapphic relationship[33]

Tintomara's unique personal charm gives us the impression that her gender is a mix of both "female" and "male." Her allure is based on her fleeting gender flexibility and other models of desire beyond the standard heterosexual cultural matrix. When an object of desire is transformed through a transvestite disguise, the dynamics of gender and desire also change.[34]

The dramaturgy of the desire present in *The Queen's Diadem* is reminiscent of trouser roles in the theatre and opera, where the attraction changes even though the disguise remains intact. Such roles can be divided into three main categories. The first includes former castrato roles in operas that can have multi-gendered casting; the second consists of characters akin to Rosalind in Shakespeare's *As You Like It*, where the performer is unambiguously female and only cross-dresses as a man; and the third has "male" characters such as Cherubino in Mozart's *Le nozze Figaro* and Octavian in Strauss's *Der Rosenkavalier*, both of whom function as young men. The dramaturgy of the trouser roles in the second category dates back to the Renaissance: the female character finds herself in a conflict from which she cannot escape as a female, although she is wise and resourceful. In male disguise she becomes an active figure and sometimes a governing character. However, masculine dress only brings short-lived freedom. Masquerading serves the task of the play, which is usually related to solving one or more conflicts of the heart. When that has been accomplished the disguise is cast off. In comedies, the pairing of one or more heterosexual couples is usually climaxed by a wedding.[35]

The classic masquerade mechanism assumes that a "correct" and "incorrect" gender exists. The correct gender identity is preferably something that is clear to both audience and actors, and so that kind of role-play is comprehensible. The dramaturgical tension is dependent on the divergence between what the audience knows and sees, and what the play's characters think they know and see. A trouser role can also be viewed from a lesbian perspective, in which case the woman in the trouser role does *not* imitate a man, but instead *is* shown as actively desiring another woman, or women in general. Contrary to the conventional "correct" interpretation, a cross-dressed character problematizes the "natural" arrangement in which desire is inexorably fixed on a body of the opposite gender.

Tintomara: The five-leaf clover and object of desire

When the five of hearts or five of spades is used as a structural symbol in *The Queen's Diadem*, Tintomara is at the center – the ace. As the young aristocrats begin a game of cards, the ace of hearts is missing from the deck and another card is in its place. Ferdinand takes the five of hearts and scrapes the small hearts from its corners, so that a single heart remains in the center. The novel plays with different configurations of cards: a four can become a five if a heart is added or a five can become a four if a heart is removed. A five can become a one if all the hearts are taken from the corners.

> Tintomara was placed on the floor among her enemies, and four guards, chosen pupils, were placed around her in a square. Adolfine, watching the group from a distance from a bench on which she had climbed, smiled at the expressive representation of a five of spades; the savage woman herself in the middle with two young men over her outstretched hands and two young girls over her feet, all on top of a white carpet spread under them, truly made a picture which resembled this ominous card.
>
> The music started, and at a sharp *fortissimo* Tintomara made a movement, a gesture with her hands and feet, so elastic but also so strong that all four guards bounced far away from her on the floor. On the instant, she was up and in flight. (QD, 68)[36]

Tintomara in the middle as the ace of hearts is desire itself, but her love is unattainable. Almqvist seems to want to depict the dissonance between undefined gender and unattainability, and also between structure and order. The setup is emphasized by the young aristocrats each having their own vocal register – bass, tenor, alto, and soprano – whereas Tintomara's register is more difficult to pinpoint in terms of gender: "A kind of alto, which would sometimes move into the range of the soprano, other times verging on a proper tenor voice" (QD, 41).[37] Each of the four has their own occupation to pass the time while hiding in Östergötland: hunting, playing the violin, singing, and reading aloud. Tintomara takes part in all of these activities.

The youths infatuated with Tintomara soon become competitors in the typical Western romantic form of a triangle. The story turns out to be one of how a lover triumphs over all others and claims the beloved – or tragically fails in the attempt.[38] Claiming the beloved always entails overcoming obstacles. René Girard highlights the centrality of competition in romantic narratives of love in his study *Deceit, Desire, and the Novel: Self and Other in*

Literary Structure.[39] He sees the phenomenon as a triangle driven by a mimetic desire, namely, the wish to ignite one's competitors more than pursue the love interest. Thus, such love is not shown in a straightforward fashion but as a triangle. Someone loves someone else who is loved by a third person, that is, an individual becomes desirable because of the desire of a third individual.

Although Girard mainly examines heterosexual desire, he alludes to same-sex desire in a passage assessing Marcel Proust. In *Between Men*, Eve Kosofsky Sedgwick suggests that English literature since Shakespeare has been structured according to an erotic triangle governed by homosocial desire between men.[40] According to Sedgwick, the homosocial triangle is so evident that a consensus between male characters is an essential part of the triangle which, in literature is founded by two men and one woman, whereby the man's true object of desire is not the woman, but the other man.

An uncertain dynamic is present between homo*social* desire and homo*sexuality*. Sedgwick states that the homosocial desire governing the triangle creates a strong bond between the men, but if that bond proves too tense (i.e., openly homosexual), the men face ideological resistance. If a man takes on the "female" role in homosexual intercourse, how can he then be differentiated from a woman? The eroticization of the bond between the men thus compromises the perception of the patriarchal gender divide between men and women.

Ferdinand and Clas Henrik invite Tintomara to their cabin in Kolmården, an unambiguously homosocial environment in which they go fishing and hunting, play cards, and walk around unshaven. Both men fall hopelessly in love with Tintomara, but only after finding out they share the secret of Tintomara's gender. Nevertheless, their relationship is equivocal. While they are hanging around the cabin longing for Tintomara, Ferdinand says to Clas Henrik: "Why shouldn't a promising young man be amusing to associate with? I confess it honestly – good, clever, lively male companionship – that's something I've always liked" (QD, 150).[41]

Male characters in narrative fiction are routinely complimented on each other's beauty and virtues, and may even describe their mutual relationship as one of love, without the reader associating it with eroticism. But references to the homoeroticism of the

Symposium and mention of the rumors about Gustav III prevent a totally heterosexual reading of the relationship between Ferdinand and Clas Henrik. The reader is left to interpret the ambiguity.

Terry Castle assesses Girard and Sedgwick's triangular models in *The Apparitional Lesbian* and offers an alternative: the lesbian counterplot.[42] Castle extends Sedgwick's model to reflect a relationship of desire between two women, posing the question of what happens to the triangle when the circumstances are broadened and another woman enters the picture. She argues that in this new arrangement a homosocial structure between the two women arises and greatly marginalizes the rapport between the men involved. In Castle's model, men can become just as isolated as women in Sedgwick's triangular model. For Castle the homosocial desire between women may be as dynamic as between men, even – at its most radical – to the extent of becoming one of lesbian desire. Borrowing two terms from Nancy C. Miller, Castle describes a plot as *dysphoric* if it has a heterosexual conclusion, and *euphoric* if it has a lesbian one. The lesbian counterplot thus challenges the standard heteronormative narrative.[43]

Adolfine, the first of the four young people who encounter Tintomara, moves freely about town and in society, even attending a masquerade ball unescorted. It is there that she meets Tintomara and clearly perceives her as a woman. The encounter takes place after the murder of the king. In the narrative Adolfine has just climbed onto the stage of the theatre and comically steps into a dreamlike world. Tintomara is in the costume that Adolfine had first thought of wearing and so Adolfine initially mistakes Tintomara for her own reflection. When Tintomara asks for her help in changing clothes, Adolfine – and the reader – can study the incredibly beautiful Tintomara. As if hit by lightning, Adolfine is lovestruck.

> Adolfine approached with a secret smile at this familiar request and unhooked the dress. She experienced a strange feeling – but we are both female, she thought, and it does not matter! – Still, she experienced a strange emotion when, in a series of quick, beautiful turnings, not just the belt, but the whole orange dress (the laced corselet was allowed to remain, untouched up to the neck), the lawn sleeves, shoes and purple stockings: everything disappeared from the figure (QD, 64)[44]

Adolfine's gaze is erotic; she continues to stare at Tintomara's beautiful figure, as it is stripped of its garments one by one. The novel depicts the encounter between Adolfine and Tintomara in far more detail than other relationships based on desire. Tintomara is only portrayed as an active temptress in her tryst with Adolfine. Her encounters with potential male love interests are far less explicit.

Although Adolfine tries to compose herself by recalling that they are both women, she sees that Tintomara's beauty far exceeds her own. Standing in such close proximity to Adolfine, Tintomara becomes an overwhelming erotic object of desire. Adolfine, thinking to herself, tries to come to terms with the idea of a love between two women:

> In a sisterly fashion, she wound her arm around its [Tintomara] black waist; and when Azouras did not refrain from putting her white arm around Adolfine's shoulders, Adolfine felt both warmth and protection from the embrace. Certain sympathies are mysterious and incomprehensible. (QD, 71)[45]

We wonder if the adjectives "mysterious" and "incomprehensible" are Adolfine's or the narrator's. The rules of propriety in same-sex relationships at the time precluded a woman from admitting that she felt warmth and a sense of security in another woman. Women were only to experience that with men.

> Adolfine kept the white hand in hers and, at the start, had difficulty finding words for what she meant: – All the way from the shoulder down to your finger tips . . . . white, quite white . . . . she said. – Yes, I believe there is much in you that is lovable . . . . whoever you are, listen to some advice from me. You're in strange company up there; I mean . . . . ugly practices . . . . a girl like you . . . . you feel . . . . you should feel it, as well as I . . . . avoid the gestures of those people when they speak of . . . . of love . . . . beware of love. Adolfine inclined her head. She didn't understand how she had come to speak in this vein. (QD, 71-72)[46]

As Adolfine recalls the wondrous evening at the opera, her heart skips a beat and she rejoices: "I'm allowed to love a girl!" (QD, 143). When Tintomara then says she was only dressed as a girl, Adolfine is startled, and tries to reassure herself that her infatuation was pure and innocent. Later as everything comes crashing down and the two sisters argue bitterly, Adolfine accuses Amanda of lying when she claimed her relationship with Tintomara was nothing more than a friendship. As Eva Borgström points out, the same can be said for Adolfine herself.[47]

The transient nature of desire

Girard, Sedgwick, and Castle all find the triangular model inadequate because it prioritizes the couple. The triangle model is based on dualistic thinking and it is confirmed each time another member enters. According to Marjorie Garber, the triangular model is untenable in itself. When bisexuality is added to the equation, the triangle is eroticized and results in the seduction scenario. The triangular structure incorporates bisexuality as one of its aspects. While bisexuality is equally directed towards two genders, multi-sexuality is a more open category. Flexible erotic displacement and the play of sexual possibilities make Tintomara a multi-sexual character. She can move in both heterosexual and homosexual contexts with equal freedom. Tintomara thus represents both multi-sexuality and androgyny.[48]

Androgyny is often associated with multi-sexuality and has figured importantly in Shakespearean study, where it has sparked two lines of discourse. The first draws on ambiguous characters who cross-dress, such as Rosalind/Ganymede and Viola/Cesario. As androgynous figures they combine femininity and masculinity, and become objects of desire for both women and men. The second line of discourse pertains to Shakespeare's androgynous world of theatre. Already in 1664, Margaret Cavendish wrote of Shakespeare's ability to empathize with both female and male thought and emotion. Later, Coleridge and other romantics discussed Shakespeare's androgynous spirit. One is reminded of Virginia Woolf's laconic comment in *A Room of One's Own* that androgyny of the mind is the source of all creativity. Woolf views Shakespeare as an example of such androgynous thinking, although she concedes that it is impossible to know what Shakespeare really thought about women.[49]

The cross-dressing and androgynous Tintomara represents restlessness, variability, quick-wittedness, and uniqueness. She sets her surroundings, including the triangles of desire, in motion. In Tintomara's case, the casting off of a disguise does not signal a return to the prevailing modes of gender and desire. J. Jack Halberstam states in *Female Masculinity* that the androgyne "represents a different form of gender variance than the masculine woman, and although the androgyne may have faced some kind of social opprobrium, it probably did not come in the form of a response to gender confusion."[50] According to Halberstam the androgyne represents some version of gender mixing, but this rarely adds up to total ambiguity.

In *The Queen's Diadem*, Tintomara's character raises questions about the external and internal dynamics between and within the sexes. She unmistakably shows that a person is neither of a specific, preordained, uncompromising gender, nor a clearly defined sexual being. Instead, a variety of factors mold people into heterosexual women and men. Tintomara personifies one way in which femininity and masculinity may be constructed. Almqvist's novel does not follow the logic of *feminine* = *womanly* = *female*, and *masculine* = *manly* = *male*. Instead, his differentiation of female, womanly, and feminine, and also of male, manly, and masculine, is surprisingly close to our contemporary perspective on gender and queer thinking, according to which these concepts are not synonymous.

On a more general level, femininity and masculinity refer to social statuses, whereas female and male are anatomical categories. Femininity embodied in a biological woman, like masculinity in a man's body, can be simultaneously true of the same person, although not necessarily. There are many types of women and femininities, as there are also many types of men and masculinities. Queer theory has taken the lead in criticizing the notion that there is only one, socially acceptable, uniform line of either femininity or masculinity that applies to every woman and man.

Tintomara's androgyny can be decoded as a continuously renewed attack against the social pressure for erotic certainties. Tintomara's person piques interest in the variations of gender on the one hand, and in the transient nature of desire on the other. She is positioned as a queer subject who questions the models of biological and hegemonic thought. Perhaps the instability of norms is most apparent when femininity is not automatically associated with a female body, or similarly when a male body does not necessarily represent masculinity.

Tintomara's death is no dysphoric solution or dramaturgical return to order. Lars Burman argues that alongside romantic aesthetics, *The Queen's Diadem* is a counterweight that embodies social criticism and an undercurrent of rebellion. It is often overlooked that near the end of the novel, Tintomara – who chooses to remain an external figure in love, gender, and class dynamics – leaves lady-in-waiting Madeleine Rudensköld an assignment. She asks her to "remember the task," which according to Burman is the banishing of the conspirator Reuterholm.[51] Tintomara is far more than a flighty child of nature, a peculiar androgyne living on her instincts, or a societal outsider, s/he is also the driving force behind rebellion and social change.

Notes

1. The abbreviation "QD" stands for *The Queen's Diadem* in English; "DJ" refers to the Swedish original, *Drottningens juvelsmycke*. "Mig finner ingen, // Ingen jag finner. /.../ Jag ler åt alla, // Alla åt mig le. – Tintomaras sång." (DJ, 171)

2. Although Tintomara's gender remains unclear, since the novel uses "she" to refer to her, we will continue that here.

3. See, for example, Doty, *Making Things Perfectly Queer*; Rosenberg, *Byxbegär*; *Queerfeministisk agenda*, 117.

4. This slight modification of Alexander Doty's definition of queer admits trans-identities into queer. See Doty, *Flaming Classics*, 6; Hall & Jagose, *The Routledge Queer Studies Reader*.

5. Westman Berg, *Studier*. See a review of her study in Bertil Romberg's "Almqvistsforskning." An extensive editor's introduction to DJ by Lars Burman may be found in the 2002 Swedish reprint of *Drottningens juvelsmycke*.

6. Hagedorn Thomsen, "Androgyneproblemet II"; Mortensen, "Till Tintomaramotivets historia." The essay was later published in an expanded form as "Tintomara" in Mortensen, *Människor och böker*. See also Holmberg, "Introduction."

7. Adolfsson, "Det androgyna skapandet."

8. Cavallin, "Androgynens kön."

9. Desertrain, "A Study of Love"; Borgström, "Musikens och erotikens harmonilära," 144.

10. "Visserligen måste det vara något eget ändå med denna varelse. Halsens och bröstets början, som jag såg, voro af en mycket behaglig, men underbar struktur, som syntes tillåta, att den förra stundom skulle höjas, jemte det senares sammandragning eller förhårdning; och tvertom, vid andra tillfällen, det sednare litet vidgas, jemte hela figurens förminskning." (DJ, 51) See also Borgström, "Musikens och erotikens harmonilära," 146.

11. "Den undersökta sägs ha försökt värja sig dels 'med det smekanda, ytterst intagande uttrycket af en lidande siren', dels 'med spotsk stolthet', som 'nästan kunde tyckas manligt.'" (DJ, 51)

12. Ibid.

13. Ibid.

14. Plato, *Om kärleken och döden*. See also the comments of translator Robin Waterfield to Plato, *Symposium*.

15. Borgström, "Musikens och erotikens harmonilära," 144.

16. Used in a derogatory sense, "androgyne" means "cowardly": a man who does not meet contemporary expectations of masculinity.

17. DJ, 54.

18. "Med androgyn förstod man något besynnerligt, ja, mystiskt. Man har trott, se ni, – och man hade flere skäl för denna tro – att menniskan ursprungligen blott skapades till *menniska*. Icke man, och ej kvinna, utan rätt och slätt *menniska*; förstår ni min vän? Jag vet likväl icke, om med Androgyn bör förstås en varelse, som är *ingetdera* könet, eller beggedera. Det förra synes ytterst melankoliskt; på det sednare, åter, hava de gamle mycket tänkt. Det vore nämligen i det senare fallet, min vän, en Helhet, som i ett väsende förenade bägges arter /.../ De gamle, som med androgyn tänkte sig ett fullkomligt, själv-tillräckligt, i deras tanke gudasällt väsende, tillade, att det var just menniskans *fall*, eller åtminstone en integrerande del av fallet, då människoväsendet klövs itu, föll sönder i *tvenne* kön, vilkas öde skulle bli, att till ve och väl jaga varann oupphörligt. Genom den ursprungligen eviga menniskovarelsens söndrande, så att den i stället

för en sfär blev tvenne hemisfärer, två slags varelser, man och kvinna; därigenom, min vän, uppkom väl möjligheten av kärlek *(Eros)*, men också av tvist *(Eris)*." (DJ, 52–53)

19. As cited in Borgström, "Musikens och erotikens harmonilära." She is referring to Page du Bois's *Sappho Is Burning*: "It [women's erotic life with other women] is allowed for as a matter of symmetry, but it is the redundant third term, male-female sex leads to reproduction, male-male sex demonstrates virility, female-female sex is not characterized," 91.

20. "Lova mig Georg, att åtminstone du icke älskar mig? /.../ Alla andra älska mig, vissna, dö, förgås, gå sönder." (DJ, 263)

21. Borgström, "Musikens och erotikens harmonilära," 99, 148.

22. Butler, *Psychic Life of Power*, 139–140.

23. Ibid.

24. For C.J.L. Almqvist's theatre traits, see Lagerroth, "Almqvist och scenkonsten"; "Amorina och Tintomara på Dramaten"; "Konsten är det enda fullt uppriktiga"; "Melodramteatern som kod"; "Selma Lagerlöf och teatern."

25. Garber, *Vested Interests*, 256.

26. Svedjedal, *Almqvist*, 26, 29, 45, 67.

27. "Tintomaras röst tvärstannade och huvudet hajade åt sidan, ty hennes skarpa syn tycktes märka, att något verkligen nalkades, och det var som om alla de, av vilka hon i sin sjungande fantasi tog avsked, kommod för att taga avsked av henne, även de. Hon såg det röra sig på de fyra vägarne: hon såg det röra sig fram emot henne ur det avlägsna svarta fjärran på en gång i alla fyra vägarne. Det nalkades avmätt, tyst, men lika i alla de svarta långa öppningarne. Det nalkades i varje av dem så försiktigt, som om varje på sitt håll icke vill vara bemärkt av någonting annat." (DJ, 218) See also Burman, "Introduction," ix.

28. Lehnert *Maskeraden und Metamorphosen*, 6; *Wenn Frauen Männerkleider tragen*.

29. "Det djuriska sättet att vara, instinktlivet, visar den harmoniskt intagande bilden av en hög enighet med sig själv. Ni har väl hört mystikernas tanke om animal celeste. Människans strävanden, påstår

man, skall verkligen vara, att till slut bliva natur igen, att bliva liksom ett djur." (DJ, 53)

30. "Hon roade sig med det hon vid sådana tillfällen ofta brukade, nämligen att sätta sina händer bredvid fötterna och så jämföra dem alla fyra." (DJ, 169)

31. Olsson, "C.J.L. Almqvist"; Holmberg, "Introduction," v–xv; Burman, "Introduction," xxii.

32. Dollimore, *Sexual Dissidence*.

33. Vicinus, "'They Wonder to Which Sex,'" 436–439.

34. In the theatre, the term for disguise is *travestia*. This concept refers first to disguising oneself, second to ridiculing, distorting, twisting or parodying, and only third to dressing up as the opposite sex. Both the French *en travesti* and the Italian *travestire* mean to disguise oneself and derive from the Latin *trans* (across) + *vestire* (to clothe). The English term "cross-dressing" is, therefore, its equivalent and is generally applied to men dressing in women's clothing or women in men's clothing. Theatre scholar Live Hov, who has studied the significance of travestia in theatre, uses the term *den grundläggande travestin* (the basic travesty) in her doctoral dissertation "Kvinnerollene i antikkens teater." Regarding trouser roles, see Rosenberg, "Transvestism och maskerad"; *Byxbegär*; "Om heteronormativ historieskrivning"; Senelick, *Gender in Performance*; *The Changing Room*. See also Blackmer & Smith, *En Travesti*; Hadlock, "The Career of Cherubino, or The Trouser Role Grows Up"; André *Voicing Gender; Listening to the Siren*. The above are all examples of a continued interest in trouser roles and queer performance.

35. Dutch historians Rudolf Dekker and Lotte van de Pol claim to have found only one example of socially acceptable female transvestism in the secluded mountain region of Northern Albania, along the border between Kosovo and Montenegro. The area was inhabited well into the twentieth century by a group of mountain people whose culture was characterized by internal contradictions and a steep hierarchy with regard to men and women. Despite this, a woman could decide to take an oath of virginity and remain unmarried. Such a woman then dressed in men's clothing, possibly even bore arms, and in effect attained a position equal to that of a man.

The best-known example of a transvestite in European theatre and literature (especially "chick lit") is probably Rosalind in *As You*

Like It. She is an archetypical tomboy who has inspired many similar characters in cinema. See also Rosenberg, *Byxbegär*.

36. "Tintomara lades på golvet midt ibland sina fiender, och fyra väktare, utvalde elever, sattes omkring henne i en fyrkant. Adolfine, som såg gruppen på afstånd ifrån en bänk där hon uppstigit, log verkligen åt den uttrycksfulla bilden av en spaderfemma; ty den vilda sjelf i midten med sina två ynglingar öfver de utsträckta händerna, och sina två flickor över fötterna, alltsammans ofvanpå en vit matta utbredd under dem, gjorde i sanningen en tafla som liknade detta ominösa kort.

"Musiken började, och vid ett skarpt fortissimo gjorde Tintomara en rörelse, en sprittning så elastisk, men tillika stark, med händer och fötter, att alla de fyra väktare studsade långt undan ifrån henne på golvet. I ögonblicket var hon uppe och flydde." (DJ, 84)

37. "En slags alt, som ena gången gick in på Sopranens område, andra gången gränsade till en ordentlig Tenor." (DJ, 51)

38. Girard, *Deceit*, 17.

39. Ibid.

40. Sedgwick, *Between Men*, 26, 86.

41. "Varför skulle icke en hoppingivande yngling vara rolig att umgås med? Det känner jag helt uppriktigt – ett gott, raskt, livligt karlsällskap – det har jag alltid tyckt om." (DJ, 192)

42. Castle, *The Apparitional Lesbian*, 66–91.

43. "Dysphoric" refers to a melancholic disposition, and its polar opposite, "euphoric", to exhilaration.

44. "Adolfine nalkades med hemligt leende över denna förtroliga anhållan, och spände upp klänningen. Hon erfor en besynnerlig känsla – men vi äro bägge fruntimmer, tänkte hon, och det gör ingenting! – en besynnerlig rörelse erfor hon likväl, när under hastiga vackra vändningar ej blott skärpet, men hela orangeklänningen (snörlivet fick bli orört kvar ända upp till halsen), lingonsärmarne, skor och purpurstrumpor, alltsammans försvann från gestalten." (DJ, 79)

45. "Systerligt lindade hon sin arm om dess svarta lif; och när Azouras icke försmådde att också lägga sin hvita arm kring hennes axlar, så tyckte Adolfine sig finna både värme och ett värn härifrån. Vissa sympatier äro hemlighetsfulla och oförklarliga." (DJ, 87)

46. "Adolfine kvarhöll den hvita handen, och hon hade i början svårt att finna ord för vad hon menade: 'Ända ifrån axeln ner till fingerspetsarna – hvitt, ganska hvitt' – sade hon – 'ja, jag tror att hos dig är mycket älskvärt – vem du är, hör också på ett råd från mig. Du är uti ett besynnerligt sällskap däruppe; jag menar – fula seder – en flicka som dy – du känner – du bör känna det, såväl som jag – undvik det där folkets gester, när de tala om.... kärlek – akta dig för kärlek –' Adolfine lutade sitt hufvud, hon förstod icke själv hur hon kommit att tala åt detta håll." (DJ, 88)

47. Borgström, "En musikens och erotikens harmonilära," 162.

48. Garber, *Vested Interests*, 431.

49. Woolf, *A Room of One's Own*, 94.

50. Halberstam, *Female Masculinity*, 57.

51. Burman, "Introduction," viii.

Works Cited

Adolfsson, Eva. "Det androgyna skapandet – en Almqvistsläsning" ("The Creation of the Androgyne – an Almqvist Reading"). In *I gränsland. Essäer om kvinnliga författarskap*, 154–188. Stockholm: Bonnier, 1991.

Almqvist, Carl Jonas Love. *Drottningens juvelsmycke* (DJ). In *Törnrosens bok, Duodesupplagan, Band IV*, edited and annotated by Lars Burman. Stockholm: Svenska Vitterhetssamfundet, 2002 [1834].

Almqvist, Carl Jonas Love. *The Queen's Diadem* (QD). *Drottningens juvelsmycke*, translated by Yvonne L. Sandstroem. Columbia, SC: Camden House, 1992 (1834).

André, Naomi. *Voicing Gender: Castrati, Travesti, and the Second Woman in Early Nineteenth-Century Italian Opera*. Bloomington: Indiana University Press, 2006.

Blackmer, Corinne E. and Patricia Juliana Smith, eds. *En Travesti: Women, Gender Subversion, Opera*. New York: Columbia University Press, 1995.

Borgström, Eva. "En musikens och erotikens harmonilära eller Hur många kön finns det i Almqvists 'Drottningens juvelsmycke?'" ("A

Musical and Erotic Theory of Harmony; or How many Genders are There in Almqvist's 'The Queen's Diadem'?"). *Res Publica* 43 (1999): 143–167.

Burman, Lars. "Introduction" to *Törnrosens bok. Duodesupplagan, Band IV: Drottningens juvelsmycke* by Carl Jonas Love Almqvist, edited and annotated by Lars Burman, vii–xxxv. Stockholm: Svenska Vitterhetssamfundet, 2002 [1834].

Butler, Judith. *The Psychic Life of Power: Theories in Subjection*. Palo Alto: Stanford University Press, 1997.

Castle, Terry. *The Apparitional Lesbian: Female Homosexuality and Modern Culture*. New York: Columbia University Press, 1993.

Cavallin, Anna. "Androgynens kön – en feministisk läsning av C. J. L. Almqvists 'Drottningens juvelsmycke'" ("The Gender of the Androgyne – a Feminist Reading of 'The Queen's Diadem' by C. J. L. Almqvist). *Tidskrift för litteraturvetenskap* 1 (1998): 3–23.

Dekker, Rudolf, and van de Pol, Lotte. *Kvinnor i manskläder. En avvikande tradition Europa 1500–1800* (The Tradition of Female Transvestism in Early Modern Europe). Stockholm: Symposion, 1995.

Desertrain, Laura Margaret. "A Study of Love. C.J.L. Almqvist's *Drottningens juvelsmycke*." Doctoral dissertation, University of Wisconsin–Madison, 1982.

Dollimore, Jonathan. *Sexual Dissidence: Augustine to Wilde, Freud to Foucault*. Oxford: Clarendon Press, 1991.

Doty, Alexander. *Making Things Perfectly Queer: Interpreting Mass Culture*. Minneapolis: University of Minnesota Press, 1993.

———. *Flaming Classics: Queering the Film Canon*. New York: Routledge, 2000.

du Bois, Page. *Sappho is Burning*. Chicago: University of Chicago Press, 1995.

Garber, Marjorie. *Vested Interests: Cross-Dressing and Cultural Anxiety*. New York: Routledge, 1995.

Girard, René. *Deceit, Desire, and the Novel: Self and Other in Literary Structure (Mensonge romantique et vérité ramanesque)*.

Translated from the French by Yvonne Freccero. Baltimore: Johns Hopkins University Press, 1990 [1961].

Hadlock, Heather. "The Career of Cherubino, or The Trouser Role Grows Up." In *Siren Songs. Representations of Gender and Sexuality in Opera*, edited by Mary Ann Smart, 67–92. Princeton: Princeton University Press. 2000.

Hagedorn Thomsen, Hans. "Androgyneproblemet II" (The Problem of the Androgyne II). *Kritik. Tidsskrift for litteratur, forskning, undervisning* 15 (1970): 91–118.

Halberstam, Judith (J. Jack). *Female Masculinity*. Durham, NC: Duke University Press, 1998.

Hall, Donald E., and AnnaMaria Jagose, eds. *The Routledge Queer Studies Reader*. New York: Routledge, 2012.

Holmberg, Olle. "Introduction" to *Törnrosens bok. Band IV*, by Carl Jonas Love Almqvist. Stockholm: Bonnier, 1921.

Hov, Live. "Kvinnerollene i antikkens teater – skrevet, spilt og sett av menn" (Women's Roles in Ancient Theatre – Written, Played, and Viewed by Men). Doctoral dissertation, University of Oslo, 1998.

Lagerroth, Ulla-Britta. "Almqvist och scenkonsten" (Almqvist and the Performing Arts). In *Perspektiv på Almqvist*, edited by Ulla-Britta Lagerroth and Bertil Romberg, 217–298. Stockholm: Rabén & Sjögren, 1973.

———. "Amorina och Tintomara på Dramaten. Två samtal med Alf Sjöberg" (Amorina and Tintomara at the Royal Dramatic Theatre. Two Encounters with Alf Sjöberg). In *Perspektiv på Almqvist*, edited by Ulla-Britta Lagerroth and Bertil Romberg, 299–322. Stockholm: Rabén & Sjögren, 1973.

———. "Konsten är det enda fullt uppriktiga. Almqvist mellan konstarter och mellan konst och liv" ("Art is the Only Fully Sincere. Almqvist Between Art Forms, and Between Art and Death"). In *I lärdomens trädgård. Festskrift till Louise Vinge*, edited by Christina Sjöblad, Mona Sandqvist, Birthe Sjöberg, and Johan Stenström, 109–125. Lund: Lund University Press, 1996.

———. "Melodramteatern som kod i Almqvists narrativa dramaturgi" ("Melodrama as a Code in Almqvist's Narrative

Dramaturgy"). *Aiolos, tidskrift för litteratur, teori och estetik*, Special edition: *Slöja och spegel – romantikens former* 14–15 (2000a): 53–78.

———. "Selma Lagerlöf och teatern" (Selma Lagerlöf and the Theatre). In *Vetenskapssocieteten i Lund Årsbok 1999/2000*, 93–113. Lund: Vetenskapssocieteten i Lund, 2000b.

Lehnert, Gertrud. *Maskeraden und Metamorphosen. Als Männer verkleidete Frauen in der Literatur*. Würzburg: Köningshausen & Neumann, 1994.

———. *Wenn Frauen Männerkleider tragen. Geschlecht und Maskerade in Literatur und Geschichte*. Munich: Deutscher Taschenbuchverlag, 1997.

Mortensen, Johan. "Till Tintomaramotivets historia" (On the History of Tintomara). In *Studier tillägnade Henrik Schück på hans 50 årsdag den 2 november 1905 af vänner och lärjungar*, edited by Oscar Levertin and Henrik Schück, 268–278. Stockholm: Geber, 1905.

———. *Människor och böcker. Studier och kritiker* (People and Books. Studies and Critics). Lund: Gleerups, 1917.

Olsson, Henry. "C. J. L. Almqvist, 'Drottningens juvelsmycke.' En diktmonografi och en orientering" ("C. J. L. Almqvist, 'The Queens Diadem.' A Poet Monograph and a Guide"). *Samlaren* 40 (1919): 85–172.

Peraino, Judith A. *Listening to the Sirens: Musical Technologies of Queer Identity from Homer to Hedwig*. Berkeley: University of California Press, 2006.

Plato. *Symposium*. Translated by Robin Waterfield. Oxford: Oxford University Press, 1994.

Romberg, Bertil. "Almqvistsforskning 1869–1966" (Research on Almqvist 1869–1966). *Svensk litteraturtidskrift* 4 (1966): 157–187.

Rosenberg, Tiina. "Transvestism och maskerad. Några nedslag i feministisk teater och teori" ("Transvestism and Masquerade. On Feminist Theatre and Theory"). In *Svenska teaterhändelser 1946–1996*, edited by Lena Hammergren, Karin Helander, and Willmar Sauter, 330–352. Stockholm: Natur och Kultur, 1996.

———. *Byxbegär* (Desiring Pants). Göteborg: Anamma, 2000.

---. "Om heteronormativ historieskrivning" ("On Heteronormative History"). In *Makalösa kvinnor: könsöverskridare i myt och verklighet*, edited by Eva Borgström, 239–284. Gothenburg: Alfabeta/Anamma, 2002a.

---. *Queerfeministisk agenda* (Queer Feminist Agenda). Stockholm: Atlas, 2002b.

Sedgwick, Eve Kosofsky. *Between Men: English Literature and Male Homosocial Desire*. New York: Columbia University Press, 1985.

Senelick, Laurence. *Gender in Performance: The Presentation of Difference in the Performing Arts*. Hanover, NH: University Press of New England, 1992.

---. *The Changing Room: Sex, Drag and Theatre*. New York: Routledge, 2000.

Smart, Mary Ann, ed. *Siren Songs. Representations of Gender and Sexuality in Opera*. Princeton: Princeton University Press. 2000.

Svedjedal, Johan. *Almqvist – berättaren på bokmarknaden* (Almqvist – the Narrator in the Book Market"). Uppsala: Almqvist & Wiksell, 1987.

Vicinus, Martha. "'They Wonder To Which Sex I Belong': The Historical Roots of the Modern Lesbian Identity." In *The Lesbian and Gay Studies Reader*, edited by Henry Abelove, Michèle Aina Barale, and David Halperin, 432–452. New York: Routledge, 1993.

Westman Berg, Karin. *Studier i C. L. J. Almqvists kvinnouppfattning* (Studies in C. L. J. Almqvist's Discourse on Women"). Gothenburg: Akademiförlag, 1962.

Woolf, Virginia. *A Room of One's Own*. London: Granada Publishing, 1977 [1929].

Hedda Gabler (Henrik Ibsen). Sonja Richter (Hedda) and Paprika Steen (Tesman). Betty Nansen Teatret, Copenhagen, 2005. Photographer: Thomas Petri. Copyright CC-BY-NC-ND: Thomas Petri, Betty Nansen Teatret, Copenhagen.

7. AGAINST LOVE: Nora and Hedda on the Contemporary Scandinavian Stage

James Bond: "A woman!"
Holly Goodhead: "Your powers of observation do you credit, Mr. Bond."
Moonraker, 1979

The left-wing enthusiasm that swept through institutions of higher learning in the 1960s was one of the most efficacious intellectual revolutions in recent history.[1] In *Eros and Civilization*, his most utopian book, Herbert Marcuse envisages a society where labor has been transformed into playful gratification and is accompanied by generalized sexual release.[2] But as feminists have pointed out, such an underground portrayal of sexual liberation is arrogantly male: women are seen as "chicks" to be spread all over the print media, the younger and "softer" the better.[3] This tradition is still alive in European theatre. Feminism has not been a dominant perspective in the works of celebrated German directors such as Frank Castorf and Thomas Ostermeier, to name only two. Neither of them appears to have been inspired by the Norwegian playwright Henrik Ibsen's liberating vision for women.

Hardly any other male dramatist has created as many major roles for women as Ibsen. However, many who have studied him tend to minimize his interest in gender. Joan Templeton examines this paradox in *Ibsen's Women*, and by emphasizing the gender issue in his plays, she reclaims him as a feminist author.[4] Another recent writer on Ibsen, Toril Moi, analyzes how Ibsen relates to the modernist tradition, and argues against those who consider his work passé.[5] She sees two different forces as having generated

---

How to cite this book chapter:
Rosenberg, Tiina 2016. AGAINST LOVE: Nora and Hedda on the Contemporary Scandinavian Stage. In: Rosenberg, Tiina *Don't Be Quiet, Start a Riot! Essays on Feminism and Performance.* Pp. 150–165. Stockholm: Stockholm University Press. DOI: http://dx.doi.org/10.16993/baf.g. License: CC-BY 4.0

resistance to Ibsen. First, the mindset that is hostile to theatre and considers it unworthy in comparison to literature, and second, the demands that some working in contemporary theatre place on theatricality, while they reject drama-based theatre.

Moi's passionate defense of Ibsen may appear unnecessary in the Scandinavian countries, where he remains celebrated and his plays are constantly performed. The 2006 Ibsen festival in Oslo on the centenary of his death featured more than 100 events, 15 foreign performances, and 9 premieres at the National Theatre. Running for three weeks, the annual festival pays tribute to Ibsen in every way imaginable. Ibsen is the theatrical bridge between Norway and the rest of the world.

Ibsen's work has no need to be rescued or recast for our time. While it arises from a nineteenth-century sensibility, it foreshadows the spirit of modernity. Hedda, Nora, Hedvig, and Ibsen's other female characters show us how human beings – women in particular – relate to love, sexuality, class, and nuclear family obligations. They are eager to fulfill the expectations of others while remaining silent about the shortcomings and failures that surround them. Ibsen's dramaturgy easily lends itself to modern adaptations, just as his themes appear neither distant nor foreign to contemporary audiences.

Ibsen appears to be the foremost critic of romantic love in European drama. Such love and the ability to express "the right feelings" have primarily been associated with women. Ibsen's female characters challenge love, relationships, marriage, and the traditional heterosexual family, even if they do not do so in explicitly feminist terms. Nora Helmer and Hedda Gabler defy the norms and conventions that nineteenth-century bourgeois women are expected to observe. As Laura Kipnis has characterized it, they each break free from their "domestic gulag, one by abandoning her household, and the other by taking her life."[6]

Over the past century, Scandinavian theatre has gone from considering Nora and Hedda immoral to finally showing understanding for them both. They are no longer seen as anomalies on today's Nordic stages as they struggle with intimacy. Love for them is more than a bolt from the blue that defies all rational understanding. It is something they wish to see manifested in an egalitarian way that allows for co-existence. Productions of Ibsen's *A Doll's House* in Gothenburg, Sweden, in 2004, and *Hedda Gabler* in Copenhagen, Denmark, in 2006, show how Scandinavian intimacy is renegotiated in heterosexual and lesbian versions of the two plays.

Henrik Ibsen, a feminist?

Mainstream interpretations of Ibsen propose that he used the women's issue as a metaphor representing freedom for all humankind. The principal evidence for this is a speech Ibsen made on May 26, 1898, at a banquet in his honor given by the Norwegian Women's Rights League.

> I am not a member of the Women's Rights League. Whatever I have written has been without any conscious thought of making propaganda. I have been more poet and less social philosopher than people generally seem inclined to believe. I thank you for the toast, but must disclaim the honor of having consciously worked for the women's rights movement. I am not even quite clear as to just what this women's rights movement really is. To me it has seemed a problem of humanity in general.[7]

Ibsen has a point: the "women's issue" does not concern women exclusively. It is part of the human condition. On the other hand, it would be naïve to pretend that the category of "woman" does not exist as a subaltern one.

The women in Ibsen's plays are very imposing. They shock by violating decorum and refusing to remain in their place according to the social mores of the time. They are not feminine in the sense of being "proper" mothers and sisters. They fire guns, abandon their homes, husbands, and children; in fact, they take over the masculine space in late nineteenth-century modern European realist drama. However, unlike Sweden's August Strindberg, Ibsen never fell into the essentialist and biological trap of the time. Late nineteenth-century Europe was saturated with a new biologism that tried to explain differences between the sexes in scientific terms. Anatomy is our destiny, as Sigmund Freud has said, and women who refused to be wives and mothers were stigmatized as abnormal. In the prevailing view, women belonged to a problematic gender that constantly needed to be explained, guided, and controlled.

Ibsen's insistence on women's autonomy makes him a modern dramatist of the first rank. He rejects the conventional dichotomy that divides femininity and masculinity into two completely different spheres. Ibsen's women are almost androgynous as they challenge the polarization of the sexes that is so much a part of patriarchal societies. While Ibsen's male characters fight to fulfill their masculinity, his female players struggle against their traditional gender script. As voices of modernity, they also come close to fulfilling the romantic ideals of women. Ibsen favors two types of women: one is sexually challenging, dangerous, and demanding, and the other is weak, friendly, and feminine, in short, paradigms of the bad and good woman.

Renegotiating Nora

A Doll's House, which premiered in 1879, is usually considered the beginning of women's liberation in international drama and society as a whole in Europe and elsewhere. Within a decade after the play was written, it had been performed in almost every Western country, and its ideas about the infantilization of women after their marriage had provoked extensive discussion and analysis. When Nora climbs onto the kitchen table and dances the tarantella, exhibiting the flesh-colored stockings under her masquerade costume to her astounded husband, something irreversible changes in modern European drama.

A Doll's House was unique in that it examined the husband–wife relationship without invoking a love triangle. Instead, it focused on women's situation in the family power structure. Nora does not leave the house to take up a role in society. She is searching for those rooms of her own that her husband denied her. Society itself is her enemy, and the patriarchal family is its instrument. Nora has been toyed with, first by her father, then by her husband, as it she were a plaything. She has never been allowed to lead her own life.

A Doll's House unequivocally contradicts the notion of idealized, bourgeois Western love. Ann Swidler has analyzed the traditional love narrative as a mythical story with a specific content and function.[8] Mythical love concerns the integrity of the individual; it constitutes a social drama in which individuals define themselves and their place in the world. This primarily involves a decisive choice. First, from out of a small circle of people, the one special person is sought. Love seems to be irrefutable, as unambiguous and true as the individual's own inner core, for it is by discovering whom you love that you discover who you really are. Second, true love must be as unique and exclusive as the individual. Third, as in Paul's letter to the Corinthians, love never fails, but endures and surmounts all obstacles, and may even continue beyond the individual's own existence.

Whether Nora's departure from her home is interpreted as a real or a metaphorical deed, it has been regarded over the decades as an immoral act. The "right" feeling (i.e., true love) not only places one in the correct position in the social hierarchy and gender order, but makes people congruous to one another. Through the enactment of the "right" feelings in the "right" way, people can establish themselves as the "right" kind of people. If so formulated, this "right" feeling appears as a form of social capital that confers the "right" social value and prestige on a person. In other words, the "right" feeling consists of something completely other than feelings. It is about conformity to social gender norms, which can only be transgressed at great cost.[9]

From the outset Nora has stood as a paradigm for a woman's liberation from a claustrophobic marriage. Her stage character once caused a sensation, and in a way it still does. Terje Maerli's 2004 adaptation of *The Doll's House* for the Gothenburg City Theatre was based on a vision of Nora as our contemporary. The production was less about women's liberation than about marriage as a social contract – even a "domestic gulag." In the space of two hours Maerli created a world not unlike that of Thomas Ostermeier's *Nora* at the Schaubühne in Berlin. We witness a busy, middle-class family using cell phones and laptops, always connected with other people, but never to those around them.

Maerli's Nora wears a red mini-skirt. Her sex appeal is very Lolita-like. The intense rhythm of the performance underlines the growing desperation in the doll's house before us. However, the ending takes a surprising turn. Just as Nora is about to leave, she appears before us properly dressed for the Scandinavian winter in boots and a warm coat. Ready to take on the world, she departs, but not without a sort of final reconciliation. Were this Strindberg, such a scene would have ended in total humiliation for the woman. Maerli, however, creates a situation in which the couple can say goodbye, if not as friends, at least on an almost equal basis. Still, this initial step toward equality only occurs after Torvald relinquishes ownership of the marriage and allows Nora her own choice.

Maerli's production focused on the possibility of an egalitarian outcome. Nora's leaving home is neither explained nor unexpected. Instead, it is the beginning of a new relationship in which the idea of an all-conquering and all-reconciling love has been exchanged for a more realistic awareness that coexistence requires constant compromise. Although such a mythic-romantic love story is rarely seen on the Scandinavian stage and belongs more to the Hollywood tradition, its allure is undeniable. The critique of romantic couples, marriage, and the nuclear family has been on the feminist agenda for a long time, but still has not managed to effectively challenge the hegemonic position of normative heterosexuality.

In the 1970s, feminists declared that romantic love afflicted women in a double sense. It stood for an ideology that was repressive, holding women captive and exploiting them in heterosexual relationships.[10] Love was an opiate for women, and it was thought that if only this false awareness were revealed it would die of itself. This did not happen. Maerli's production transposed the discussion to a more realistic, democratic, and equitable vision of love. According to Anthony Giddens, we are generally moving in the direction of a society with a new kind of democratic, equal intimate relationship at its core. This is a possibility open to everyone, since it is not based on compelling economic arrangements or social conventions.[11]

Giddens regards the women's liberation movement as one of the driving forces behind this development. However, it may be wishful thinking on his part. There is little evidence that people nowadays are engaged in a self-reflecting process of shaping themselves and their identity through love relationships. There is even less reason to assume that heterosexual relationships in the West or elsewhere are increasingly characterized by democratic love and intimacy. On the contrary, economic disparity and a lack of genuine equality continue to intrude into the everyday reality of intimate relationships.

A more democratic version of the classic love story has emerged as a counterpart to previous ones. Echoing social changes and the evolution of new ideals, modern theatre is trying to keep up with contemporary intimacy by portraying it from different perspectives. The story line in the Gothenburg production of *A Doll's House* does not tell us whether Nora and Helmer will find their way to a more equitable intimacy, but there is at least an opening for renegotiation of their heterosexual relationship. The problem appears to be that the tender aura of love may get thrown out with the divorce.

"Good god! People don't do such things!"

Hedda Gabler is the silent heroine who quietly walks into the next room and shoots herself. She does not say much in the play; she has few lines and not a single monologue. Nevertheless, her inner voice screams out to us throughout the drama. Her marriage to Jörgen Tesman is hateful to her, and what she craves more than her conventional life are horses and weapons. She is the proud daughter of General Gabler and as such is never referred to as "Hedda Tesman," her married name. To the end she remains Hedda Gabler, the general's daughter, rather than Tesman's wife. Whatever could have induced her to marry Tesman in the first place? Hedda's enigmatic answer is only, "I had finished dancing. My time was up!"

Although Hedda distains traditional women's activities in favor of masculine pursuits, the men in the play nevertheless treat her as a sexual object. Tesman steadfastly hold to the belief that Hedda is madly in love with him. Brack takes it for granted that she will be his mistress, and Lövborg cannot forgive her for not wanting to have sex with him. Although Hedda is pregnant, there is nothing maternal about her. She does not want to live *for* a man, but *like* a man. There seems to be some gender ambiguity here.

The prospect of having a child revolts her. She challenges the consensus of the bourgeoisie to which she belongs. It is not a coincidence that the final words in the play, "Good God! People don't do such things!" are spoken by a male observer. The male characters in *Hedda Gabler* are literally blind. Tesman does not even comprehend that Hedda is pregnant, thinking that their honeymoon has made her fat. Rainer Werner Fassbinder once said that women's attitudes and behavior say more about society than men's, since men often live as though everything is as it should be.[12] This is certainly true of Jörgen Tesman.

If Hedda once seemed like a tragic impossibility, over the years she has come to symbolize how a patriarchal world refuses to share power. Hedda's burden is that she is expected to function as wife, childbearer, and hostess. But she is also General Gabler's daughter, a sophisticated woman who cannot suffer bourgeois bigotry. She rules mainly on the strength of her sexuality, flirting with everyone except her husband. Her primary target is Eilert Lövborg, a strong, intelligent man who has managed to overcome his alcoholism. But he refuses to be conquered by her and so must be crushed.

Hedda Gabler is Ibsen's reply to Strindberg's *Miss Julie*. Hedda, too, is a "man-woman," raised by her father and equipped with two pistols, often interpreted in the Freudian tradition as wielding a pair of threatening erections. She has also been read intertextually as a hysterical version of Mrs. Alving in *Ghosts*, a "frigid" woman who is incapable of having a heterosexual love relationship.

By not choosing to fall for any of the men around her, Hedda breaks the norm that Francesca Cancian calls the feminization of love.[13] The term refers to a process that took place in the nineteenth century. In Europe it led to love being identified as an inner emotion. It was linked to the home and to those bourgeois women who were relegated to that sphere. It was bound up with descriptions of women requiring intimate tenderness, while men wanted sex. Women and men's lives are obviously more complex than that, but Cancian holds that these narratives encourage men to downplay, and women to exaggerate, their emotional needs. This, in turn, has served to undermine women's power, while maximizing the power of men.

Because Hedda breaks the heterosexual matrix, she has often been interpreted as a destructive character, a man-hating lesbian monster. Hedda's acute desperation rests on several elements: her impending role as a mother– which will chain her to her femininity;

her way of using sex to manipulate and dominate men; and her upper-class origins. She can be called a disaster waiting to happen. In contrast to Thea Elvsted's "normal" femininity, Hedda's phallic non-femininity seems aggressive, hostile, and out of place. Thea, whose magnificent hair Hedda is constantly pulling, leaves the man she does not love for the one she does, something Hedda is not prepared to do. And so she must die!

The Western theatrical tradition seems to hold that the best woman on stage is a dead woman. A visit to the theatre is like going to one's own funeral, Hélène Cixous once wrote.[14] Western classical drama and opera celebrate women's death as a part of the pleasure of the total performance. Especially despicable women are sacrificed with great fanfare. The Western theatre as a whole perpetuates a social order that requires either domestication of the female protagonist or her death.[15]

Queering Hedda in Copenhagen

"I always felt that Hedda Gabler was a terrible character," wrote the Swedish theatre critic Leif Zern in his review of the Stockholm City Theatre's production of *Hedda Gabler* in 2007.[16] Hedda has just returned from her honeymoon and moved into her new home. Her husband, Jörgen Tesman, is in high spirits. He is on his way out the door to a gentlemen's dinner. When he returns he will work on his book about Flemish crafts of the Middle Ages. Meanwhile, Hedda is going mad. What kind of life is this? Hedda cannot cope with having to compromise, and Zern, the reviewer, wonders aloud why she married Tesman in the first place.

In another production of *Hedda Gabler* directed by Peter Langdal at the Betty Nansen Teatret in Copenhagen in 2006, Hedda marries a woman instead of a man. This innovative theatre has been exploring Ibsen for some time now. They staged a version of *A Doll's House* that was expressive and violent, and their *Peer Gynt* was performed as a stand-up comedy act including rap music. In the case of *Hedda Gabler* their mise-en-scène was spectacular. The director used sexuality to investigate who is in love with whom and why. His approach was founded on a queer analysis that literally turned the play on its head: the stage was built above the auditorium, and the audience was seated around the Tesman's minimalist contemporary home, which resembled a boxing ring. Everything was hi-tech: laptops, cell phones, large-screen TV, air-conditioning – even the human relations seemed to be electronically controlled.

While the director made no major alterations in Ibsen's text, he did change the gender of the characters. He presents Hedda and Tesman as a young, newly-married lesbian couple. The roles were played by two prominent Danish actresses, Sonja Richter and Paprika Steen. Thea Elvsted, now also a male, is married to another man whom he wishes to leave in order to engage in a relationship with Lövborg, who turns out to be bisexual. As in Ibsen's original straight casting, the drama centers about the re-union of Hedda and Lövborg, despite the destructive love affair they once had.

Hedda, already bored with marriage, plays with her guns in a terrifying way, simulating a number of frightening death scenes. She suffers from a divided self that fluctuates between gay/straight/bisexual inclinations, something she has tried to cover up by intensive engagement in sexual activities. Tesman, here a woman, does her best to keep things going. She is a modern, politically aware, intellectual lesbian who seeks social acceptance for her middle-class lesbian marriage, and who also desperately needs peaceful surroundings for her research and writing. She is so overeager in her quest for recognition and assimilation that she fails to recognize Hedda's frustration and existential angst. The lesbian couple is also threatened by the aggressive masculinity of Brack, the lawyer, who expresses his deep-rooted lesbophobia when drunk. Brack seems to suggest there is room for a "real" man in this lesbian thing, a fairly common attitude towards lesbians.

Langdal's production not only breaks with the heteronormative tradition of Hedda Gabler interpretations, but also demonstrates that not everyone is able to cope with instabilities, a code word for modern urban lifestyles. The portrayal of the protagonists as a lesbian couple also highlights heterosexual love as the culturally and socially dominant matrix that organizes the way relationships are supposed to be initiated, conducted, and experienced in order to be comprehensible to the characters and to society in general.

There have been few cultural representations of non-heterosexual love in films, on stage, and in novels, since relationships are usually structured upon heterosexuality, although modeling on same-sex relationships is increasing. However, Langdal's transposition of *Hedda Gabler* from heterosexuality to homosexuality does not necessarily mean that the heterosexual matrix has been broken.[17]

Langdal's production was probably not so ambitious as to challenge the heterosexual matrix that is also actively at work in same-sex relationships. Hedda is unhappy regardless of whether she is a lesbian or a heterosexual woman. While her partner is preoccupied with forging political alliances and the democratic acceptance of lesbian relationships in the world around her, Hedda could not care less. She takes no interest in having their relationship appear "good" and acceptable in the eyes of society, and she seems even less interested in the sexual politics that have broadened to include same-sex couples in Scandinavia.

Inclusion, however, comes at a price. Apart from the practical challenges of creating intimacy, lesbian and gay male couples still live in a society dominated by homophobia. The heterosexual matrix that shapes the love narratives and ideals of intimacy today is just as exclusionary and normative as before. Only respectable same-sex twosome relationships are acceptable in the public eye. Hedda's sexual dissatisfaction, appropriated from Ibsen's heterosexual version, is now carried over to the lesbian relationship. In this case, however, it is no salvation and leads to a renegotiation of the intimacy that defines sexual relationships, regardless of orientation.

Hedda Gabler in Copenhagen renews the discussion of emotion in Ibsen's work. Emotions have long been considered the hardest part of human personality to control, and for that reason the truest and most universally valid. The idea that emotions are exponents of truth is a contemporary Western belief. It views the individual as a unique being whose emotions are thought to communicate the inner core of one's being.

It may be very difficult to identify a feeling if we do not already know what it feels like and how it should be expressed. Like other emotions, love cannot thrive in isolation: it is a social and cultural construct. Michelle Rosaldo has written that emotions are "embodied thoughts." They are culturally specific, social practices, organized by narratives that we both enact and retell, and which shape and are shaped by our experiences.[18]

Focus on emotions

No matter how we interpret *A Doll's House* or *Hedda Gabler*, it is clear that frustration is crushing Nora and Hedda. Both characters convince us that something is fundamentally wrong with the world. Recent Scandinavian presentations of these two dramas have consequently challenged the structures that shape the emotional life of the individual. Hedda Gabler, who has existed for over a century as a destructive – although seductive – femme fatale, is no longer portrayed in that way, and has not been for many years. In our times, when divorce is the rule rather than the exception, Nora no longer strikes us as an anomaly, but as rather commonplace. Ibsen's ordinariness continues to appeal to Scandinavian audiences. In his day and in ours he reveals fundamental social injustices that society faces the lack of sexual equality being just one example.

In *The Cultural Politics of Emotion,* Sara Ahmed reminds us that injustice is also a question of how bodies come into contact with other bodies. We need to respond to injustice in a way that shows the complexity of the relation between violence, power, and emotion, rather than denying it.[19] If injustice is not simply about feeling bad, then justice is not only a matter of feeling good, overcoming pain, or even achieving happiness since being happy is not in itself a sign of justice. No one can be promised happiness as a return on their investment in social norms. Lauren Berlant considers this fantasy of happiness an ignorant form of optimism that believes "adjustment to certain forms or practices of living and thinking will secure one's happiness."[20] Such optimism does not originate from a subject, but is generated by promises made to the subject, which then may circulate as "truths" in public culture.[21]

Martin Heidegger has given a systematic account of how emotions influence our relationship to the world in § 29 of *Sein und Zeit*. He calls emotions *Befindlichkeit*, our way of existing in body and world in a way that makes life relevant to us. Without emotion, Heidegger says, there is no will, no thought, and no meaningful world in which to act. Emotions are not superficial attributes; they are the foundation of our interrelations with other human beings.[22]

The emotions and love relationships that Ibsen portrays are inextricably bound up with social structures and power constellations beyond the individual. Those structures intersect and diverge in a nexus of gender, sexuality, class, race, and other power axes. One factor that seems to have disappeared from the emotional agenda of representation, however, is the dream of an all-consuming and all-conquering romantic love that Ibsen has so effectively deflated. Still, the dream is probably stronger than reality, and thus may persist in the imagination. As Laura Kipnis writes in *Against Love*: "Who would dream of being against love? No one. Love is, as everyone knows, a mysterious and all-controlling force, with vast power over our thoughts and life decisions. Love is boss, and a demanding one too: it demands our loyalty. . . . There's no way of being against love precisely because we moderns are constituted as beings yearning to be filled, craving connection, needing to adore and be adored, because love is vital plasma and everything else in the world is just tap water."[23]

Notes

1. Scruton, *Thinkers*, 1, 87.

2. Segal, *Straight Sex*, 17.

3. Ibid., 22.

4. Templeton, *Ibsen's Women*.

5. Moi, *Henrik Ibsen*.

6. Kipnis, *Against Love*, 52–104.

7. Finney, "Ibsen and Feminism," 90.

8. Swidler, *Talk of Love*.

9. Nordin, *Man ska ju vara två*, 57–60.

10. Jackson, *Heterosexuality in Question*; Pearce & Stacey, *Romance Revisited*.

11. Giddens, *Transformation of Intimacy*, 128.

12. Bensoussan, "Wir sitzen auf einem Vulkan," 570.

13. Cancian, "Feminization of Love."

14. Cixous, "Aller à la mer."

15. Clément, *L'opéra*.

16. Zern, "Magisk Hedda."

17. The heterosexual matrix is defined by Judith Butler as "a hegemonic discursive/epistemic model of gender intelligibility that assumes that for bodies to cohere and make sense there must be a stable sex expressed through a stable gender (masculine expresses male, feminine female) that is oppositionally and hierarchically defined through the compulsory practice of heterosexuality." *Gender Trouble*, 151, note 6.

18. Nordin, *Man ska ju vara två*, 58–59; Rosaldo, "Anthropology of Self."

19. Ahmed, *Cultural Politics*, 196.

20. Berlant, "Two Girls," 75.

21. Ahmed, *Cultural Politics*, 196.

22. Martin Heidegger, *Sein und Zeit*.

23. Kipnis, *Against Love*, 3.

Works Cited

Ahmed, Sara. *The Cultural Politics of Emotion*. New York: Routledge, 2004.

Bensoussan, Georges. "Wir sitzen auf einem Vulkan: Rainer Werner Fassbinder über Deutschland, Antisemitismus und Homosexualität." In *Fassbinder über Fassbinder: Die ungekürzten Interviews*, edited by Robert Fischer, 557–578. Frankfurt: Verlag der Autoren, 2004.

Berlant, Laurent. "Two Girls, Fat and Thin." In *Regarding Sedgwick: Essays on Queer Culture and Critical Theory*, edited by Stephen Barber and David Clark, 71–108. New York: Routledge, 2002.

Butler, Judith. *Gender Trouble: Feminism and the Subversion of Identity*. New York: Routledge, 1990.

Cancian, Francesca M. "The Feminization of Love." *Signs: Journal of Women in Culture and Society* 11 (1986): 692–709.

Cixous, Hélène, "Aller à la mer." *Le Monde*, 28 April 1977.

Clément, Catherine. *L'opéra ou la défaite des femmes*. Paris: Grasset, 1979.

Finney, Gail. "Ibsen and Feminism." In *The Cambridge Companion to Ibsen*, edited by James McFarlane, 89–105. Cambridge, UK: Cambridge University Press, 1994.

Giddens, Anthony. *The Transformation of Intimacy*. Oxford: Polity Press, 1992.

Heidegger, Martin. *Sein und Zeit*, Tübingen: Niemeyer, 2006 [1927].

Jackson, Stevi. *Heterosexuality in Question*. London: Sage, 1999.

Kipnis, Laura. *Against Love: A Polemic*. New York: Pantheon, 2003.

Moi, Toril. *Henrik Ibsen and the Birth of Modernism: Art, Theatre, Philosophy*. Oxford: Oxford University Press, 2006.

Nordin, Lissa. *Man ska ju vara två: Män och kärlekslängtan i norrländsk glesbygd* (Two Is Better than One. Men, Love, and Longing in Northern Rural Areas). Stockholm: Natur och Kultur, 2007.

Pearce, Lynne, and Jackie Stacey, eds. *Romance Revisited*. London: Lawrence & Wishart, 1995.

Rosaldo, Michelle Z. "Toward an Anthropology of Self and Feeling." In *Culture Theory: Essays on Mind, Self, and Emotion*, edited by Richard A. Shweder and Robert A. Levine, 137–157. Cambridge: Cambridge University Press, 1984.

Scruton, Roger. *Thinkers of the New Left*. London: Longman, 1985.

Segal, Lynne. *Straight Sex: The Politics of Pleasure*. London: Virago Press, 1994.

Swidler, Ann. *Talk of Love: How Culture Matters*. Chicago: University of Chicago Press, 2001.

Templeton, Joan. *Ibsen's Women*. Cambridge: Cambridge University Press, 1997.

Zern, Leif. "Magisk Hedda." *Dagens Nyheter*, 21 April 2007.

Alexandra Dahlström rehearsing her role as Alexandra/Julie at The Schoolhouse Theater, Croton Falls, New York. Still from Fia-Stina Sandlund's film *She's Staging It*, 2012. Photographer: Marius Dybwad Brandrud. Copyright CC-BY-NC-ND.

8. From Here to Eternity: Miss Julie Strikes Back and Refuses to Die

Arrange for the bored and possibly clueless daughter of a count to find herself in the presence of a handsome servant with social ambitions. Add a maid who represents order, morality, and common sense. Immerse them in the Swedish midsummer night with its atmosphere of sexuality and magic. The result is the August Strindberg classic, *Miss Julie*, a play that has never ceased to fascinate directors, actors, and audiences since it was first staged in Copenhagen in 1889.[1]

It has long been claimed that *A Doll's House* was the world's most performed play. Today *Miss Julie* seems about to edge Henrik Ibsen's drama from the top position. European theatres have recently presented *Miss Julie* in a variety of interpretations, including a British update by Patrick Marber directed by Natalie Abrahami at Young Vic in London; a multimedia version by Katie Mitchell and Leo Warner at the Schaubühne in Berlin; and a French mise-en-scène by Frédéric Fisbach, in which Juliette Binoche makes one of her rare appearances on stage. The Schaubühne's director and CEO, Thomas Ostermeier, has set his *Miss Julie* in contemporary Moscow. As in the same director's earlier productions of *A Doll's House* and *Hedda Gabler*, Miss Julie is trapped in a claustrophobic middle-class setting from whose social patterns she is unable to break free. The Russian Julie is the spoiled daughter of a former KGB officer who is now a nouveau-riche businessman living in luxury and opulence. We have watched Ostermeier's Nora and Hedda go under, and now it is Julie's turn to die.

When Sweden observed the centennial of Strindberg's death in 2012, some greeted the upcoming celebration with skepticism and an air of boredom. There had already been a wide-ranging

---

How to cite this book chapter:
Rosenberg, Tiina 2016. From Here to Eternity: Miss Julie Strikes Back and Refuses to Die. In: Rosenberg, Tiina *Don't Be Quiet, Start a Riot! Essays on Feminism and Performance*. Pp. 166–174. Stockholm: Stockholm University Press. DOI: http://dx.doi.org/10.16993/baf.h. License: CC-BY 4.0

discussion about women playwrights whose works, after being performed in the 1880s, were then overshadowed by Strindberg, and had only recently been rediscovered and brought to the stage once more. What could possibly be new about Strindberg? Mounting Strindberg in Sweden has mainly come to mean two things: first, performing the canonized repertoire, and second, having one of the players impersonate Strindberg himself. No other Swedish playwright or author has been so identified with his characters as Strindberg. For a long time, it was axiomatic that male protagonists in productions of Strindberg's plays wore the Strindberg mask: a mustache, a trim goatee, and a suspicious gaze.[2] In foreign productions audiences are typically given a wider breadth of interpretation as directors and actors can move more freely outside the Swedish national tradition. But the centennial has not been as predictable as one might have imagined. Three exciting feminist multimedia productions of *Miss Julie*, the play that has been one of the year's darlings, bear a closer look.

In Strindberg's own performance space, Intima Teatern (The Intimate Theatre) in Stockholm, Anna Pettersson offered a virtuoso solo performance in 2012, in which she played the actress-director and the three roles of Julie, Jean, and Kristin. The audience entered to find an open curtain that revealed a classic *Miss Julie* setting: a kitchen table, an open window with curtains stirred by a summer breeze, and Swedish midsummer music playing in the background. But as soon as Pettersson came out the atmosphere changed radically. As she cleared all the props from the stage, a straight razor was projected on a large screen, and she began to wonder aloud how she will ever make it through the play. She waved a symbolic Strindberg about in the form of a book, raising questions about certain passages in the drama, performing parts of scenes, and testing the characters – all in a lively exchange with the audience.

In a theatre talk that followed the show, Pettersson revealed that she had originally intended to stage *Miss Julie* with three actors, but then decided to perform all three roles herself. She subsequently added the character of Anna, an actress, director, and contemporary woman who raises her voice in protest, but still engages with the Strindberg legacy. Pettersson's production of *Miss Julie*, given as part of the artistic research program at the Stockholm Academy of Dramatic Arts, examined the convention of Miss Julie and her compulsory suicide. On stage Pettersson asked angrily, "Why should Julie always have to kill herself? Why does Jean not commit suicide?" Since Jean also had sex with her, his shame and guilt ought to be as heavy as hers.

It is a question the audience carries home with them. Does Julie really have to die in the end? It seems to depend on one's point of view. The end is only half-explicit in the play: both Julie and Jean are hesitant, but when Jean admonishes Julie that, although it is terrifying, she has to go through with it, she numbly walks off-stage with the razor. There is a power and dramaturgic seduction in Strindberg's play that makes the audience hang on every word of Strindberg's, whether they like it or not. In order to oppose this force, Pettersson built in a certain distance between the stage and the audience. In an innovative, simultaneous approach that did not undermine the power of the play, she performed *Miss Julie* as a chain of segments in which she both acted out and reacted to today's challenges.

Another feminist project built on the theme of *Miss Julie* is Fia-Stina Sandlund's art film trilogy, *Save Miss Julie*: *She's Blonde Like Me* (2010), *She's Staging It* (2011), and *She's Wild Again Tonight* (2015), focusing on a contemporary couple, Julie and Jean, living in New York. Sandlund is a feminist art activist who became known to a wider Swedish public in 2001 through the Slimy Old Men action (*Gubbslem*) in which she and fellow artist Joanna Rytel attacked the Miss Sweden beauty contest. Sandlund has been involved in performance and direct action ever since. For the role of Julie in the Saving Miss Julie project she chose Alexandra Dahlström, known from the film *Show Me Love* (1998), a groundbreaking examination of teenage lesbian love in a small Swedish town.

In *Save Miss Julie: She's Blonde Like Me,* Sandlund meets Dahlström at Arlanda airport in Stockholm for an audition. Three days later, they put on a performance at the Venice Art Biennale in the form of an interview. The two discuss *Miss Julie* and their own experiences as younger women, and find they have a lot in common with the characters they portray in the film. In the second part of the trilogy, *She's Staging It,* Dahlström travels to New York, where rehearsals of Sandlund's version of *Miss Julie,*

She's Wild Again Tonight (a line from the play and also the title of the third part of the trilogy), are taking place. The screenplay is by Josefin Adolfsson, who wrote Lisa Aschan's film *She Monkeys* (2011). An African-American trans-butch actor, Lea Robinson, plays Jean. By bringing in female masculinity Robinson turns the play into a lesbian plot. This approach has been more popular in contemporary productions of Ibsen (Hedda Gabler has become a favorite lesbian character) than in performing Strindberg. The race-related dramaturgy had already been done in South Africa, again with a white Julie and a black Jean. A production in Canada sets the story in a native Canadian context.

Sandlund's *Miss Julie* is about power, but it is also about shame and sexuality. Although the trilogy is composed of art films, they are constructed in the action-documentary-analysis style Sandlund prefers. Her feminist conception shares its point of departure with that of Anna Pettersson. By rescuing Miss Julie from an obligatory suicide, both playwrights oppose the tradition of dead women's theatre. Feminists have become frustrated with this convention, which goes back to ancient Greek drama, where women were routinely murdered or sacrificed.[3] When asked why a feminist activist like herself would bother to work with Strindberg's play, Sandlund responded:

> People have questioned the fact that I am dealing with Strindberg, instead of dealing with one of his female colleagues. But it is not Strindberg himself who is interesting; it is our interpretations of his work that are exciting because I think he has great plays and stories. Strindberg was ahead of his time and saw these structures and these problems, although he had a different attitude towards them. So it is easy to identify with him. He felt that the personal was political: he was upset and questioned the existing power structures.[4]

Sandlund's mission is to rescue *Miss Julie* from death, and she characterizes her project by three key words: gender, comedy, and sadomasochism. The inspiration for her interpretation is taken from feminism and the psychoanalytic work of Jessica Benjamin, who also appears in the film *She's Staging It*. In addition to sexuality and shame, Sandlund considers class and gender to be the main themes of *Miss Julie*. She places the story in a contemporary setting and wants to show that these issues still persist for women.

Strindberg calls Julie a 'half-woman,' that is, a woman brought up to believe that she has the same rights and freedoms as a man, and this drives her to her death.[5] Sandlund, born in the 1970s, reminds us that although "we now live in a feminist conscious society that claims to accept 'half women', there still remains tremendous resistance."[6] She finds *Miss Julie* especially relevant because it deals with both class and gender. Sandlund identifies herself with the character of Julie and wants all the 'half women' to unite in a world where women believe they can become anything they want. "A hard awakening," Sandlund notes dryly.[7]

British director Katie Mitchell and video artist Leo Warner have created a strikingly radical interpretation of *Miss Julie*. The Schaubühne originally mounted their production in 2010. It was among the main attractions of the Avignon Theatre Festival of 2011, reaching Stockholm and the Bergman Festival in May 2012. A young German ensemble performs *Miss Julie* in an impressive blend of film and theatre. The stage action is simultaneous, but not identical, with a film projected on a screen above it. Jean (Tilman Strauss), Julia (Louise Wolfram), and Kristin (Jule Böwe) enact Strindberg's tragedy in an atmospheric mansion kitchen as a technician selects certain film sequences and projects them on the screen. Combining performance, video, and live music on stage is an approach Mitchell and Warner have previously applied in productions of Virginia Woolf's *Waves* and Dostoyevsky's *The Idiot* at the National Theatre in London. They transform the stage into a movie studio, and the actors appear in close-ups on the screen.

The sequences in *Miss Julie* that are shown on the screen are full of Nordic nostalgia reminiscent of Ingmar Bergman. Bergman's influence over the play's visual composition becomes clearer when *Miss Julie* is performed in Sweden. Mitchell, who grew up with Bergman's films, has stated that the opportunity of working with Bergman's actors brought her to Sweden a few years ago to direct *Easter*, her first Strindberg production, at the Royal Dramatic Theatre in Stockholm.[8]

Mitchell and Warner's cinematic treatment opens new perspectives on Strindberg. Julie thrusts herself into the picture like a knife slipping in between Kristin and Jean. In one scene Kristin is alone in the foreground, looking out of a window, while Jean and Julie are preoccupied with each other in the background. While Kristin sleeps the ensemble takes the stage and creates a suggestive cinematic dream sequence that includes water and lighting effects. Gareth Fry's music, performed by the cellist Chloe Miller, dynamically unifies the mise-en-scène.[9]

In this interpretation, *Miss Julie* is filtered through Kristin, a working class woman, who changes the dynamic from traditional productions of the play. She rapturously picks midsummer flowers and looks on as the increasingly frivolous game between her unfaithful fiancé and the daughter of her upper-class employer intensifies. Alone in her room Kristin listens to them quarreling in the kitchen and is overcome with grief.[10] By contrast, most productions depict Kristin as a woman of limited emotional range, as though her imagination could neither rise above the mundane nor be touched by any sense of romance or heartbreak.

While technology may tend to keep an audience at a distance, in this case frequent tight camera shots projected on the screen bring Kristin close to the audience: they see the reddened hands of a domestic worker, her drawn skin, tired eyes, and anguish as she overhears Jean in the act of betraying her. Theatergoers are drawn into her consciousness and see the drama through her eyes. In an unusual arrangement, three actors perform the role of Kristin. One sometimes takes up a position at a separate microphone and reads poems by Inger Christensen as Kristin's internal monologue. The production says little about who these three aspects of Kristin are. It is rather a midsummer night's rhapsody of emptiness where mute cameras register inner and outer actions on stage as a human tragedy unfolds.

None of the three multimedia productions described above are based on traditional conceptions. The technique of integrating film sequences has become a commonplace in contemporary theatre. The Swedish critic Leif Zern finds that this slights the work of actors: not only is the constant presence of electronic equipment stressful for the performers, but there are sometimes more screens than actors on stage.[11]

Nevertheless, technology used creatively in these productions has facilitated new interpretations. Mitchell says she wanted to stage something as technically sophisticated as a feature film in order to bring the story closer to the audience and disclose elements that may reawaken our interest in Strindberg. A breath of fresh air may just be what the performing arts need in a high-tech era where live theatre has ceased to be a priority for many people. The generation born just before the millennium lives in a transnational, mobile world linked via the Internet, while the performing arts remain linguistically and spatially bound to the local environment. Mitchell hopes that her productions will kindle enthusiasm among young audiences and draw them to the theatre, either as participants or spectators.[12]

Anna Pettersson, Fia-Stina Sandlund, and Katie Mitchell have succeeded in combining a vision of Strindberg with a creative application of technology. To the concern that technology may overwhelm actors, Mitchell responds, "I am attempting to keep the integrity of the live experience and also enhance the complexity and nuances."[13] All three directors have envisioned the characters in *Miss Julie* in their unique ways. When Mitchell heard about Pettersson's one woman *Miss*, she exclaimed, "It's wonderful that the two of us, from two different countries, independently of each other, challenge Strindberg. He should not end up in a museum!"[14]

Notes

1. Ring, "Genial Fröken Julie." See also Strindberg, *Miss Julie*.

2. Zern, "Sju mustacher."

3. Cixious, "Aller à la mer."

4. Quoted in Gelin, "De vill rädda livet."

5. Gustavsson, "Julie måste inte dö."

6. Quoted in Gelin, "De vill rädda livet."

7. Ibid.

8. Ångström, "Multimedia ger Julie nytt liv."

9. Zern, "Två sällsynta mästerverk."

10. Benér, "Dramatisk urkraft bäddar."

11. Zern, "Kroppen är teaterns hus."

12. Ångström, "Multimedia ger Julie nytt liv."

13. Ibid.

14. Ibid.

Works Cited

Ångström, Anna. "Multimedia ger Julie nytt liv" (Multimedia Give Julie New Life). *Svenska Dagbladet, Kultur*, 13 May 2012.

Benér, Theresa. "Dramatisk urkraft bäddar för nytolkningar" (Dramatic Primordial Beds for New Interpretations). *Svenska Dagbladet, Kultur*, 28 May 2012.

Cixous, Hélène. "Aller à la mer." *Le Monde*, 28 Apr 1977. English translation in *Twentieth Century Theatre: A Sourcebook*, edited by Richard Drain, 133–135. London: Routledge, 1995.

Gelin, Martin. "De vill rädda livet på fröken Julie" (They Want to Rescue Miss Julie). *Dagens Nyheter, Kultur*, 16 Oct 2011.

Gustavsson, Andreas. "Julie måste inte dö" (Julie Must Not Die). *ETC Stockholm*, 11 May 2012.

Ring, Lars. "Genial Fröken Julie." (A Brilliant Miss Julie). *Svenska Dagbladet*, 22 Apr 22 2012.

Strindberg, August. *Miss Julie and Other Plays*. Translated by Michael Robinson. Oxford: Oxford University Press, 2009.

Zern, Leif. "Kroppen är teaterns hus" (The Body Is the Home of Theatre). *Dagens Nyheter, Kultur*, 10 Dec 2009.

———. "Sju mustacher, tre hattar, men bara en skald." (Seven Mustasches, Three Hats, but Only One Author), *Dagens Nyheter, Kultur*, 22 Jan 2012.

PART 3:
ON FEMINIST ACTIVIST AESTHETICS

Valerie Solanas for President of the United States (Sara Stridsberg). Ingela Olsson (Valerie Solanas) and Noomi Rapace (Cosmogirl). Royal Dramatic Theatre, Stockholm, 2006. Photographer: Roger Stenberg. Copyright CC-BY-NC-ND, Royal Dramatic Theatre, Stockholm.

9. Still Angry After All These Years, or Valerie Solanas Under Your Skin

> Every man, deep down, knows he's a piece of shit.
> —Valerie Solanas, *S.C.U.M. Manifesto*

On April 30, 1988, the body of Valerie Solanas was found at the Bristol Hotel, a single-room occupancy in the Tenderloin District of San Francisco. According to the terse police report she was kneeling beside the bed in the tidy room with papers carefully arranged on her desk. The report goes on to state that Solanas had died around April 25 and that cadaverous worms had invaded her body. The hotel staff had seen her writing at her desk a few weeks earlier.

The image of the neat room with piles of manuscripts and the dead body of Solanas fascinated Sara Stridsberg, a Swedish playwright and novelist. She decided to find out who Solanas was, just as Isabelle Collin Dufresne, one of Andy Warhol's superstars, had done almost two decades earlier. In the 1960s, Dufresne, better known as Ultra Violet, had phoned people who knew Solanas. By the time Solanas died only a few of them were still alive. They had warned Ultra Violet about Solanas. She is dangerous, they said.[1]

Stridsberg was intrigued by everything she found out. Solanas literally got under her skin. Stridsberg's novel, *The Dream Faculty: An Addition to the Theory of Sexuality* (2006) and her play *Valerie Jean Solanas for President of the United States* (2006) both center around Solanas. Characteristic for Stridsberg's work are her heroines, whom she depicts in a vulnerable and deplorable state, although they continue to maintain their dignity. Stridsberg's play tells of Solanas's wounded childhood, how she sold her body to finance her studies in psychology, why she shot Andy Warhol, and

---

How to cite this book chapter:
Rosenberg, Tiina 2016. Still Angry After All These Years, or Valerie Solanas Under Your Skin. In: Rosenberg, Tiina *Don't Be Quiet, Start a Riot! Essays on Feminism and Performance.* Pp. 176–182. Stockholm: Stockholm University Press. DOI: http://dx.doi.org/10.16993/baf.i. License: CC-BY 4.0

about her death in the hotel room in San Francisco. The playwright also translated Solanas's *S.C.U.M. Manifesto* from English into Swedish in 2003 and provided the text with an extensive introduction. The acronym *S.C.U.M.* stands for Society of Cutting Up Men, a fictitious organization whose founder and sole member was Solanas. The original Swedish version of the *S.C.U.M. Manifesto* was performed in Stockholm in 2003, staged as a chorus of angry women reciting it like an act of political agitation.

Stridsberg knew the *S.C.U.M. Manifesto* by heart. She had laughed and cried over this irresistible wild and crazy satire of patriarchy that resembled nothing a feminist had ever written before. The language of the manifesto is harsh and its ideals completely beyond reach. Its intense tone does not belong to any school of rhetoric, politics, art, or philosophy. It is a fantastically desperate and euphorically mad text. Stridsberg believes that the *S.C.U.M. Manifesto* is all about poetry, not politics in the traditional sense. She places Solanas in the same company as Sylvia Plath, Courtney Love, Gertrude Stein, Yoko Ono, Billie Holiday, and Tracey Emin.

Writing about Solanas was Stridsberg's attempt to communicate with the woman whose turbulent life had produced the most outlandish utopia ever. Stridsberg describes Solanas's childhood as a *dance macabre* of violence and brutality, and her end as the contrast between the frenzied voice of the manifesto and a lonely death in a cheap hotel room. Solanas's complicated life embraced things we are used to regarding as incompatible. Stridsberg finds her "the intellectual whore, the utopian misanthrope. She is the victim who refuses to excuse herself. She is the child without childhood; she is the women's movement without women. She is the absolute triumph and the definitive defeat."[2] Stridsberg was also determined to find out why Solanas, the anti-violence activist, would shoot Andy Warhol. Those attending Stridsberg's play received no answer to that question; they only learned that Solanas regretted she had not been a better shot.

The real Valerie Solanas (1936–1988) was born in Ventnor City, New Jersey. Very little is known about her life until 1966 when she moved to Greenwich Village and published the play *Up Your Ass*. It featured a man-hating heroine who managed to survive as a sex worker and beggar, as Solanas had done. Andy Warhol liked *Up Your Ass* and they began to socialize. In 1967 Solanas wrote the *S.C.U.M. Manifesto*. Then, one year later, she suddenly shot Andy Warhol. There are many interpretations of her action. Some have seen it as a feminist attack on Warhol as the master vampire of the arts. This is how the story is told in the film *I Shot Andy Warhol* (1996), which presents Solanas as a feminist heroine. After Solanas was released from jail in 1971, her reputation oscillated between feminist martyr and madwoman. During the times when she was not hospitalized, she lived alone in run-down hotels and spent her time writing.

As Stridsberg mulled over the piles of papers and manuscripts on Solanas's desk in her imagination, a dream play began to emerge. In this play she saw Solanas as a brilliant but confused bag lady dressed in a silver coat. As the play *Valerie Jean Solanas for President of the United States* opens, Valerie is dying in a hotel room. Now and then she rises from her deathbed and enacts dream sequences, hallucinations, and scenes from her life. Valerie is the driving force of the play. She appears before us as its explosive element, while the other characters are merely pale figures. Valerie is depicted as standing against the world, pushing beyond all limits. She moves rapidly from the hopeful young student to the drug-addicted street person. She talks nonstop; her genre is monologue and her tempo *furioso*. Whether we see her in prison or in a mental institution, she is hysterically repeating her mantra that men are superfluous and inferior to women in every respect. In one ultra-rapid discourse Valerie appears to be fleeing from a pursuer. Her words function as both a weapon and music.

Stridsberg's interest in Solanas may be viewed in the context of the socially committed Swedish theatre of the 1990s and early 2000s, although the political performing arts scene in Sweden has links back to earlier decades. Taking an open political stand on gender, sexuality, ethnicity, class, and other social issues were hot topics in the Swedish theatre during the late 1990s, but the most pressing issue was and remains today the downscaling of the Swedish welfare state. Leftist feminists felt that the world-renowned Swedish project of a social democratic, egalitarian, and open society had changed beyond recognition.[3]

The public reading of the *S.C.U.M. Manifesto* was strongly challenged by men, who saw neither the irony of the text nor what the point of such an event was altogether. The historical context in which the performance took place was significant: all the political parties in Sweden, with the exception of the Conservatives and Christian Democrats, had declared themselves feminist parties. At this moment of presumed feminist consensus, the *S.C.U.M. Manifesto* resounded like a declaration of war. Sweden was a country in which pragmatic gender equality politics could not afford to have angry lesbian feminists making explicit proclamations in a public space, or anywhere else for that matter.

Looking back on that time, it becomes clear that what took place was a political misunderstanding in which mainstream gender equality politics were taken for feminism. The price of mainstreaming is always a certain degree of adjustment to hegemony. Feminism occupied a paradoxical position in the early 2000s; it was at once integral to hegemonic gender equality politics, and at the same time marginal, feared, and ridiculed. It had become a victim of its own success. A bored bourgeoisie picked out the parts of feminist and leftist subculture that they found amusing, consumed it, but did not "buy" it.

This was the moment when feminist artists turned to revolutionaries like Valerie Solanas or Ulrike Meinhof, rather than looking to mainstream politics for support. Stridsberg reveled in a figure who could never become mainstream: the angry lesbian feminist. There is no social space that such a character may inhabit. Stridsberg's main concern was resistance, as Meinhof had succinctly defined the term in her 1967 article "From Protest to Resistance" in the journal *konkret*. "Protest," Meinhof wrote, "is when you say that something does not suit you. Resistance is when you see to it that the thing not suiting you stops."[4] The logic here is that there is not necessarily anything wrong with angry women, but there is something wrong with a heterosexist world. Angry women are generally not well received, but the history of anger gives feminist politics its edge. Anger is a form of 'against-ness' akin to the way Meinhof defines resistance. It is not only a sign of protest, but seeks to put an end to the thing you are protesting against.

Valerie Solanas is not easy to shake off. "She is a state of mind," Stridsberg writes, "a play, an invasion, a mirror, a wonderland, and a promise of absolutely nothing. Her heart becomes an insatiable pulsating wound. Valerie is both a utopist and a romantic."[5]

Stridsberg has entitled her play *Valerie Jean Solanas for President of the United States* because she envisions a black utopia. She addresses life and death, expressing, in Jill Dolan's words, "a rather melancholic yearning for a different future, fueled by wistful but persistent hope."[6] Dolan terms this militant optimism.

Stridsberg's play and novel are her postmortem gifts to Solanas, the fulfillment of a wish to give her everything she failed to obtain when alive: an army of lovers in silver coats, her life as a dream and a nightmare. Stridsberg has written that she never loved any text as much as she did the *S.C.U.M. Manifesto*. "It has changed my way of thinking, my heart, and my cunt, my way of moving through the city; it has taught me everything worth knowing."[7] Stridsberg writes that the *Manifesto* is impossible to forget once you have read and absorbed it. Patriarchy has every reason to be fearful of it because it is a dangerous text. Clarity (the text forces you to see) and mercilessness (the text has no loyalty to men) are its gift to the reader. When Solanas was a little girl her father raped her. She later lived for a long time as a sex worker. The street is the loneliest place in the world and it is the heart of patriarchy: "a puffing, screaming, black hole of misogyny and sticky bodily fluids. *S.C.U.M.* is written of that experience. What is said about patriarchy from that position is the only thing that is worth knowing about patriarchy."[8]

In creating the Valerie character Stridsberg takes Solanas seriously and also demonstrates her own retrospective solidarity with the author. Valerie is the kind of person we have all seen begging on the street, talking to themselves, frightening passers-by. You can recognize a Valerie lookalike by her worn-out coat and bag full of unassorted curiosities. Lipstick may be smeared on her face and she may be carrying on an endless conversation with herself on all kinds of topics. If you stop for a moment and listen to what such a person is saying, you may hear anything from hardcore poetry to absolute nonsense to brilliant political analysis. It may be incomprehensible but also extraordinarily beautiful, and may range from obscure to crystal clear. "Everything is made up and poetry makes it obvious," Stridsberg says about the *Manifesto*.[9] It is a text without compromises. "This is an agenda for eternity and utopia," Stridsberg concludes, as she reminds her readers that, "It is now or never. The future is *S.C.U.M.* The future is already here."[10]

Notes

1. Violet, *Famous for 15 Minutes*.
2. Stridsberg, "Den svarta utopin."
3. Rosenberg, "Revival," 413.
4. Meinhof, "Von Protest zum Widerstand." For a comprehensive list of Meinhof's publications see: www.jutta-dirfurth.de and www.oekolinx-arl.de
5. Stridsberg, "Den svarta utopin," 11.
6. Dolan, *Utopia in Performance*, 142.
7. Stridsberg, "Förord," 7.
8. Ibid., 10–11.
9. Ibid., 11.
10. Ibid., 29.

Works Cited

Dolan, Jill. *Utopia in Performance: Finding Hope at the Theatre*, Ann Arbor: University of Michigan Press, 2005.

Rosenberg, Tiina. "The Revival of Political and Feminist Performance in Sweden in the 2000s." In *Gender Delight. Science, Knowledge, Culture and Writing*, edited by Cecilia Åsberg, 411–424. Linköping, Sweden: Linköping University, 2009.

Stridsberg, Sara. *Introduction to* S.C.U.M. Manifesto *by Valerie Solanas*. Stockholm: Modernista, 2003.

———. "Den svarta utopin – anteckningar om en amerikansk superflicka" (The Black Utopia – Notes on an American Super Girl). In *Valerie Solanas ska bli president i Amerika*, 5–11. Stockholm: Kungliga Dramatiska teatern, 2006.

Ultra Violet. *Famous for 15 Minutes: My Years With Andy Warhol*. New York: Harcourt, 1988.

Meinhof, Ulrike. "Von Protest zum Widerstand." *Konkret*, May 1967.

D Muttant (Maya Hald) and Y Puss (Åse Fougner) performing D Muttant's Mission in 2005. Photographer: José Figueroa. Copyright CC-BY-NC-ND.

10. Solidarity Lost and Found: Reflections on Contemporary Feminist Performance

As the millennium began, performance and art have shown a resurgence of interest in politics, everyday life, and the documentary. A political agenda has been reinstated that intends to not only portray but also challenge the post-political *Zeitgeist* and the vision of politics as a consensual form of democracy. However, nothing "just suddenly" becomes political. Political performance had not entirely disappeared from Sweden at the end of the 1970s. Theatre companies and projects with a political orientation could always be found, although political tendencies in Swedish theatre grew stronger in the late 1990s and were increasingly noticeable by the turn of the new century.

The background of contemporary feminist performance in Sweden can be located in the shift from a social democratic state to a neoliberal one. In civil society, the distinction between the two can be assessed by the extent of personal freedom enjoyed by the populace, including sexual and reproductive rights, and whether interpersonal civic transactions are typified by commercialization and favoritism, or by mutuality and equality.[1] Some scholars who have tried to summarize the era of postmodernism have pointed to the September 11th attacks of 2001 as the symbolic reason for a major shift in political theory and practice.[2] Aggressive neoliberal right-wing economic politics, the war against terrorism, climate change, increasing global inequality, poverty, and the lack of social justice are the principal reasons for the reappearance of class issues in critical theory, feminist politics, and performance. The third way of thinking beyond the political left and right is dismissed by Chantal Mouffe in *On the Political* (2005), where she urges passion

---

How to cite this book chapter:
Rosenberg, Tiina 2016. Solidarity Lost and Found: Reflections on Contemporary Feminist Performance. In: Rosenberg, Tiina *Don't Be Quiet, Start a Riot! Essays on Feminism and Performance.* Pp. 184–205. Stockholm: Stockholm University Press. DOI: http://dx.doi.org/10.16993/baf.j. License: CC-BY 4.0

in politics and stresses the importance of creating forms of anti-essentialist collective identification around democratic objectives.[3]

Hope in negative times

Postmodern theory and performance have insisted on depression and negativity to such an extent that one hardly knows where to launch a counterargument. As theatre scholar José Estaban Muñoz points out, it is difficult to advocate hope or critical utopianism when cultural analysis is dominated by the opposite.[4] Queer theorist Lee Edelman's famous polemic, *No Future: Queer Theory and the Death Drive* (2004), is only one example of this obsession with negativity. In it he speaks of "the structuring optimism of politics of which the order of meaning commits us. Installing as it does the perpetual hope of reaching meaning through signification, is always, I would argue, a negation of this primal, constitutive and negative act."[5] Political hope fails queers because it is heteronormative and resonates only on the level of reproductive futurity. Giving up futurity and the death drive is what Edelman recommends. He advocates identification with the negative: the enemy of the future, the enemy of the state, and the enemy of the child as a symbol of the future.

A critical intellectual, however, need not be a negative one. Negativity strongly influences the contemporary intellectual opinion industry, which profits from rapid consumption of all kinds of cultural products. An objection to this overtly negative trend should not be based on the populist ideology of happiness and compulsory optimism that is created by the feel-bad-becomes-feel-good formula of popular psychology and consumerist capitalism. While negativity is an important artistic technique, it is not necessarily a criterion for art. When the Austrian Nobel Prize-winning playwright and novelist Elfriede Jelinek announced that her creativity comes out of negativity and that she could not write anything positive, it sounded like a manifesto. "There is nothing programmatic in writing about negative things. Unfortunately, I only see negative things; and I can only describe what I see, what I have experienced, and what I know about the world."[6]

Another example of an extremely negative aesthetic is the work of British dramatist Sarah Kane, whose dark, brutal visions have already achieved mythical status. In five dramas, she radically criticizes a culture that anaesthetizes rather than questions our contemporary state of mind.[7] *Blasted* (1995) opens with Ian and Cate in a hotel room in Leeds. Suddenly the drama explodes: Ian rapes Cate. A war begins and the hotel is bombed. The dialogue consists of lyrical, rhythmic, short sentences. When the play is over, Ian concludes the performance by saying, "Thank you." Kane also invokes an ancient past in her *Phaedra's Love* (1996), in which Hippolytus refuses to participate in the corruption around him, but is finally brought down by self-hatred. Kane continues in the tradition of Samuel Beckett, but with an important difference: While Beckett sought to work out a drama for post-war Europe after Auschwitz and the Holocaust, Kane only sees darkness, and her vision for postmodern times carries with it very little hope.

Kane's provocations encourage her audience to react. For her, theatre is not an escape from the world but a confrontation with it. Everything can be (re)presented on stage. To say that something cannot be performed on stage is, in Kane's theatre, like saying one dare not mention it. That denial is an ethical statement. Our human relations are the networks that keep us alive in a world where we find ourselves tormented, weak, and helpless. Kane's play *Cleansed* (1998) is perhaps the best metaphor for this. The world is all about darkness, and in that darkness we must learn how to love in order to survive.

As in Edelman's *No Future*, religious overtones may also be found in Kane's writing. After the cataclysm a little light, such as that glimpsed at the end of Kane's play *Crave* (1998), may be seen. God is dead and the remaining human beings are trying to find some meaning in life by relating to other humans. It is not the first time theatre has been used to represent existential and religious issues. Pain and isolation can be bridged by communication, if communication is even possible. "It is my belief," Muñoz writes, "that minoritarian subjects are cast as hopeless in a world without utopia. That is not to say that hope is the only modality of emotional recognition that structures belonging; sometimes shame, disgust, hate and other 'negative' emotions bind people together."[8]

Our communication culture, and especially the genre of outspokenness, has changed in recent years. The culture of rudeness and cruelty in Facebook's hate pages is a socially accepted form of bullying. Kane, who died by her own hand in 1999 at the age of

28, must have had some faith in communication or she would not have bothered writing. Her experimental language and the image of suffering in her writing comes close to Jill Dolan's "moments of liminal clarity and commission, fleeting, briefly transcendent bits of profound human feeling and connection, [that] spring from the alchemy between performers and spectators and their mutual confrontation with a historical present that lets them imagine a different, putatively better future."[9]

Paradise lost: The social democratic utopia

The climate for taking a political stand was not entirely absent from the postmodern 1980s and early 1990s. Then, after the turn of the century, Sweden experienced an explosion of feminist performance as direct actions, theatre, shows, and events with a distinctive approach emerged in force. Many feminist cultural festivals were held, and individual feminist performance, dance, and theatre events sometimes attracted even broader audiences than festivals. This popularization of feminist performing arts is related to the lively climate of feminist activism in Sweden. Just as activism in the 1990s was reshaped by the political climate of the decade, activist art also reflects the art and theatre world of the 2000s. However, as Mouffe cautions, with the increasing acceptance of their feminist activist work, artists must resist being neutralized by capitalism. One of the most urgent and contentious issues the feminist left has had to deal with is the downscaling of the Swedish welfare state. For many, the Swedish project of establishing a social democratic, egalitarian, liberal, and open society has changed beyond recognition.

The assassination of the social democratic Prime Minister Olof Palme in 1986 meant a loss of Swedish innocence in many ways. It also affected the public's confidence in the future. Palme was the subject of two 2001 plays, *Olof Palmes leende* (Olof Palme's Smile) by Malin Lagerlöf at the Länsteatern in Örebro, and *Palme dör innan pausen* (Palme Dies Before the Intermission) by Stefan Lindberg at Teater Bhopa in Gothenburg. The Swedish band Latin Kings put music to Olof Palme's speech on social exclusion and discrimination, and the feminist artist Malin Arnell's series *Jag ser vad du säger* (I See What You're Saying), a slide presentation of slogans, included a photo of "I shot Olof Palme" scribbled in Swedish on a wall in Barcelona. At the Academy of Art in Malmö, Olof Palme gazed with a Che Guevara stare from a blood red t-shirt created by the artist Olaf Unnar. One of the latest outraged reactions against the Swedish right-wing government was the 2010 election video *Gråt allians av vårt hat* (Crying out to a government we hate) by the Queer Institute in Gothenburg. The term alliance refers to "Alliansen", as the right-wing coalition calls itself. The video is a rallying cry for action against the government and its policies. In works such as these, young dramatists and artists have called into question the downsizing of the social democratic project and the fading dream of a model welfare society that greeted their generation as it reached adulthood.

Interest in Olof Palme has reemerged in a number of biographies, and in director Carolina Frände's 2009 collage production of *Palme* at the Uppsala City Theatre. It appears to represent not only nostalgia for Palme, but the public mourning of the lost vision of a social democratic nation as well. For younger Swedes the story of Olof Palme begins with his assassination on Sveavägen in central Stockholm in 1986. This brutal act, the confused and confusing police investigation that followed, the various conspiracy theories that flourished in the media, and the eventual capture of a murder suspect who was later released, constitute a national trauma that has never entirely healed.

Thanking Olof Palme

Lo Kauppi, a feminist performer, is grateful for her upbringing in social democratic Sweden. Her performance, *Bergsprängardottern som exploderade* (The Rockblaster's Daughter Who Exploded), was one of the most successful shows of the 2004–2005 season. In it Kauppi delivered a naked, powerful, and candid account of her life and class origins, conveying to her audience both social reportage and the energy to keep going: "It felt like I had gone through drama school just to be able to tell this story," she has said.[10] Many who were present wanted to hear it.

Kauppi's life story was not just a private anecdote, but also a fierce political criticism of cutbacks in social programs and the curtailment of health services. Her fury drove her presentation. Kauppi pointed out that no one at drama school understood what she meant by political theatre: "I felt so lost—what if I had chosen the wrong profession? And now it has all fallen into place. I was able to do political theatre after all."[11] Her one-woman show sums up how much she has cost society and how much cheaper it would have been had she been given proper treatment when she began having medical problems around the age of fourteen. In her teens she tried to resolve her inner chaos by dieting. Her eating disorder increased in the midst of a working-class family of addicts who used to argue about who was the sickest. This was followed by years of drug abuse and other social problems. "I'm incredibly grateful that I grew up in Olof Palme's Sweden. It doesn't matter what the Conservatives say. I would never have survived in a more competitive society," she states, thanking Sweden's social democratic system for her life.[12]

With her performance in *Bergsprängardottern som exploderade*, Kauppi felt she was able to obtain forgiveness and acceptance at last. Performance was her means of expressing her feelings. Fully aware that it would require her to put her body on stage – the body that she had been trying to alter since she was fourteen – she took the risk.

> I have done so many stupid things in my life; robbed, fought, and injured myself in lots of different ways, and I always thought everything was my own fault, that I only had myself to blame. But now that I'm older, I realize that everything might be connected and that perhaps we do things simply because we have to when we are small, and that everything was really just a cry for help that was about making dad stop drinking. I'm not trying to avoid responsibility, just trying to explain. To explain why I did all those things. To show that there might be a reason why some people behave like idiots and one shouldn't get mad at those who fail. To show what it's like to be a teenager and realize that you're not actually a human being, but a woman condemned to be an object to make old men horny that everybody has the right to criticize and put down, and how hard it is to defend yourself against the constant advertisements with anorexic models, when everything is chaos at home and there's nobody who can tell you you're fine just

the way you are. How that sort of thing affects your life and gets too heavy for some of us.[13]

Kauppi's leftist-feminist performance was televised in 2010, and she has continued to work in this political direction since then. Her more recent performances discuss themes such as sexism, power, and poverty in a society that has lost its focus on solidarity. Kauppi's anger can be understood in the sense, as Mouffe points out, that Europe is now faced by the unchallenged hegemony of neo-liberalism that claims there is no existing order.[14] This view has been accepted by social democratic parties which under the pretense of modernizing, have been steadily moving to the right, while at the same time redefining themselves as center-left. According to Mouffe, rather than profiting from the crisis of its old communist antagonist, social democracy has been dragged until it collapsed.[15]

In this way, a great opportunity has been lost for (social) democratic politics. The events of 1989 in Europe should have been the occasion for a redefinition of the Left, now relieved of the pressure previously put upon it by the Soviet system. Mouffe suggests that there was a real chance for a deepening of the democratic project at the time, since traditional political frontiers had been shattered and could have been redrawn in a more progressive way. Unfortunately, this chance has been missed in Sweden and everywhere in Europe. "Instead we hear triumphalist claims about the disappearance of antagonism and the advent of a politics without frontiers, without a 'they': a win-win politics in which solutions could be found favoring everybody in the society."[16]

Activist aesthetics and the street

Feminist, queer, anti-racist, and class-based performances take us onto the streets. Since the breakthrough of New Circus in the 1980s and 1990s, the performing arts has become a realm where the borders between dance, acrobatics, and acting have been dissolved. Theatre and performance have been enticed and seduced by reality; Shakespeare alone is not enough. Social movements seeking gender, sexual, class, racial, and ethnic liberation have taken the form of demonstrations, protests, guerrilla theatre, music, poetry, visual culture, and media events unfolding on the "street", that is, in public space.[17] Art historian Nina Felshin points out that the hybrid cultural practice called art activism is shaped as much by the "real world" as by the art world. Writing in 1995, she stated that

> activist art represents a confluence of the aesthetic, sociopolitical, and technological impulses of the past twenty-five years or more that have attempted to challenge, explore, or blur the boundaries and hierarchies traditionally defining the culture as represented by those in power. This cultural form is the culmination of a democratic urge to give voice and visibility to the disenfranchised and connect art to a wider audience. It springs from the union of political activism with democratizing aesthetic tendencies originating in Conceptual art of the late 1960s and early 1970s.[18]

Activist art requires community or public participation in order to effect social change and promote social justice. This can be accomplished by working in a variety of organizations, feminist, radical, or solidarity groups, labor unions, cultural task forces of small leftist parties, environmental, pacifist, LGBTQ, and anti-racist organizations – all groups offering ways to connect with those who share a common interest.[19] Activist art, in the forms it takes and in the methods it uses, is process rather than an object or product-oriented endeavor. It takes place at public sites outside the context of the art world. In practice, it often appears as temporal interventions, such as performance or performance-based activities, media events, exhibitions, and pop-up installations.

Feminists in Sweden and abroad have used spectacular means to dramatize the many ways in which women are objectified by the prevailing cultural and social representation systems. For example, feminist action groups have organized counter-performances in connection with the Miss World and other beauty pageants by outfitting their own bodies with flashing lights attached to their breasts and crotches, or by decorating shop dummies with signs denigrating women. The "No More Miss America" demonstration in August 1968 launched the popular image of feminists as bra burners. Such an action was once again used by the Swedish feminist activist group Unfucked Pussy (Joanna Rytel and Fia-Stina Sandlund) in their *Gubbslem* (Slimy Old Men) action against the Miss Sweden pageant in 2001. The early street demonstrations and direct actions of the 1960s and 1970s triggered the body-centered critique of gender and sexual representations that dominated feminist theatre, theory, and practice in the 1980s.[20]

When Swedish feminist artists adopted performance art as a legitimate form of stage presentation, it gave them greater freedom. Focus shifted from text and craftsmanship to thoughts and ideas. In performance art one may use whatever form of expression that most effectively conveys the topic at issue. The presentation centers on direct action, mixing such styles and genres as spoken word poetry, music, dance, circus, and elements of popular culture – with various impromptu pranks and tricks thrown in. However, it also utilizes text-based traditions of theatre when required. The political arena is a space of power, conflict, and antagonism. Valid political questions always require one to choose between conflicting alternatives.

Next to antagonism, the concept of hegemony is a key notion for addressing the question of the "political." Mouffe links the political to the acts of hegemonic institutions. In this sense one has to differentiate the social from the political.[21] Every order is political and based on some form of exclusion. There are usually other possibilities that have been repressed but can be reactivated. The articulatory practices through which a certain order is established and the meaning of social institutions is fixed are hegemonic. Every hegemonic order is susceptible to being challenged by counter-hegemonic practices, i.e., those that attempt to disarticulate the existing order in order to install another form of hegemony.[22]

Actions in public space

The heteronormative boundaries for women's bodies, and narrow definitions of femininity, are the central themes for the group of artists who call themselves the High Heel Sisters who physically explore concrete social settings. In their critiques of power, they seek to renegotiate the rules that determine social games. The group's methods – cooperation based on sisterhood – encourage women to support each other and finally lay to rest the myth of the genius male artist. On the assumption that gender is performative, the High Heel Sisters present exaggerated behaviors in diverse situations to emphasize how everything is a matter of social codes, and in this way they seek to undermine those codes.

The High Heel Sisters met at an art exhibition: "We were standing next to each other at an opening and discovered we had the same physical traits: we are taller than 1.78, older than 30, we take more than a 41 size shoe, and we had beautiful, hairy legs. We felt that this was power."[23] The artistic method of the High Heel Sisters consists in the group setting themselves a particular assignment or choosing a situation to be explored. For their first performance they assigned themselves tasks to solve in the course of one day, namely, how long could they hang from a tree together and stand still together under specific circumstances that would allow them to study their own physical limitations and the confining normalization mechanisms of society: What determines whether something is art or not?

To Walk Together Across a Square (2003) was a work in which the High Heel Sisters invited women to assemble and walk with assurance across Sergel's Square in Stockholm for a given period of time. The invitation read:

> The High Heel Sisters invite you and all other women to walk back and forth with determined steps across Sergel's Square for an hour. Devote one hour to walking together across a plaza. You are welcome to take part on Wednesday, 27 August, from 12 to 1 pm. Instructions: walk with determined steps, slowly and proudly, towards a fixed point on the other side of the plaza. When you reach it, turn around and fix your gaze on a new point, etc. Do not speak while doing this. Feel that we own the place.[24]

The purpose of the action was to create an ownership relationship vis-à-vis Sweden's most public space, to gain a physical experience of redefining gender, and to give other women an opportunity to share this experience. Another work, *Never Too Much* (2004), reverses the striptease. The High Heel Sisters started the performance nude, reading aloud from books by Gertrude Stein, Judith Butler, and Julia Kristeva, then eventually got up on stage and put their clothing on. The group's actions and activities are used as a way of creating and then inhabiting social situations to reveal power relationships at different levels.

Malin Arnell of the High Heel Sisters and Fia-Stina Sandlund also organized a public reading of Zoe Leonard's 1992 manifesto *I Want a President*. Standing on the steps of Sergel's Square, they gathered women together to recite and sing a slightly modified version of the following lines on the day before national elections were held in Sweden in September 2010:

> I want a dyke for president. I want a person with AIDS for president and I want a fag for president and I want someone with no health insurance and I want someone who grew up in a place where the earth is so saturated with toxic waste that they didn't have a choice about getting leukemia. I want a president that had an abortion at sixteen and I want a candidate who isn't the lesser of two evils and I want a president who lost their last lover to AIDS, who still sees that in their eyes every time they lay down to rest, who held their lover in their arms and knew they were dying. I want a president who has stood on line in a clinic, at the DMV, at the welfare office, and has been unemployed and laid off and sexually harassed and gay-bashed and deported. I want someone who has spent the night in the tombs and had a cross burnt on their lawn and survived rape. I want someone who has been in love and hurt, who respects sex, who has made mistakes and learned from them. I want a black woman for president. I want someone with bad teeth and an attitude, someone who has eaten that nasty hospital food, someone who cross-dresses and has done drugs and been in therapy. I want someone who has committed civil disobedience. And I want to know why this isn't possible. I want to know why we started learning somewhere down the line that the president is always a clown: always a john and never a hooker. Always a boss and never a worker, always a liar, always a thief and never caught.[25]

Jane Mansbridge calls this "practice-oriented activist knowledge" or "street theory," in contrast to theories produced within the academy. Street theory is created in and by communities. Sometimes these ideas are picked up by academic scholarship, rearticulated, redefined, and end up meaning something other than they did in their street period. It is problematic that historians who chronicle political movements rarely address parallel currents in academic writing, and academic theorists are not consistent about acknowledging the influence of direct-action politics on their scholarship.[26]

Humor

The idea of combating repression with pranks and wry humor has ancient roots. In contemporary feminist art activism, the Guerrilla Girls, who by now are veterans of feminist cultural resistance, describe themselves as fighting discrimination with facts, humor, and fake fur. Another activist group, Absurd Response To An Absurd War, proclaims that the way to maintain today's anti-war message is through humor, theatre, music, flamboyance, irony, and fun. The Plutonium Players, a performance group, were aware of this when they launched their project "Ladies Against Women" (LAW) in the US in the 1980s. Dressed as drag queens who, in turn, were dressed as Nancy Reagan and her friends, LAW used the familiar activist tactics of satire, coup, and parodying the enemy. Their favorite settings were Republican gatherings such as Reagan's prayer breakfasts, where they blended in with the crowd and inserted slogans listing ingredients such as "white sugar, white flour, white power" in the pies.

Political agitation often uses humor because it is so disarming. Although frustration may help drive the feminist activist, humor is communicative and makes the audience feel included rather than accused. Common to most of these acts, and setting them apart from 1970s feminist theatre, is their unique form of political agitation that includes a considerable amount of monologue, performance, and elements of popular culture. The performance artist Maya Hald's alter ego, D Muttant, is an example as she raps her message:

> I want women who see my show to feel encouraged by the fact that D Muttant does what she does. But they don't have to agree with everything. But I want to convey an allowing message that "I can do anything at all." There are more and more of us. There are masses of feminist performing artists who are beginning to be established, but also a multitude of up-and-coming ones who will

carry on the work. This is not something that will disappear in the next few years.²⁷

In the mid-2000s D Muttant has sometimes appeared with Y Puss (Åse Fougner) as a double feminist hip-hop act, although the duo preferred not to be pigeonholed. Their music was based on simple beats produced by a toy drum machine. The sound was monotonous, with rough cuts and sudden changes. Their concept was that feminism comes first and that hip-hop is a secondary tool for shouting out their message. In this case that message was unmistakable: women continue to be marginalized. Y Puss/D Muttant wanted to change the balance of power. D Muttant was dressed in net stockings under a red latex dress with a triangular hole over her crotch. On her head, she wore a green hat emblazoned with the Swedish word *subba* (bitch). Y Puss wore pink trousers with pockets and studs, a pink glittery vest, and a woolly hat.

Following in the footsteps of older feminist sisters, the younger feminist generation has given the cunt a face, as the name of the activist group Unfucked Pussy and the 2005 show *Lilla Fittan på prärien* (Little Cunt on the Prairie) by the comedy group PomoDori both demonstrate. Now as before, feminists present the female genitalia to show that this is still a sensitive subject. Little Cunt on the Prairie echoes the popular *Little House on the Prairie*, where everyone was always so good and kind; but here the similarities end. The group culled their material from actual situations they had experienced in daily life. A great deal concerned the insistence on being a happy person and the dominant social norms for women. The group tried to articulate the way many people go around feeling that they are some kind of fake. PomoDori wanted to get at the "loser" we all have inside us. Although their humor was sophisticated, PomoDori also took the liberty to be rude, physical, ugly, and coarse in the same way men are. They also challenged the fact that men write much of what is performed by women in mainstream theatre. This causes women to remain the lackeys of men, rather than have the freedom to rebel. PomoDori resolved this in their own case by working as an all-women ensemble.

The activist artist as an organic intellectual

Mouffe asks whether artistic practices can still play a critical role in a society where the difference between art and advertising has become blurred, and where artists and cultural workers have been co-opted and made part of capitalist production. She notes that while artistic endeavors can figure in the struggle against capitalist domination, this would require understanding the dynamics of democratic politics.[28] Cultural democracy is as much a right as economic and political democracy. One way to achieve this is to practice solidarity. Sara Ahmed classifies feminist emotions as anger, wonder, and hope, resulting in solidarity. Anger awakens the feminist and keeps her going. Wonder lets her see the world as if for the first time. Hope reminds her that concern for the future must be bound up with the legacy of the feminist past. "For feminists, a political and strategic question remains: When should we let go? And what should we let go of? Such a question has no immediate resolution: we must decide, always, what to do, as a decision that must be made again, and again, in each present we find ourselves in."[29] Hence, one should not make feminism the object of our hope, even if it does give us hope. Ahmed sees Chandra Talpade Mohanty's vision of transnational solidarity as one way to approach feminist strategies for the future.

For Mohanty, political scientist Jodi Dean's notion of reflexive solidarity as an interaction involving three people is helpful. The thematizing of the third voice is to reconstruct solidarity as an inclusive ideal, rather than an "us versus them" dichotomy.[30] Mohanty praises Dean's idea of a communicative in-process understanding of the "we," since solidarity is always an achievement – the result of the active struggle to construct the universal on the basis of particulars and differences.[31] "It is the praxis-oriented, active political struggle embodied in this notion of solidarity that is important to my thinking – and the reason I prefer to focus attention on solidarity rather than on the concept of 'sisterhood,'" Mohanty writes.[32] She finds feminist solidarity the most principled way to cross borders, decolonize knowledge, and practice anti-capitalist criticism. While not implying that women's lives and struggles are the same everywhere, she nevertheless finds them comparable. Therefore, Mohanty argues for political solidarity, which she understands as a community or collectivity among women workers that reaches across class, race, and national boundaries, and is based on shared material interests and common ways of reading the world. For this reason she sees solidarity as the basis for mutually accountable and equitable relationships among different communities of women.[33]

If one takes feminist activist artists together with Mohanty's notion of practiced and decolonized solidarity and combines them with Antonio Gramsci's idea of the intellectual, we arrive at one possible way to engage with social movements, the academy, and the arts. Gramsci saw the intellectual as essential to countering hegemony, and he identified two types of intellectuals: traditional and organic.[34] This distinction may be applied to artists as well.

The first type would consist of artists who regard themselves as autonomous. The general population views them as independent of the dominant social group. Traditional intellectuals give themselves an aura of historical continuity, despite the social upheavals they might have experienced. They are essentially conservatives, allied to and assisting the ruling group in society. The second type, the organic intellectual, includes activist artists. This group grows as a matter of course alongside the dominant social group, for which it acts as its thinking and organizing element. Gramsci saw that organic intellectuals were produced by the educational system to perform a function for the dominant social group, for through them the ruling class maintains its hegemony.[35] In his *Prison Notebooks* from 1929 to 1935 Gramsci wrote that not only should a significant number of traditional intellectuals join the revolutionary cause, but that the Left should produce its own organic intellectuals. He considered it one of his roles to assist in the creation of such individuals from the working class, while winning over as many traditional intellectuals as possible. The intellectual realm, as he understood it, was not confined to an elite but grounded in everyday life. "The mode of being of the new intellectual can no longer consist in eloquence . . . but in active participation in practical life, as constructor, organizer, permanent persuader, and not just a simple orator."[36]

Agonistic struggle

The ideal for a feminist performer is to combine Mohanty's notion of solidarity with Gramsci's idea of the organic intellectual. The organic feminist artist is the activist guerrilla performer connecting the art world with social movements and politics in a broad sense. Political mobilization, Mouffe writes, requires politicization, but politicization cannot exist without the production of a conflictual representation of the world.[37] People in general, including artists, identify with different political camps. Organic feminist artists can contribute to the political struggle via passionate performances as a way to mobilize audiences politically within the spectrum of the democratic process.

The primary object for feminist organic artists is to make social conflicts visible. Mouffe points out that in order for a conflict to be accepted as legitimate, it needs to have a form that does not destroy its political association. Therefore, a common bond must exist between the parties in conflict, so that they will not simply treat their opponents as enemies to be eradicated.[38]

Mouffe makes a distinction between agonistic and antagonistic. An agonistic struggle is a conflict between opposing hegemonic projects that can never be reconciled rationally. According to Mouffe, the antagonistic, which is always present, is a real confrontation, but is played out under conditions regulated by democratic procedures accepted by the adversaries.[39] She believes that instead of trying to design institutions that would reconcile all conflicting interests through supposedly impartial procedures, an effective exercise of democracy for theorists and politicians would be to envision a vibrant agonistic public sphere, where hegemonic political projects could freely confront one another.[40]

Conclusion

Feminist performers, particularly in Sweden, have challenged the supposedly post-political Zeitgeist of our time. The shortcomings of the post-political approach should force us to think beyond Left and Right. However, the critical utopianism of the Left has been difficult to promote at the present moment, when cultural analysis is so dominated by anti-utopianism. Nevertheless, feminist performers do contribute to sustaining that utopianism. It has been recommended that the feminist performer identify herself as a feminist organic artist invested in a feminist understanding of solidarity. This approach to performance and politics should be from an agonistic, rather than antagonistic, perspective by providing legitimate forms of expression for political conflicts. In this way social dissent would not undermine democracy, but would be a challenge that invigorates democratic politics.[41]

Notes

1. Walby, *Globalization*, 279.

2. Anderson, *Origins of Postmodernity*; Eagleton, *After Theory*; Cusset, *French Theory*; Davis, *After Poststructuralism*; Hill & Birchall, *New Cultural Studies*; Jameson, *Postmodernism*.

3. Mouffe, *On the Political*.

4. Muñoz, *Cruising Utopia*, 9.

5. Edelman, *No Future*, 3.

6. Quoted in Schueler, "Allt ljus på Jelinek."

7. Kane, *Complete Plays*.

8. Muñoz, *Cruising Utopia*, 97.

9. Dolan, *Utopia in Performance*, 168.

10. Quoted in Skawonius, "På korståg."

11. Ibid.

12. Ibid.

13. Quoted in Poppius, "Förebilden."

14. Mouffe, *On the Political*, 31–32.

15. Ibid.

16. Ibid.

17. Felshin, "Introduction," 11.

18. Ibid., 10.

19. Lippard, "Trojan Horses."

20. Aston, *Feminist Theater Practice*, 5; Rosenberg, "Stockholm Interventions."

21. Mouffe, *On the Political*, 17.

22. Ibid., 18.

23. E-mail from High Heels Sisters, 26 Aug 2003.

24. Ibid.

25. Leonard, "I Want a President." www.a.s.b.com. Accessed 29 Sept 2010.

26. Mansbridge, "What Is a Feminist Movement?" 29.

27. Kalmteg, "Feministiska föreställningar."

28. Mouffe, "Artistic Activism", 1.

29. Ahmed, *The Cultural Politics of Emotion*, 188.

30. Dean, *Solidarity of Strangers*, 3.

31. Mohanty, *Feminism Without Borders*, 7.

32. Ibid.

33. Ibid., 193.

34. Gramsci, *Prison Notebooks*.

35. Ibid., 10.

36. Ibid., 10.

37. Mouffe, *On the Political*, 24–25.

38. Ibid., 20.

39. Ibid., 21.

40. Ibid., 3.

41. Ibid., 4.

Works Cited

Ahmed, Sara. *The Cultural Politics of Emotion*. New York: Routledge, 2004.

Anderson, Perry. *The Origins of Postmodernity*. London: Verso, 1998.

Aston, Elaine. *Feminist Theater Practice: A Handbook*. London: Routledge, 1999.

Cusset, Francois. *French Theory: How Foucault, Derrida, Deleuze and Co. Transformed the Intellectual Life of the United States*. Minneapolis: University of Minnesota Press, 2008.

Davis, Colin. *After Poststructuralism: Reading, Stories, and Theory*. London: Routledge, 2004.

Dean, Jodi. *Solidarity of Strangers: Feminism after Identity Politics*. Berkeley: University of California Press, 1996.

Dolan, Jill. *Utopia in Performance: Finding Hope at the Theater*. Ann Arbor: University of Michigan Press, 2005.

Eagleton, Terry. *After Theory*. London: Allen Lane, 2003.

Edelman, Lee. *No Future: Queer Theory and the Death Drive*. Durham, NC: Duke University Press, 2005.

Felshin, Nina, ed. "Introduction." In *But Is It Art? The Spirit of Activism*. Seattle: Bay Press, 1994.

Gramsci, Antonio. *Selections from the Prison Notebooks*. London: Lawrence & Wishart, 1971.

Hallin, Eva. "Med motstånd mot förändring: Samtal med Sapphos döttrar, High Heel Sisters, Johanna Gustafsson och Fia-Stina Sandlund" ("Resistance and Change: A Conversation with Sappho's Daughters, High Heel Sisters, and Fia Stina Sandlund"). In *Konstfeminism: Strategier och effekter i Sverige från 1970-talet till idag* (Feminism in the Arts. Strategies and Effects in Sweden from the 1970s until Present), edited by Anna Nyström, Louise Andersson, Magnus Jensner, Anna Livion Ingvarsson, and Barbro Werkmäster, 158–159. Stockholm: Atlas, 2005.

High Heel Sisters. Personal communication (e-mail), 26 Aug 2003.

Hill, Gary, and Clare Birchall, eds. *New Cultural Studies: Adventures in Theory*. Athens, GA: University of Georgia Press, 2007.

Jameson, Fredric. *Postmodernism, or the Cultural Logic of Late Capitalism*. Durham, NC: Duke University Press, 1991.

Kalmteg, Lina. "Feministiska föreställningar fyller salongerna" ("Success for Feminist Performances"). *Dagens Nyheter*, 24 Aug 2005.

———. "Feminister på scen senaste året" ("Feminists on Stage in the Past Year") *Dagens Nyheter*, 24 Aug 2005.

Kane, Sarah. *Complete Plays: Blasted, Phaedra's Love, Cleansed, Crave, 4.48 Psychosis, Skin*. London: Methuen Drama, 2001.

Leonard, Zoe. "I Want a President." Typewritten broadsheet widely circulated on the Internet. Original publication data unclear (1992?).

Lippard, Lucy. "Trojan Horses: Activist Art and Power." In *Art After Modernism: Rethinking Representation*, edited by Brian Wallis, 341–358. New York: New Museum of Contemporary Art, 1984.

Mansbridge, Jane. "What Is the Feminist Movement?" In *Feminist Organizations: Harvest of the New Women's Movement*, edited by Myra Marx Ferree and Patricia Yancey Martin, 27–34. Philadelphia: Temple University Press, 1995.

Mohanty, Chandra Talpade. *Feminism Without Borders: Decolonizing Theory, Practicing Solidarity*. Durham, NC: Duke University Press, 2003.

Mouffe, Chantal. *On the Political*. London: Routledge, 2005.

———. "Artistic Activism and Agonistic Spaces." *Art and Research* 1 (2007): 1-5.

Muñoz, José Esteban. *Cruising Utopia: The Then and There of Queer Utopia*. New York: New York University Press, 2009.

Poppius, Kristoffer. "Förebilden: Lo Kauppi har en pjäs för att unga tjejer inte ska känna sig så fula och otillräckliga" ("The Role Model: Lo Kauppi Presents a Play for Young Girls who Should not Feel Ugly or Inadequate"). *Dagens Nyheter*, 20 Jan 2004.

Rosenberg, Tiina. "Stockholm Interventions: Feminist Activist Performance." In *Staging International Feminisms*, edited by Elaine Aston & Sue-Ellen Case, 76–85. New York: Palgrave Macmillan, 2007.

Schueler, Kaj. "Allt ljus på Jelinek" ("Jelinek in the Spolight"). *Svenska Dagbladet*, 9 Dec 2004.

Skawonius, Betty. "På korståg mot den sjuka vården: Lo Kauppis självbiografiska succépjäs går ut på turné" ("A Crusade Against Health Care: Lo Kauppi's Autobiographical Success Play on Tour"). *Dagens Nyheter*, 18 Aug 2004.

Stjernö, Steinar. *Solidarity in Europe: The History of an Idea.* Cambridge, UK: Cambridge University Press, 2005.

Walby, Sylvia. *Globalization and Inequalities: Complexity and Contested Modernities.* London: Sage, 2009.

Makode Linde at a demonstration in support of endangered artists and writers at the Kulturhuset City Theatre in Stockholm, 14 February, 2015. Photographer: Frankie Fouganthin. Copyright Creative Commons Attribution-Share Alike 4.0 International license, CC-BY-SA. https://sv.wikipedia.org/wiki/Makode_Linde#/media/File:Makode_Linde_in_Feb_2015.jpg

11. Against Tolerance: Thoughts on Contemporary Scandinavian Racism

Over the last few decades, traditionally "tolerant" northern Europe has witnessed the rise of populist and neo-fascist movements. These have resulted in political parties such as the Finns (Perussuomalaiset), the Danish People's Party (Dansk Folkeparti), the Sweden Democrats (Sverigedemokraterna), and the Norwegian Progressive Party (Fremskrittspartiet). Such factions have effectively interpreted the ongoing economic situation as a "national identity crisis." It is as if politicians had nothing to offer people other than a national identity, rather than engaging in a political analysis of the decline of the Nordic welfare state.

The emergent right-wing parties have cultivated troubling thoughts about an unambiguous, monolithic national culture and history. These fantasies of "pure" nations cleansed of immigrants echo Europe's darkest past and recirculate nationalism as a model for the future in many European countries. In 2010, German Chancellor Angela Merkel gave a historic speech whose essence may be summed up in a few words: "Multikulti ist absolut gescheitert" (Multiculturalism has absolutely failed). Merkel, perhaps the most powerful politician in Europe, was not the only one declaring that multiculturalism in Europe was dead. Nicholas Sarkozy, the French president at the time, along with British Prime Minister David Cameron both shared Merkel's view.

According to them, multiculturalism gives rise to violence. Merkel emphasized the word *Leitkultur*, a national core culture. Sarkozy, himself a descendant of Hungarian immigrants, conjured up a threat to French culture, and Cameron spoke of muscular liberalism. All three agreed that the Achilles heel of multiculturalism

---

How to cite this book chapter:
Rosenberg, Tiina 2016. Against Tolerance: Thoughts on Contemporary Scandinavian Racism. In: Rosenberg, Tiina *Don't Be Quiet, Start a Riot! Essays on Feminism and Performance*. Pp. 206–217. Stockholm: Stockholm University Press. DOI: http://dx.doi.org/10.16993/baf.k. License: CC-BY 4.0

is the Muslim population in Europe. This discourse creates an imaginary national virginity, which gives people a sense that they belong to a single collective "we." Michael Warner calls processes of these types appellative energy based on a loss of social memory and willful ignorance of inequality and marginalization.[1]

In *Inszenierte Wirklichkeit*, Joachim Fiebach investigates global cultural performance as theatrical and symbolic acts. Inspired by Victor Turner, Fiebach sees symbols as social processes whereby groups become adjusted to internal changes and adapt to their external environment.[2] The Nordic countries are used to holding themselves out as prime examples of the welfare state, and will eagerly admonish others in this regard. Jasbir K. Puar labels this phenomenon exceptionalism that "paradoxically signals distinction from (to be unlike, dissimilar) as well as excellence (imminence, superiority), suggesting the departure from (yet mastery of) linear teleologies of progress."[3] Scandinavian exceptionalism means that "we" have things under control, while the rest of the world is still busy fighting inequality. Fiebach emphasizes the power of the symbolic and of the mythical. Two recent events, *Tintin in the Congo* and the Cake Scandal, are performative examples of these phenomena.

Tintin in the Congo

In 2012 a heated debate about structural racism took place in Sweden when Behrang Miri, the artistic director of the children's division of the Stockholm Culture Center (Kulturhuset), removed the comic book *Tintin in the Congo* from the reading room. He said he acted because of the racist and colonialist descriptions of the African, Turkish, and Russian characters in the book. Others conjectured that if children's literature were to be analyzed from a post-colonial, anti-racist perspective, not many books would be left on public library shelves. Civil conversation on this topic quickly turned into heated exchanges and hate speech in social media with calls to "Remove Behrang Miri!" It was a classic whistler blower scenario in which the message is lost and vituperation is directed at the messenger – in this case someone who had wanted to make a point about a valid social issue.

Tintin comics have come under criticism for a long time. Their author, cartoonist Georges Remi (pen-name Hergé), has been denounced in his home country of Belgium for his Nazi sympathies. A trial against *Tintin in the Congo* took place there in 2011, but the outcome was inconclusive. It was argued that since the book was written in 1931, the author could not help adopting the racial stereotypes of the time. In Sweden the book's publisher, Bonnier Carlsén, was similarly charged in 2007. There have been other controversies about recent children's literature. Even Ingrid Vang Nyman's classic drawings for Astrid Lindgren's *Pippi Longstocking in the South Pacific* (Pippi i Söderhavet) have been criticized, as was the content of the book, in which Pippi's father is the "negro king" of the mysterious Kurrekurredutt Island. The list goes on and includes many classics of children's literature.[4]

The cry of racism in bitter media debates is often cited as the irrational attitude of a disturbed individual. Nevertheless, postcolonial scholarship has shown that racialized stereotypes are structurally produced and perpetuate racism. Stereotypes recycle a particular iconography of otherness, seeking to explain diverse everyday experiences by very simple means. The debate over Tintin inevitably raises the question of how people transmit stereotypes of those they do not know, homogenizing otherness into a single entity in their skewed descriptions of human beings.

Postcolonial studies examine power structures related to colonialism, imperialism, and racism. Ever since the seventeenth century, Europeans have exploited other nations. Even the Nordic countries, although often disclaiming colonialism, have had a colonial past. Compared to the UK, France, and Portugal the history of Nordic colonialism may seem modest, but one should remember the very tenuous Nordic critique of Nazism in the World War II era. To this day discrimination continues in Scandinavia against the Roma and Sami people. One should also not forget the Swedish State Institute for Racial Biology (Rasbiologiska Institutet) in Uppsala, which only closed in 1958, and other institutions based on race, ethnicity, or colonialism in the Nordic countries.

At its core, racism has a structure that relies on fabrications to categorize otherness. It produces a metaphorical darkness whose paradigmatic expression has been found it Joseph Conrad's *Heart of Darkness*. Although Conrad's darkness was existential and went deeper than a literal reading of black Africa, its setting was the same colonial landscape in which Tintin's adventures took place. This symbolic Congo, and beyond it the whole of Africa, is considered a place of otherness, legitimizing the exploitation of Africa and keeping it the "dark" continent.

The Cake Scandal

At the same time that *Tintin in the Congo* was being debated, another race-related cultural event took place in Sweden, the so-called Cake Scandal, also referred to as Cakegate, in homage to Watergate. It began as an installation by the artist Makode Linde, who created an actual cake in a shape of an African woman wearing a blackface mask. The occasion was a celebration of World Art Day at the Museum of Modern Art in Stockholm. The cake was part of Linde's *Afromantics*, a work that examined Western stereotypes of contemporary Africa and Africans.

At the reception, the edible creation was offered to the Swedish Minister of Culture, Eva Adelsohn Liljeroth, and representatives of other cultural organizations. Liljeroth cut the first piece, not realizing the symbolism of what she was doing. The distinguished guests were unnerved as the cake "woman" screamed whenever a piece was cut off. As it turned out, behind the blackface was the artist himself. Photos and videos of the event circulated widely, showing white people laughing and enjoying themselves as they dismembered the portentous black body. The consequence was a huge cultural debacle.[5] In the midst of it all, Linde declared that the artist's responsibility is to experiment.

> If we wish, there can be a wide spectrum of representations of blackness in Swedish culture. Artists should be allowed to experiment with colors, figures, forms, expressions, and meanings. The power of art is in its ability to turn our ideas and concepts upside down and invest old symbols with new meanings.[6]

Art and popular culture capture our contemporary moment, along with its problems and delights. But art in itself is an ideologically charged ritual, since everything has a history and a context, and we all stand on the shoulders of others. Sweden's Minister of Culture was acting in the presence of countless ghosts of the colonial past, and generations of invisible African ancestors who metaphorically winced each time the knife bore down. The inevitable question was whether someone so naïve as to take part in such a ceremony was the right person to serve as Sweden's cultural minister. Was Liljeroth blind to the connection between white people nonchalantly cutting off pieces of a black marzipan body, and all the black bodies that have been violated in countless acts of brutality down through the centuries?

In 1955, Aimé Césare wrote a critical analysis of colonialism, *Discours sur le colonialisme*, in which he discusses different types of racism.[7] Césaire points out that there is a tendency to view European manifestations of evil as accidental events of some kind. It is as if European racism were a reminder of some barbarous, long-forgotten past whose memory may suddenly rekindle the sacrificial fires. He describes how the French bourgeoisie reacted to Nazism during the World War II. According to Césaire, they did not oppose anti-Semitism because the Nazi invaders were too close at hand and were threatening their own lives. They also looked the other way when it came to the racism suffered by Africans, Asians, and indigenous people, since those inequities were directed at people who were geographically far removed from France, and therefore difficult to identify with.

After the Cake Scandal, the author and literary critic Stefan Jonsson commented that what the artist had shown was that the white woman who cut a piece of a black woman was, in fact, just *a white woman who cut a piece of a black woman*. "And all of a sudden we see it. White people cut black people. Our Minister of Culture participates in it, and this is part of the order of things, still a natural part of the order in which white people are laughing while cutting up the fake body of a black woman."[8]

Against tolerance

Europe has always been a complex and multi-cultural part of the world, but in recent decades it has become evident that European societies are unable to handle blatant, increasingly visible racism. At stake is a value-based conservatism, political populism, and neo-fascism. Behind Tintin and the Cake Scandal is the old but newly-recovered cultural biologism, or essentialism as it has been called, the idea of a genetically inherited repulsive culture that in Europe today encompasses all immigrants, but especially Muslims and Africans.

Democracy and human rights may be abstract concepts to some, but to others they are the concrete foundation of political activity. Democracy loses its power if it is turned against human rights and equality. The situation is problematic, as French philosopher Alain Badiou has said, because democracy is the self-appointed emblem of the West – a badge of honor.[9] A democrat only respects another democrat. However, when non-Western immigrants are discussed, there is not much talk about democracy, humanism, or human rights. Instead, the discourse shifts to identity cards, national borders, refugee camps, and police raids. According to Badiou, the world is divided into the "good" democratic world, and the "bad" anti-democratic communities. While human interaction is rarely so simple, because of such bias one person's notion of the social hierarchy does not match another's.

Democratic and anti-democratic tendencies work side by side, and affect each other in different ways. If conservative and nationalist ideas form social practices, we can also think and act to the contrary. Democratic actions are implemented to create new and more equitable social practices. Minorities and corresponding majorities do not exist in a vacuum, but are socially and historically produced. Social boundaries create minorities and vice-versa. The majority of the population has the power to define what culture, democracy, and the nation are about, and can make a variety of legislative proposals in the name of tolerance.

Feminist theorist Wendy Brown has stated that tolerance is based on the concept of aversion towards the tolerated ones.[10] As a concept, tolerance contains within it the power to tolerate or fail to tolerate an individual or a community. The cultural biologism that underpins racism defines those people who are considered obnoxious, and those communities who cling to their identity and resist becoming like the majority. As a result, the active social presence of minorities – especially unwanted migrants – is perceived as a threat to the nation.

For decades cultural studies and critical theory have insisted that culture is constantly in a state of change. Its boundaries are not permanent, and so national culture can never be precisely defined.

Culture has always been a construction, just as much as politics and the writing of history. It is something produced by people themselves and for that reason should be analyzed as an ideological, not an essentialist, phenomenon. Social ills cannot be defined or justified by biologism or genes, or even less by a *Leitkultur*.

Fiebach points out that it is impossible to overestimate the change in global politics that followed the September 11 attacks in New York in 2001.[11] The subsequent "war on terror" introduced a new political climate. Muslim countries were no longer orientalist cultures, but acute threats to the West. In the post-9/11 world mistrust has spread far beyond populist and neo-fascist parties and communities. Immigrants and radicalized extremists have now become the major political challenge to Europe.

Those who have analyzed the period after the 2001 attacks agree that both politics and theory changed at the time. Samuel P. Huntington's *Clash of Civilizations* declared in 1996 that the ideological struggle of the Cold War was over.[12] Future conflicts would now be between different civilizations, and the struggles would be cultural. Huntington emphasized the relationship between Muslims and non-Muslims. He wished to introduce a new reading of history, claiming that Islam has always threatened the West. The pages of Western history are filled with descriptions of bloody clashes against Muslims. Huntington's historiographical point of departure was the West's "eternal struggle" against Islam, coupled with the Eurabia conspiracy theory that Muslims are invading the West through immigration.

Affect economy

In order to understand the emotional debates over *Tintin in the Congo*, the Cake Scandal, Angela Merkel's desire to strengthen German core culture, growing political populism, and neo-fascism in Europe, one must be aware of the *affects* involved. Sara Ahmed writes about affect economy and views contemporary social boundaries from an intersectional perspective. Thus, social phenomena such as gender and race do not create meaning by themselves, but always in combination with location, time, and context. Affect economy is not primarily a matter of personal experience or individual emotions. It encompasses the entire spectrum from love to hate. The way to the hearts of people traverses affects: put simply, what "feels" right, is right.[13]

Looking upon so-called authentic feelings as suspect is not a new idea, but a classic attitude of critical theory. Ahmed connects feminist, postcolonial, and queer critique, focusing on the question of how socially defined intersections change and develop through various encounters, emotions, and bodily interactions. Mobility between nations depends upon the affect economy creating an order that allows certain privileged people to move freely from one place or country to another, while others are unable to do so. Borders cannot simply be crossed by anyone at any time. Ahmed reminds us that not all tourists, immigrants, or foreigners are defined as guests or strangers, as the case may be. Many of them are more "at home" than others and are not asked questions about their family's national origin. Even holding the "right" passport will not help in a situation where one has the "wrong" name or skin color.

Ruined self-image

Sometimes what looks on the surface like a meeting is actually an encounter with one's own mirror image. If one looks at the Tintin and Cake affairs and the controversy surrounding them, it appears that media debates have become a ritual. The purpose of the debates was not to come up with new insights or interpretations, but to use the "others" as a tool with which to strengthen the national community.

One needs an external enemy who can validate the raison d'être of one's own group. It is a human all-too-human behavior, but problematic nevertheless. The attempt at censoring *Tintin in the Congo* and the entrapment of the Cake Scandal were exploited by the media to show the madness of trying to say something about structural racism. The events functioned as occasions to trigger ritualized actions that might secure national identity, rather than promote a meaningful exchange of ideas.

Both *Tintin in the Congo* and the Cake Scandal exposed the cluelessness of the insiders as well as the dangers to outsiders. While people fumed over the attempt to censor *Tintin*, and literature in general, the cultural elite saw their self-image ruined in the

Cake Scandal: 'We are good people with good values. No one has been hurt!' the noble self-image proclaims. 'We like diversity!' – although their practice tells otherwise. In the end both events were about superiority and inferiority. Fiebach states that one possible way out of the dilemma is to consider how strongly and in what ways "symbolic bodies" manifest themselves in the most varied non-media public spaces, beginning with the street and extending to open or closed meeting rooms – how they are present there, and how they experience, suffer, and treat the world there.[14] Alternative spaces and alternative ways of expressing oneself have always offered breathing room for artists. In those spaces the ideas of Behrang Miri and Makode Linde might make sense after all. Thus, *Tintin in the Congo* and the Cake Scandal can be seen as welcome contributions that provoked eye-opening revelations into the majority's crueler side. Few horror movies are as scary.

Notes

1. Warner, *Publics and Counterpublics*, 89. See also Anderson, *Spectre of Comparisons* and, by the same author, *Imagined Communities*.

2. Fiebach, *Inszenierte Wirklichkeit*, 21.

3. Puar, *Terrorist Assemblages*, 3.

4. Habel, Ylva: "Den svenska vithetens blinda fläck"; Jensen, "Kom inte här och kom"; Mellgren, "Kort bannlysing av Tintin"; Söderling, "Tintin bannlyst på Kulturhuset" and, by the same author, "Nu får barnen läsa Tintin igen" and "Lilla Hjärtat kvar på biblioteket."

5. Barkman, "Krav på avgång"; Helgesson & Ekman, "Motsägelsefull och meningslös"; Hjort, Svanell, & Loman, "Avgångskrav efter tårtkalas"; Kempe, "Rastänkandet effektivt punkterat"; Loman & Hjort, "Nu står gallerierna på kö"; Monnakgotia, "Afrosvenskarna delvalverar ordet rasism"; Neuman, "Makode slår till igen"; Schottenius, "Makode Linde."

6. Linde, "Tusen nyanser av svart."

7. Césaire, *Discours*.

8. Jonsson, "När de vita skär i den svarta tårtan."

9. Badiou, "L'emblème démocratique."

10. Brown, *Regulating Aversion.*
11. Fiebach: *Inszenierte Wirklichkeit,* 10–11.
12. Huntington, *Clash of Civilizations?*
13. Ahmed, "Affective Economies."
14. Fiebach: *Inszenierte Wirklichkeit,* 285.

Works Cited

Ahmed, Sara. "Affective Economies." *Social Text* 22 (2004): 117–139.

Anderson, Benedict. *Imagined Communities. Reflections on the Origin and Spread of Nationalism.* London: Verso, 2006.

———. *The Spectre of Comparisons. Nationalism, South East Asia, and the World.* London: Verso 1998.

Badiou, Alain. "L'emblème démocratique." In *Démocratie dans quel état?,* edited by Giorgio Agamben, Alain Badiou, Daniel Bensaïd, et al., 19–27. Paris: Broché, 2009.

Barkman, Clas. "Krav på avgång efter tårtskandal" (Resignation Demanded after Cake Gate). *Dagens Nyheter,* 18 Apr 2012.

Brown, Wendy. *Regulating Aversion: Tolerance in the Age of Identity and Empire.* Princeton, NJ: Princeton University Press, 2006.

Césaire, Aimé. *Discours sur le colonialisme.* Paris: Éditions Présence Africaine, 1955.

Fiebach, Joachim. *Inszenierte Wirklichkeit. Kapitel einer Kulturgeschichte des Theatralen.* Berlin: Theater der Zeit, 2007.

Habel, Ylva. "Den svenska vithetens blinda fläck" (The Blind Spot of Swedish Whiteness). *Svenska Dagbladet,* 12 Sept 2012.

Helgesson, Stefan, and Kajsa Ekis Ekman. "Motsägelsefull och meningslös. Rasism är inte en fråga om gester och utseende" (Contradictory and Meaningless: Racism is Not a Matter of Gestures and Appearance). *Dagens Nyheter,* 25 Apr 2012.

Hjort, Mira, Adam Svanell, and Stina Loman. "Avgångskrav efter tårtkalas" (Resignation demanded after Cake Gate). *Svenska Dagbladet,* 18 Apr 2012.

Huntington, Samuel P., ed. *Clash of Civilizations? The Debate.* New York: Foreign Affairs, 1996.

Jensen, Emil. "Kom inte här och kom" (Don't Come Here to Provoke!). *ETC Stockholm*, 5 Oct 2012.

Jonsson, Stefan. "När de vita skär i den svarta tårtan" (When Whites Slice into the Black Cake). *Dagens Nyheter*, 22 Apr 2012.

Kempe, Jessica. "Rastänkandet effektivt punkterat" (Racism Effectively Punctuated). *Dagens Nyheter*, 12 May 2012.

Linde, Makode. "Tusen nyanser av svart" (A Thousand Shades of Black). *Dagens Nyheter*, 28 Sept 2012.

Loman, Stina, and Mira Hjort. "Nu står gallerierna på kö" (The Galleries are Lining Up). *Svenska Dagbladet*, 19 Apr 2012.

Mellgren, Fredrik. "Kort bannlysing av Tintin" (A Brief Ban on Tintin). *Svenska Dagbladet*, 26 Sept 2012.

Monnakgotia, Tebago. "Afrosvenskarna delvalverar ordet rasism" (African Swedes Devalue the Word Racism). *Dagens Nyheter*, 24 Apr 2012.

Neuman, Ricki. "Makode slår till igen – i Kungsträdgården" (Makode Strikes Back – in Kungsträdgården). *Svenska Dagbladet*, 8 Jun 2012.

Puar, Jasbir K. *Terrorist Assemblages: Homonationalism in Queer Times.* Durham, NC: Duke University Press, 2007.

Schottenius, Maria. "Makode Linde är nominerad till DN:s kulturpris" (Makode Linde is Nominated for the DN Cultural Award). *Dagens Nyheter*, 31 Jan 2012.

Söderling, Fredrik. "Tintin bannlyst på Kulturhuset" (Tintin Banned by Kulturhuset). *Dagens Nyheter*, 25 Sept 2012.

———. "Nu får barnen läsa Tintin igen" (Now Children are Allowed to Read Tintin Again). *Dagens Nyheter*, 26 Sept 2012.

———. "Lilla Hjärtat kvar på biblioteket" (*The Little Heart* is Still in the Library). *Dagens Nyheter*, 23 Nov 2012.

Warner, Michael. *Publics and Counterpublics.* New York: Zone Books, 2005.

Pussy Riot, Moscow, 2012. Photographer: Igor Mukhin. Copyright Creative Commons Attribution-Share Alike 3.0 Unported license, CC-BY-SA. https://en.wikipedia.org/wiki/Pussy_Riot#/media/File:Pussy_Riot_by_Igor_Mukhin.jpg

12. Don't Be Quiet, Start a Riot! On Feminist Activist Performance

On February 21, 2012, a group of five young women calling themselves Pussy Riot appeared at the Cathedral of Christ the Savior in Moscow. Their guerrilla performance was part of a democracy movement focusing on human rights, freedom, and equality that continues to this day. A month after the above action the three members of Pussy Riot sat in a packed courtroom in Moscow. They were accused of hooliganism and anti-religious propaganda for performing their now world-famous punk prayer, "God save us from Putin."

In April of the following year a mute Vladimir Putin stood beside Angela Merkel at an industrial event in Germany. In the front of him bare-breasted women with slogans such as "Fuck Putin, dictator!" painted on their bodies were shouting. The rigidly composed Russian president did not know where to look. The startling action was perfectly timed, and the photographers present could not get enough of the show. However, this was not a Pussy Riot event. It was their Ukrainian colleagues, Femen, firing off one of their anti-Putin actions. A global audience was able to witness a political provocation by feminist activists because media technology relayed the event to the world.

Pussy Riot and Femen illustrate how contemporary transnational feminist activist performance theatricalizes a provocation in public space as an anarchistic method of directing attention to issues. It is no coincidence that the actions of Pussy Riot and Femen are theatrical and executed as performative events. The methods are old, but the immediate impact is new. Social media and modern technology provide these actions with the transnational visibility they never had before. As Judith Butler notes, gender is

---

How to cite this book chapter:
Rosenberg, Tiina 2016. Don't Be Quiet, Start a Riot! On Feminist Activist Performance. In: Rosenberg, Tiina *Don't Be Quiet, Start a Riot! Essays on Feminism and Performance.* Pp. 218–238. Stockholm: Stockholm University Press. DOI: http://dx.doi.org/10.16993/baf.l. License: CC-BY 4.0

performative, a certain kind of enactment. No one is first one's gender and then decides to enact it. Enactment is part of its ontology.[1]

Pussy Riot's performance style and Femen's topless actions contain four elements characteristic of activist art: 1) performance, 2) provocation, 3) location, and 4) manifestos. Pussy Riot chose the Cathedral of Christ the Saviour as the stage for its prayer to the Virgin Mary, imploring that Putin be ousted from power. Femen generally uses public spaces to stage their political actions. While this is accepted by most feminists, it has also created complications within the feminist movement. Femen, for example, has been accused of both Islamophobia and white, able-bodied Western dominance by Muslim feminists. Such conflicts have arisen from the open display of the naked body by protestors and the ensuing controversy over whether it is an appropriate direction for all feminists to take.

Pussy Riot

News of Russia appearing in Western media has been dominated by reports of corruption, a lack of democracy, Putin's increasingly authoritarian methods, the invasion and intimidation of neighboring states, and discrimination against minorities, especially LGBTQ people.[2] The world witnessed how the Ukrainian revolution began in November 2013 when protestors occupied Maidan Square in Kiev. It was followed by a massacre that launched one of the most remarkable European political developments in recent memory. In February of the following year the Russians captured Crimea, a farcical referendum was held, and before people realized what was happening, the Crimean peninsula had become Russian again. Civil war broke out in 2014 in the Ukraine, which since then has been unlike any other European country.

Civil society in Russia is strictly controlled, but it continues to thrive through various forms of everyday solidarity. Those who want to catch a glimpse of the new civil society in Moscow can look at the recently opened cafes, small publishers, groups of artists, and other alternative associations where a fresh spirit flourishes. Pussy Riot is a part of that growing scene. Founded in August 2011, it is a Russian feminist art collective whose members prefer to remain anonymous. That anonymity was broken when three of its members, Maria Alyokhina, Nadezhda Tolokonnikova, and Yekaterina Samutsevich were arrested. Samutsevich was released, while Tolokonnikova was imprisoned at Correctional Colony Number 14 in Mordovia and Alyokhina at Correctional Colony Number 28 in the Urals until December 2013.

Since that time, members of Pussy Riot have campaigned for improved conditions in Russian prisons. They have also carried out activist interventions during the Sochi 2014 Winter Olympics, where police herded them away. Responding to questions about why they chose to become political performance artists, Tolokonnikova stated that while it might be possible in the West to be an independent artist, Russian artists do not have the legal channels to freely express critical views. Pussy Riot was offered a world tour after their release, but they declined. In *Words Will Break Cement: The Passion of Pussy Riot*, Masha Gessen rejects labeling Pussy Riot colorful "punk girls." Instead, she sees them as a conscious part of the Russian democracy movement and an element in larger resistance efforts.³

Femen

While members of Pussy Riot are based in Moscow, Femen was founded in Kiev in 2008 by students protesting discrimination against women, poor prenatal care, sex tourism, trafficking, sexual harassment in the workplace, and other forms of sexism. Femen had originally intended to work on building civil society in the Ukraine, but moved its base to Paris when the recent political upheaval in the Ukraine made it impossible to remain there.

Widely known for its bare-breasted actions, the group has expanded over the years to several countries where members take issue with practices they perceive as unfair and misogynistic. Femen has always used performance to present its message. In a deliberate theatrical transnationalization of its political mission, Femen presents naked or half-naked women and men in its protests. In its outreach across the borders of nation states, the group's objective is total victory over patriarchy. It seeks to achieve this through its bare-breasted activism (which it terms "sextremism") by provoking patriarchy into open conflict; undermining its fundamental institutions (such as dictatorships); abolishing the sex industry and the church (both of which it sees as controlling and oppressing people); and creating an effective, worldwide feminist combat movement.

Rebecca Schneider, writing about the concept of the explicit body, states that feminist performance art accentuates the body in political purpose.[4] In appearing topless, members of Femen use their bodies as scenes in which protest literally unfolds. Their slogans are written directly on bare skin to make a political point. However, another performance scholar, Peggy Phelan, cautions that visibility can entrap people by provoking voyeurism and fetishism. Because a colonial, imperialist hunger after ownership persists in our society, visibility remains a peculiar political enticement.[5]

By making its bodies explicit, Femen connects with the activist feminist tradition. Bodies are presented by Femen in such a way that they become provocative and confusing, something which might evoke hostility, but also empathy, from the audience. According to Femen's website, it sees itself as the premier force of feminism: its militant advance movement, and a contemporary incarnation of the free and fearless spirit of the Amazons.[6] However, the group has also been accused of sensationalism and craving media attention.[7] Critics deride Femen as young, white, able-bodied, topless exhibitionists who lack any ideological driving force. Femen, in turn, argues that in confronting men they use male sexist strategies, such as writing their messages on their breasts where men cannot help but read them.

Anarchism revisited

It is an open question whether the actions of Pussy Riot and Femen should be considered artistic performances with a political purpose, or political activity pursued through artistic means. Anarchism has become a point of departure in recent discussions on politics. In *Gaga Feminism: Sex, Gender, and the End of Normal*, J. Jack Halberstam reformulates the concept of revolution. Examining popular culture as embodied in Lady Gaga (including anarchism, surrealism, feminism, queer, and gender theory, as well as such social movements as Occupy Wall Street), Halberstam concludes that "going gaga" means something other than revolution as Karl Marx or Valerie Solanas would have defined it. The kind of revolution

Halberstam has in mind is a contemporary way to connect a punk sort of anarchist feminism to stylize and express protests today.

As we have seen in the 2011 riots, protests, and occupations happening around the world, especially in urban centers, we seem to have entered a new era of anticorporate anticolonial struggle in which the form matters as much as the content. No longer satisfied with simply marching or issuing a list of demands, these new movements turn politics into performance and combine anarchist mistrust of structure with queer notions of bodily riot and antinormative disruption.[8]

Using performance as a revolutionary method is not new. The theatricality of everyday life and public demonstrations are matters that scholars of performance studies have discussed for decades. The things that have happened in various parts of the world have revitalized transnational protest cultures and taken advantage of anarchist suspicions against capital and the state. Halberstam counters both traditional feminism and capitalism in conjuring up a vision of gaga feminism in which mom wants an anarchist revolution instead of an expensive new handbag.[9]

Butler, who focuses on human rights, ethics, and anti-war politics, has recently written on anarchism.[10] The letters of Emma Goldman, known for her anarchist political philosophy, have been published in a new edition. In *Two Cheers for Anarchism*, sociologist James C. Scott analyzes contemporary society from an anarchist perspective.[11] In 2013 the Museum of Modern Art in New York City presented an exhibition entitled "PUNK: Chaos to Couture" in which underground, agitprop, and do-it-yourself (DIY) activism were all juxtaposed with made-to-measure fashions. The contributors to *The Anarchist Turn*, an anthology of papers from a 2011 conference of the same name at the New School for Social Research in New York City, try to convince readers that anarchy is in the air and that it is especially suited to our times.[12]

The Arab Spring, the Occupy Movement in the US, anti-austerity protests in Greece, pro-democracy demonstrations in Hong Kong, the fight of indigenous people for land, and the Blockupy Movement in Europe are all examples of contemporary global protest movements with anarchist agendas.¹³ Against this background, the connection between anarchism and feminist public protests such as Pussy Riot's punk prayer and Femen's actions is evident. The style, shock value, and to some extent the philosophy of these movements have similarities. Nina Gurianova writes that the relationship between concepts of culture and politics, and between aesthetics and anarchy, has changed radically over the past century.¹⁴ In a 1973 study entitled *L'esthétique anarchiste,* André Rezler was the first to develop a methodology that considers avant-garde aesthetics "anarchist," as opposed to Marxist interpretations of the arts.¹⁵

Ontological anarchism and the avant-garde

The performative roots of Pussy Riot and Femen may be found in the tradition of the Russian avant-garde and feminist performance. Gurianova's study, *The Aesthetics of Anarchy: Art and Ideology in the Early Russian Avant-Garde,* shows how Russians in the 1910s were influenced by the nineteenth-century anarchism of Mikhail Bakunin and his idea of destructive creation.¹⁶ The root of the term anarchism comes from the Greek *an* (without) and *arche* (beginning or rule). Thus, *an* + *archos* means "without a ruler." The avant-garde's common denominator has been an aesthetic and philosophical ethos that Gurianova calls ontological anarchism, in contrast to political anarchism. The avant-garde developed in parallel with the revolutionary political movement that emerged in Russia just before World War I.

Ontological anarchism is anti-authoritarian and radically individualistic. It rejects the legacy of ready-made systems of thought in order to make space for creativity, but it does not endorse any specific political utopia. In Russia the avant-garde began with the formation of the artists association *Bubnovi Valet* (Jack of Diamonds), whose principal members were Mikhail Larionov and Natalia Goncharova. The latter challenged established notions of art in her search for a new national Russian style. Because she broke taboos, Goncharova was accused of pornography and blasphemy. Artists of the avant-garde deliberately shocked and provoked people by introducing unexpected gaps in the flow of words, images, or tones, forcing their audience to think and react, while offering them no final answers.

The avant-garde flourished in the atmosphere of strong political tensions as the war approached. In Russia an apocalyptic mood was intensified as a result of the country's political system, which had become increasingly authoritarian after the 1905 Revolution failed. Unlike political revolutionaries, the artists of the period were socially engaged. They followed no narrow political tradition, but thought that art should liberate a society stuck in old patterns of thought.

Most avant-garde artists supported the Bolshevik Revolution, but reacted quickly against restrictions placed upon freedom of expression, and they resisted political attempts to take control of cultural life. When that did happen, artists began to cooperate with political anarchists. Goncharova and others contributed articles to *Anarkhia*, the newspaper of the Moscow Federation of Anarchist Groups, whose first issue was published in 1917. *Anarkhia* directly opposed the policies of the Bolsheviks in 1918, and so the newspaper was shut down.

The avant-garde tradition of ontological anarchism remains alive in feminist performance. However, rather than revive the 1910s avant-garde style, a common anarchist ethos was adopted that shocked and incited the public in order to challenge established ideas. With laughter, irony, parody, and taking things to extremes, contemporary feminist artists provoked the dismantling of power, along with its symbols and concepts.

Russian Riot Grrrls

"Hey Girlfriend, I got a proposition for you. It goes something like this: dare ya to do what you want, dare ya to be who you will, dare ya to cry right out loud," sings the group Bikini Kill in "Double Dare Ya." The Riot Grrrl movement, insofar as it can be considered a single movement, was born in the Pacific Northwest during the early 1990s. Bikini Kill became one of its first and most famous bands. The movement encouraged young women to take their place in rock music without apologizing for their presence. As the phenomenon spread, a variety of fanzines and, later, webpages were founded by young angry Grrrls who created music with a furious sound. They developed an aesthetic that was to reclaim femininity with outfits consisting of stereotypical girlish features,, including short doll dresses, lipstick, and Hello Kitty accessories.

The three members of Pussy Riot who are known through international media grew up sharing their frustration over the marginalization of feminism in post-Soviet society. Inspired by feminist theory and the Riot Grrrl movement, they founded the band Pisia Riot (*pisia* meaning pussy in Russian). They set lyrics addressing the daily struggles of women to a track from the British punk group Cockney Rejects, and called on women to rebel and kill sexists. In this way, the idea of Pussy Riot was born.

The Pussy Riot performance style combines mini-dresses and colorful balaclavas with and powerful, extroverted body language encoded in harsh (rather than classically feminine) tones and gestures. Their words are delivered in a style that approaches screaming, accompanied by kicks and flailing arm movements, while their politically conscious lyrics address feminism and sexual politics. The main enemies of Pussy Riot and Femen are Vladimir Putin and his authoritarian regime.

Performing provocations

Social movements have their specific aesthetic formats. These may be demonstrations, protests, guerrilla theater, music, poetry, visual arts, media events, or actions that play out in the streets. The concept of public space presupposes that a line is drawn between what is public and what is non-public. The same distinction applies to works of art, where we distinguish between public (generally outdoor) and private (indoor) art. The public sphere is a place where democracy can be exercised, with the government guaranteeing security. As public space has come under the control of politicians, social groups have relocated away from urban settings, although officials continue to describe those spaces as "available." Butler cites Hannah Arendt's comment that politics requires the space of appearance. Spaces make people explicit, and according to Butler we should rethink this notion: "In order to understand the power and effect of public demonstrations for our time, we will need to understand the bodily dimensions of action, what the body requires, and what the body can do, especially when we must think about bodies together, what holds them there, their conditions of persistence and of power."[17]

Pussy Riot maximized the visibility of their prayer action by choosing to stage it in a cathedral, knowing that their provocation would be filmed and quickly gain media attention, including their protest song. Its lyrics claim that if the Virgin Mary were alive today, she would become a feminist and denounce Putin. While the punk prayer of Pussy Riot contains the irreverent words "the Lord's shit," it regards the religious figures it invokes positively, in contrast to Putin and Patriarch Kirill of Moscow, whose secular name was Vladimir Mikhailovich Gundyaev. The Virgin Mary is petitioned as a feminist to save the people from Putin, and in the English version of the lyrics Patriarch Kirill is urged to withdraw his trust from Putin and place it in God instead. Pussy Riot's performance was a conscious public provocation whose consequences might have been anticipated.

(Chorus)
Virgin Mary, Mother of God, put Putin away,
Put Putin away, put Putin away!

(Petitioner)
Black robe, golden epaulettes,
All parishioners crawl and bow;
The phantom of liberty is in heaven,
Gay pride sent to Siberia in chains.

The head of the KGB, their chief saint,
Leads protesters to prison under escort.
In order not to offend His Holiness,
Women must give birth and love.

Shit, shit, the Lord's shit!
Shit, shit, the Lord's shit!

(Chorus)
Virgin Mary, Mother of God, become a feminist,
Become a feminist, become a feminist!

(Petitioner)
The church's praise of rotten dictators,
The crossbearing procession of black limousines.
A teacher-preacher will meet you at school:
Go to class – bring him money!

Patriarch Gundyaev believes in Putin.
Bitch, better believe in God instead!
The belt of the Virgin can't replace mass meetings;
Mary, Mother of God, is with us in protest!

(Chorus)
Virgin Mary, Mother of God, put Putin away!

Halberstam stresses the meaning of popular culture and the performative strategies used in conjunction with public manifestations: songs, shows, poetry readings, chanted slogans, and other elements belonging to cultural demonstrations. Inspired by Lady Gaga's "Gaga Manifesto," in which a gagapocalypse was envisioned, Halberstam advocates not reform, but anarchist revolution – and preferably now. Halberstam states that while popular culture is often criticized for its superficiality and commercialism, those elements are the keys to understanding and liberating society as it is constituted today.[18]

Manifestos

Pussy Riot's prayer was a manifesto, the poetry of revolution rooted in the tradition of Marx and Engels, whose 1848 *Communist Manifesto* has been described as the single most influential text of the nineteenth century. Terry Eagleton has pointed out that very few thinkers have changed the course of history in such a decisive manner with a single document as Marx and Engels.[19]

In his history of manifestos, Martin Puchner notes that the genre began with Marx and Engels. Puchner finds that modern manifestos do not analyze the past; they wish to make history.[20] A manifesto is an agonistic speech act that characterizes a monumental conflict and presents a radical utopian solution. Manifestos are both performative and theatrical acts, and are familiar to us from futuristic, Dadaist, and surrealist proclamations. The avant-garde of years past has performed and published a great number of manifestos, many of them satirical. Filippo Tommaso Marinetti wrote a futurist manifesto that was published in *Le Figaro* in 1909.

Examples of more recent manifestos connecting feminism with sexual politics are Valerie Solanas's *S.C.U.M. Manifesto*, a cult text of the 1960s, whose famous opening words are "Life in this society being, at best, an utter bore and no aspect of society being at all relevant to women, there remains to civic-minded, responsible, thrill-seeking females only to overthrow the government, eliminate the money system, institute complete automation and destroy the male sex."[21] Further examples of manifestos are "Queers Bash Back" by Queer Nation, "The Advantage of Being a Woman Artist" by Guerilla Girls, and "The Riot Grrrl Manifesto: Revolution Girl Style Now!" These texts were all born out of anger, although they avail themselves of humor and irony in order to make a political point. Halberstam invokes Lady Gaga's "Monster Mother's Manifesto" to push us further into the crisis, and quotes The Invisible Committee's slogan, "In a crisis, in this crisis, don't remain calm: get agitated and add to the chaos."[22]

The Topless Jihad Day

Provocations, like spaces and manifestos, are complex matters. When Pussy Riot was accused of blasphemy they insisted that they were not against religion as such, but against organized religion and the Russian Orthodox Church. But actions can sometimes miscarry, and the feminist desire to create solidarity does not always succeed. Femen's ideology is based on sextremism, feminism, and atheism, and one dubious provocation was their call for a Topless Jihad Day in solidarity with the Tunisian activist Amina Sboui, who in March 2013 posted topless pictures of herself on Facebook with the text, "My body belongs to me."

The idea behind a Topless Jihad Day was to launch an international campaign of unity and have topless women march through the streets of several European cities. Femen's initiative met with opposition by the Facebook page "Muslim Women Against Femen," which featured pictures of fully-clothed Muslim women with slogans like "Too cool to be oppressed" and "I do not need to be rescued." Sofia Ahmed, a Muslim feminist and student activist in Manchester, UK, was of the opinion that Femen's campaign was counterproductive and that the group was using stereotypes that expressed Islamophobic views of Muslim women. Femen countered that "You can use as many scarves as you wish, if you have the freedom to take them off when you wish and put them back on when you wish."

Another action, a hijab manifestation, was conducted in Sweden in the summer of 2013. The campaign was aimed at everyone who normally does not wear a hijab, but was willing to do so for one day. Both women and men participated in this action. Even so there was a lively debate about whether a feminist defense of the hijab was possible. Others were critical of white middle-class people playing at being Muslims for a day and then returning to their own secure lives. Heated discussions over the veil showed that in a diverse society some people like to wear certain clothes, while others feel that wearing compulsory garments is an affront to their liberty.

Having relocated from Kiev to Paris, Femen International, as the organization is now called, operates in a country where a 2004 law has banned school children from wearing "explicit signs" of religious affiliation in the public schools. Although the law applies to all religious groups, it is primarily directed against Muslim girls wearing headscarves. Supporters of the law regard the veil as indicative of Islam's inability to modernize, and claim that upholding the ban defends France's secular and republican values.

In *The Politics of the Veil*, Joan Wallach Scott sharply rejects this approach. Based on an analysis of the issues that underlie the ban debate – racism, secularism, individualism, and sexuality – she shows how, rather than facilitating coexistence between different religious and cultural groups, the law has exacerbated such divisions in French society.[23] Scott and others who have studied the outrages of Islamophobia in the West since 9/11 believe that the traditional idea of national unity ("one size fits all") is no longer a viable model for Western democracies.

A new approach, in which diversity is accepted as a necessary component of national and transnational communities, is badly needed. Unfortunately, the political current in European politics is not going in that direction. Instead, there is a resurgence of neo-fascist and right wing populist parties fostering Islamophobic and anti-migrant agendas. Such parties have one thing in common: the dream of a mono-cultural nation, free from migrants, as their political utopia. Femen appears not to have realized how complex this political question is when they declared their vision of veil-free Muslim sisters.

Feminist aesthetic strategies

The avant-gardists of the early twentieth century were intent on destroying the bourgeois art marketplace that largely focused on selling art or finding artwork that was best suited to be exhibited in museums. Instead, they wished to replace the commercial art business with art activism that would have a direct impact on society and everyday life. Their artistic efforts were directed against social power structures and they thereby created a new aesthetics of the commonplace. They designed fashion, cars, furniture, and other objects of everyday life. Their aim was to create a totally new concept of art's place in human life.

Those ideas have since inspired generations of feminist artists. The legacy of the avant-garde, with its unconventional attention to ordinary phenomena, was a form of impure aesthetics that produced "ugly," fragmentary, and chaotic work. Such issues again emerged in the 1960s as the Western world was moving into a new and radical era. From these beginnings a feminist avant-garde developed. Central to this emerging movement and its theoretical underpinnings were issues of representation, power, gender, and politics, but also the relationship between art and daily life.

Activists in the feminist tradition have employed naked protests before Femen appeared. Pioneers of body art, beginning with such artists as Carolee Schneeman, Hannah Wilke, and Yanoi Kusama, all performed bodily acts. Schneeman's *Interior Scroll* (1975) is a classic in which where she drew a long strip of paper containing a poem written to a structuralist filmmaker out of her vagina and read it aloud in performance. Other classic examples of body actions are Marina Abramovic's works *Rhythm 2* and *Rhythm 0*, both created in 1974. In *Rhythm 2* Abramovic took drugs and then gave her body to the audience in a state of vulnerability and passivity. In *Rhythm 0* she experimented with passive aggression by standing on a table and offering her body to the audience along with razor blades, scissors, knives, needles, candles and other items to use in any way they wished. At the end of the performance her body was decorated with various accessories, but it was also damaged by sharp objects. A similar experience was presented in Yoko Ono's *Cut Piece* (1964), where she investigated passive aggression by letting the public cut up the clothing she wore on her body. The initially reserved crowd became more and more aggressive as the event progressed. The lesson to be drawn from Abramovic and Ono's early performances is that the cruel reactions those events elicited probably apply to audiences at large.

Vulnerability

Stacy Alaimo discusses corporeal feminist theories and material feminisms in relation to the many naked protests that have taken place worldwide. She sees the enacting of nakedness as an ethical performance of vulnerability, and uses the term trans-corporeality to emphasize the imbrications of human bodies – with one another, and with non-human creatures and physical landscapes.[24] Protests such as those of Pussy Riot and Femen redefine modes of representation and gendered scenarios of visibility. Both groups act out vulnerability between human corporeality, geographical places, and networks of power. Like feminist body theorists Elizabeth Grosz and Elizabeth Wilson, Alaimo reconnects with the materiality of the body, literally with the "flesh."

The interpretation of subversive feminist bodily strategies in different art forms is highly context dependent. When protesters show their naked bodies, they expose their vulnerability from a political and ethical standpoint. Their human flesh and the indications of life it reveals are sensitive because of their bodily existence and presence. Using the group La Tigresa as an example, Alaimo states that naked protests are effective at directing attention to certain political issues. When protesters undress they challenge the limitations of being human for a brief period. Trans-corporeal ethics, according to Alaimo, is one way for feminist cultural studies to take these actions seriously, allowing us to seek a more complex and sustainable interpretation of the flesh we humans consist of and the places we live and move in.[25]

On utopia

Pussy Riot has made their voices heard through speeches, letters, and other written materials. Masha Gessen has interviewed members of the group and documented their trial. In 2013 The Feminist Press in New York published *Pussy Riot! A Punk Prayer for Freedom. Letters from Prison, Songs, Poems, and Courtroom Statements, Plus Tributes to the Punk Band that Shook the World*. The book was issued in Pussy Riot's name, although not by the group. Publication rights were negotiated through Pussy Riot's attorneys Mark Felgin, Nikolai Plozovin, and Violetta Volkova. The book includes correspondence between Pussy Riot and their lawyers that was never intended for publication. Included in the collection is the now legendary performative speech act that Nadezhda Tolokonnikova delivered as her closing argument at the Moscow trial in August 2012. She ended her testimony with the following statement:

> In conclusion, I would like to read the words of a Pussy Riot song that, strange as it may seem, proved to be prophetic. We foresaw that "the head of the KGB and Chief Saint of the land would place the protesters under guard and take them to prison." Neither I myself, Alyokhina, nor Samutsevich were found to have powerful and stable affects, or other psychological values that could be interpreted as hatred toward anything or anyone. So, "Open all the doors, tear off your epaulettes. Come, taste freedom with us!"
> That's it.
> (Applause)
> The judge (irritated): Ladies and gentlemen, we are not in a theater![26]

The judge's admonition was an attempt to reestablish order in the courtroom. He feared it might be turned into a theater, a place of make-believe and illusion, although in fact trials tend to be theatrical by nature. The well-worn metaphor that the world is a stage and the notion of *theatrum mundi* have a seductive ability to let reality appear as theater, hence as a kind of play. Daily life and its ritualized situations may seem imbued with theatricality, although that does not mean they can be explained as theater. The exasperated judge wanted to show the world how Russia handles feminist rebels by sending them to penal institutions, a contemporary form of Gulag.[27]

Through the activist feminist tradition of our times we can hear the voice of Antigone resounding. She was an anti-authoritarian figure who might have stood as an anarchist role model if that tradition had had such figures. Although condemned to death, there was still power in her forceful protest. The present feminist revolution encompasses diverse political struggles and should be regarded as an unstable process through which change occurs. The politics of the everyday, trivial to some, are the foundation for protest movements today.

Jill Dolan and José Estaban Muñoz have both written about performing arts and utopia.[28] The term utopia, from the Greek *ou* (not) and *topos* (place), i.e., "no place," was coined as the name of an imaginary land by Sir Thomas More in 1516. Neither Dolan nor Muñoz describe the precise location or specific appearance of their future utopia. For them performance is an arena in which alternative worlds and experiences are created and can be communicated. Dolan calls this "militant optimism": keeping one's hope up, come what may.

Feminist activism has always used hi-volume provocative performance in spaces open to the public as a part of its militant optimism. The time spent in prison did not break Pussy Riot's spirit, and Femen continues its bare-breasted actions. It is both a conjecture and a hope that feminist artists and activists will continue to create material as vehicles for the urgent stories that need to be told. The anarchist approach, typical of our time, concentrates on resistance and processes; the objectives evolve from the action. The goals are thus indistinguishable from the method, and the outcome is less important than the process.

Notes

1. Butler, "Bodies in Alliance," 12.

2. Gessen, *Words Will Break Cement* and, by the same author, *Man Without a Face*; Hill & Gaddy, *Mr. Putin*.

3. Gessen, *Words Will Break Cement*.

4. Schneider, *Explicit Body*.

5. Phelan, *Unmarked*.

6. www.femen.org

7. "Muslim Women Against Femen," www.facebook.com

8. Halberstam, *Gaga Feminism*, 133.

9. Ibid.

10. Butler, "Palestine."

11. Scott, *Two Cheers for Anarchism*.

12. Blumenfeld, Bottici, & Critchley, *Anarchist Turn*.

13. van Gelder, *This Changes Everything*. See also Graeber, *Direct Action* and, by the same author, *The Democracy Project*.

14. Gurianova, *Aesthetics of Anarchy*, 7.

15. Ibid., 9; Reszler, *L'esthétique anarchiste*.

16. Gurianova, *Aesthetics of Anarchy*; Jonson, "Pussy Riots metoder."

17. Butler, "Bodies in Alliance," 2.

18. Halberstam, ix–x.

19. Eagleton, *Why Marx was Right*.

20. Marx & Engels, *Communist Manifesto*, "Introduction".

21. Solanas, "S.C.U.M Manifesto."

22. Halberstam, *Gaga Feminism*, 133.

23. Scott, *Politics of the Veil*.

24. Alaimo, "Trans-Corporeal Ethics." See also Reilly & Nochlin, *Global Feminisms*.

25. Alaimo, "Trans-Corporeal Ethics," 35.

26. *Pussy Riot!* 103; Tolokonnikova, *Slutplädering*, 31–32.
27. Ibid.
28. Dolan, Utopia; Muñoz, *Cruising Utopia*.
29. Boden, "Femen in på livet."

Works Cited

Alaimo, Tracy. "The Trans-Corporeal Ethics of the Protesting Body." *Women & Performance: A Journal of Feminist Theory* 20 (2010): 15–36.

Blumenfeld, Jacob, Chiara Bottici, and Simon Critchley, eds. *The Anarchist Turn*. New York: Pluto, 2012.

Blumenkranz, Carla, Keith Gessen, Mark Greif, Sarah Leonard, and Sarah Resnick, eds. *Occupy!: Scenes from Occupied America*. New York: Verso, 2011.

Bodin, Anna. "Femen in på livet" (Down to the Skin in Femen). *Nyheter Lördag*, 15 Nov 2014.

Butler, Judith. "Palestine, State Politics and the Anarchist Impasse." In *The Anarchist Turn*, edited by Jacob Blumenfeld, Chiara Bottici, and Simon Critchley, 203–24. New York: Pluto, 2012.

———. "Bodies in Alliance and the Politics of the Street." *#Occupy Los Angeles Reader* 1–3 (2011): 2–12.

Dolan, Jill. *Utopia in Performance: Finding Hope at the Theater*. Minneapolis: University of Minnesota Press, 2005.

Eagleton, Terry. *Why Marx was Right*. New Haven: Yale University Press, 2011.

Gessen, Masha. *The Man Without a Face: The Unlikely Rise of Vladimir Putin*. New York: Riverhead, 2013.

———. *Words Will Break Cement. The Passion of Pussy Riot*. New York: Riverhead, 2014.

Graeber, David. *Direct Action. An Ethnography*. Oakland, CA: AK Press, 2009.

———. *The Democracy Project. A History. A Crisis. A Movement*. London: Penguin, 2013.

Gurianova, Nina. *The Aesthetics of Anarchy: Art and Ideology in the Early Russian Avant-Garde*. Berkeley: University of California Press, 2012.

Halberstam, J. Jack. *Gaga Feminism: Sex, Gender, and the End of Normal*. New York: Beacon Press, 2012.

Hill, Fiona, and Clifford Gaddy. *Mr. Putin: Operative in the Kremlin*, Washington, DC: Brookings Institution, 2013.

Jonson, Lena. "Pussy Riots metoder har gamla anor" ("Pussy Riot's Methods Are Not New"). *Svenska Dagbladet*, 17 Aug 2012.

Marx, Karl, and Friedrich Engels. *The Communist Manifesto and Other Writings by Karl Marx, Friedrich Engels*. Introduction and Notes by Martin Puchner. New York: Barnes and Noble, 2005.

Muñoz, José Estaban. *Cruising Utopia: The Then and There of Queer Futurity*. New York: New York University Press, 2009.

Phelan, Peggy. *Unmarked: The Politics of Performance*. London: Routledge, 1993.

Pussy Riot! A Punk Prayer for Freedom: Letters from Prison, Songs, Poems, and Courtroom Statements, Plus Tributes to the Punk Band that Shook the World. New York: Feminist Press, 2013.

Reilly, Maura, and Linda Nochlin, eds. *Global Feminisms: New Directions in Contemporary Art*. London: Merrell, 2007.

Remmets, Anna. "Kritik mot Putinstyre fick punkbönens form" ("Critic Against Putin got the Shape of a Punk Prayer"). *Arbetaren* 35 (2014): 10–11.

Rezler, André. *L'esthétique anarchiste*. Paris: Presses universitaires de France, 1973.

Schneider, Rebecca. *The Explicit Body in Performance*. London: Routledge, 1997.

Scott, James C. *Two Cheers for Anarchism: Six Easy Pieces on Autonomy, Dignity, and Meaningful Work and Play*. Princeton, NJ: Princeton University Press, 2012.

Scott, Joan Wallach. *The Politics of the Veil*. Princeton, NJ: Princeton University Press, 2007.

Solanas, Valerie. *S.C.U.M. Manifesto*. Oakland, CA: A.K. Press, 2013 [1968].

Tolokonnikova, Nadezhda. *Slutplädering*. Stockholm: Norstedts, 2012. [Tolokonnikova's closing argument from the Pussy Riot trial in Swedish translation.]

van Gelder, Sarah, ed. *This Changes Everything: Occupy Wall Street and the 99% Movement*. San Francisco: Berrett-Koehler, 2011.

Homepages

www.femen.org

www.freepussyriot.org

"Muslim Women Against Femen," www.facebook.com

www.womynkind.org

Index of Persons

A

Abbate, Carolyn: 11, 12, 17, 18, 26, 46, 48, 76, 77
Abel, Sam: 4, 5, 9, 16, 18, 28, 43, 44, 47, 48
Abelove, Henry: 149
Abrahami, Natalie: 167
Abramovic, Marina: 232
Adelsohn Liljeroth, Eva: 210
Adolfsson, Eva: 122, 145
Adolfsson, Josefin: 170
Ahmed, Sara: xii, xv, 84, 94, 96, 109, 113, 114, 162, 164, 198, 202, 213, 214, 216
Ahmed, Sofia: 230
Alaimo, Tracy: 233, 235, 236
Almqvist, Carl Jonas Love: viii, ix, xiii, 118, 119, 121, 122, 123, 124, 125, 126, 128, 129, 131, 132, 134, 139, 140, 142, 143, 145, 146, 147, 148, 149
Alperson, Philip: 97, 115
Alyokhina, Maria: 221, 233
Anderson, Benedict: 201, 203, 215, 216
Andersson, Perry: 203
Andersson, Louise: 203
André, Naomi: 4, 16, 18, 76, 77, 115, 143, 145
Ångström, Anna: 189, 190

Arendt, Hannah: 226
Aristotle: 25, 46, 49, 105, 109, 124
Arnell, Malin: 188, 195
Aschan, Lisa: 170
Ascheid, Antje: 81, 82, 93, 96
Aston, Elaine: 92, 202, 203, 204
Augustine: 3, 146
Austen, Jane: 129
Austin, Gayle: 24, 46, 48
Ayame, Yoshizawa: 65

B

Badiou, Alain: 212, 215, 216
Baez, Joan: 105
Baker, Roger: 75, 77
Barale, Michèle Aina: 149
Barber, Stephen: 164
Barkman, Clas: 216
Barthes, Roland: xi, xv, 8, 9, 11, 12, 15, 16, 17, 18, 68, 16, 17, 18, 20, 26, 27, 46, 48, 49, 75, 77, 107, 108, 113, 114
Baylin, Bernard: 61
Benér, Theresa: 173, 174
Benjamin, Jessica: 170
Benjamin, Walter: 8
Bensoussan, Georges: 164,
Bergman, David: 109
Bergman, Ingmar: 171

Berlant, Lauren: 113, 114, 162, 164
Bikini Kill: 225
Binoche, Juliette: 167
Birchall, Clare: 201, 203
Blackmer, Corinne E: 4, 5, 16, 17, 19, 20, 76, 77, 143, 145
Blackwood, Evelyn: 77, 78
Blumenfeld, Jacob: 235, 236
Blumenkranz, Carla: 236
Boëthius, Maria-Pia: 94, 96
Borgström, Eva: 123, 124, 126, 138, 141, 142, 145, 149
Bottici, Chiara: 235, 236
Brandryd, Marius Dybwad: viii, 166
Brecht, Bertolt: 72
Broch, Hermann: 90, 95, 96, 113, 114, 216
Brontë, Charlotte: 129
Brown, Wendy: 212, 216
Bubnovi Valet: 224
Budde, Antje: x
Bullough Bonnie: 75, 77, 78
Bullough, Vern: 75, 77, 78
Burman, Lars: 140, 142, 143, 145, 146
Butler, Judith: 12, 17, 19, 70, 71, 72, 73, 77, 78, 127, 128, 142, 146, 164, 194, 219, 223, 226, 235, 236
Byström, Malin: vii, 6
Bäcker, Mats: ii, vii, 2
Böwe, Jule: 171

C
Cameron, David: 207
Cancian, Francesca M: 158, 164, 165
Carter, Erica: 85, 86, 87, 94, 95, 96
Case, Sue Ellen: xv, 10, 14, 17, 18, 19, 25, 35, 48, 78, 204
Castle, Terry: 15, 18, 19, 41, 130, 136, 138, 144, 146
Castorf, Frank: 151
Castro, Fidel: ii, 114
Cavallin, Anna: 122, 141, 146
Cvendish, Margaret: 138
Césaire, Aimé: 211, 215, 216
Christensen, Inger: 172
Cixous, Hélène: xii, xv, 3, 25, 44, 46, 48, 159, 164, 165, 174
Clark, David: 164
Clément, Catherine: xv, 4, 10, 14, 16, 17, 19, 26, 46, 48, 164, 165
Cleto, Fabio: 94, 95, 96, 114
Cockney Rejects: 226
Coleridge, Samuel Taylor: 138
Conrad, Joseph: 209
Cook, Sam: 103
Critchley, Simon: 235, 236
Cusset, Francois: 201, 203
Cvetkovich, Ann: 113, 114

D
Dahlström, Alexandra: viii, 166, 169
Dame, Joke: 13, 14, 17, 19
Davis, Colin: 82, 201, 203

Dean, Jodi: 198, 202, 203
Dekker, Rudolf: 16, 19, 143, 146
de Beauvoir, Simone: 24
de Lauretis, Teresa: 6, 16, 19, 45, 48
Desertain, Laura Margaret: 139
Deutschmann, David: 114
Diamond, Elin: xv, 14, 15, 18, 19, 224
Dickens, Charles: 129
Diderot, Denis: 123
Dietrich, Marlene: 82
D Muttant & Y Puss: viii, 184, 196, 197
Dolan, Jill: 181, 182, 188, 201, 203, 234, 236
Dollimore, Jonathan: 132, 143, 146
Dostoyevsky, Fyodor: 171
Doty, Alexander: 140, 146
Drain, Richard: xv, 48, 174
du Bois, Page: 126, 142, 146
Dufresne, Isabelle Collin (Ultra Violet): 177, 182
Dunbar, William: 61
Dyer, Richard: xi, xv, 83, 96, 110, 114
Dylan, Bob: 105

E

Eagleton, Terry: 201, 203, 228, 235, 236
Ebert, Georg: vii, 80
Edelman, Lee: 186, 187, 201, 203
Ekenstam, Claes: 93, 95, 96
Ekman, Kajsa Ekis: 215, 216

El General (Hamada Ben Amor): 104
Eliot, George: 129
Elkin, R. H: 79
Emin, Tracy:178
Engels, Friedrich: 237
Eyerman, Ron: 115

F

Farmer, Brett: 61, 85, 86, 94, 95, 96
Fassbinder, Rainer Werner: 158
Felgin, Mark: 233
Felshin, Nina: 192, 201, 203
Felski, Rita: 88, 95, 96, 115
Femen International: xiv, 219, 220, 221, 222, 224, 226, 229, 230, 231, 232, 234, 235, 236, 238
Ferree, Myra Marx: 204
Ferris, Lesley: 75, 76
Fetterley, Judith: 49
Feuer, Rosemary: 104
Fiebach, Joachim: x, 208, 213, 215, 216
Figueroa, José: viii, xiv, 184
Finney, Gail: 163, 165
Fisbach, Frédéric: 167
Fischer, Robert: x, 164
Fischer-Lichte, Erika: x
Fisher, Tom: 88
Flaubert, Gustave: 3, 15, 19, 110
Foucault, Michel: 3, 12, 146, 203
Fouganthin, Frankie: viii, 206
Fougner, Åse: viii, 197, 184
Freccero, Yvonne: 147

Freud, Sigmund: 9, 102, 108, 112, 113, 116, 146, 153, 158
Fry, Gareth: 172
Frände, Carolina: 189

G

Gaddy, Clifford: 235, 237
Garber, Marjorie: 18, 19, 65, 66, 70, 73, 76, 77, 78, 128, 138, 146
Garbo, Greta: 82
Garland, Judy: 82, 83, 94, 96
Gelin, Martin: 174
Gessen, Keith: 236
Gessen, Masha: 221, 233, 26
Giacosa, Giuseppe: 53, 79
Giddens, Anthony: 156, 164, 165
Giesz, Ludwig: 92, 95, 96, 115
Gilbert, Sandra: 75, 78
Goethe, Johann Wolfgang: 29, 93, 122
Goldman, Emma: 223
Goncharova, Natalia: 224, 225
Girard, René: 134, 135, 136, 138, 144, 146
Graeber, David: 235, 236
Gramsci, Antonio: 111, 114, 115, 199, 200, 202, 203
Grigorian, Asmik: vii, 52
Gronau, Barbara: x
Grosz, Elizabeth: 232
Gubar, Susan: 75, 78
Guerilla Girls: 229
Guevara, Ernesto (Che): vii, 100, 101, 106, 107, 189
Gundyaev, Vladimir Mikhailovich (Patriarch Kirill of Moscow): 227
Gurianova, Nina: 224, 235, 237
Gustav III: 121, 128, 129, 136
Gustavsson, Andreas: 173, 174
Gårder, Marcus: vii, 22

H

Habel, Ylva: 215, 216
Hadlock, Heather: 4, 16, 19, 143, 147
Hagedorn Thomsen, Hans: 122, 140, 147
Halberstam, Jack (Judith): 85, 94, 96, 139, 145, 147, 222, 223, 228, 229, 235, 237
Hald, Maya: viii, 184, 196
Hall, Donald E: 147
Hallin, Eva: 203
Halperin, David: 149
Hammergren, Lena: 148
Harris, Daniel: 86, 94, 97
Harvey, Lilian: 81
Hawley, John C: 75, 78
Hebdige, Dick: 113, 115
Heidegger, Martin: 162, 163, 164, 165
Heinonen, Timo: ix
Helander, Karin: 148
Helgesson, Stefan: 215, 216
Hellquist, Annie: 113, 115
High Heel Sisters: 193, 194, 195, 202, 203
Hill, Fiona: 235, 237
Hill, Gary: 203

Higgins, Kathleen: 92, 95, 97, 114, 115
Hirschfeld, Magnus: 64, 76
Hjort, Mira: 215, 216, 217
Holiday, Billie: 115, 178
Holm, Michael: 94, 97
Holmberg, Olle: 122, 131, 140, 143, 147
Honolka, Kurt: 46, 49
Hov, Liv: 76, 78, 143, 147
Huntington, Samuel P: 213, 216, 217
Hwang, David Henry: xiii, 53, 54, 57, 58, 59, 65, 66, 67, 68, 69, 74, 75, 76

I

Ibsen, Henrik: viii, x, xiv, 150, 151, 153, 154, 158, 159, 160, 161, 162, 163, 165, 167, 170
Illica, Luigi: 53, 79
Ilmonen, Kaisa: x
Ingvarsson, Anna Livion: 203
Irigaray, Luce: 11, 12, 13, 15, 17, 19 20

J

Jackson, Stevi: 163, 165
Jagose, Annamarie: 71, 77, 78, 140, 147
Jameson, Fredric: 201, 203
Jamison, Andrew: 113, 115
Jardine, Alice A: 11, 17, 20
Jelinek, Elfriede: 186, 201, 204
Jensen, Emil: 215, 217
Jensner, Magnus: 203
Jonson, Lena: 235, 237

Jonsson, Stefan: 211, 215, 217
Jostedt, Madeleine Ulrici: vii, 2

K

Kalmteg, Lina: 202, 204
Kane, Sarah: 186, 187, 201, 204
Kaplan, Ann: 25, 46, 49
Kauppi, Lo: 189, 190, 191, 204, 205
Kekki, Lasse: x
Kempe, Jessica: 215, 217
Kenney, Alexander: vii, 6, 8, 52
Kerman, Joseph: 4, 16, 20
King, Martin Luther Jr: 105
Kipnis, Laura: 152, 163, 164, 165
Klinga, Elin: viii, 118
Klöcke, Anja: viii
Knight, Deborah: 89, 95, 97, 115
Knopp, Guido: 84, 94, 97
Koestenbaum, Wayne: 20, 30, 31, 32, 33, 34, 36, 59, 62, 63, 65, 102, 113, 128, 130, 131
Kolesch, Doris: 27, 33, 36, 62, 65
Kondo, Dorinne K: 91, 94
Kraus, Chris: 111, 113
Kristeva, Julia: 27, 210
Kulka, Thomas: 111, 113, 131
Kupfer, Joseph: 105, 111, 113, 131
Kusama, Yanoi: 247
Kuzniar, Alice A: 103, 107, 110, 111, 112, 113

L

Lady Gaga: 238, 239, 244, 245, 251, 253
Lagerlöf, Malin: 204

La Tigresa: 249
Langdal, Peter: 175, 176, 177
Latin Kings, 204
Lagerroth, Ulla-Britta: 144, 158, 163
Larionov, Mikhail: 240
Leander, Zarah: 5, 7, 9, 13, 14, 96, 97, 98, 99, 100, 101, 102, 103, 104, 106, 107, 108, 109, 110, 111, 112, 113, 114, 123, 126
Lehnert, Gertrud: 22, 32, 36, 147, 158, 164
Leonard, Sarah: 220, 252
Leonard, Zoe: 211, 220
Levertin, Oscar: 148
Levine, Robert A: 181
Lewis, Matthew: 137
Lindberg, Stefan: 204
Linde, Makode: 8, 222, 226, 231, 233
Lindgren, Astrid, 225
Lippard, Lucy, 217, 220
Loman, Stina: 232, 233
Lorenz, Gottfried: 110, 114
Love, Courtney: 194
Lynskey, Dorian: 121, 129, 131

M

Madonna: 98
Maerli, Terje: 171, 172
Mahler, Gustav: 102
Mansbridge, Jane: 211, 218, 220
Marber, Patrick: 183
Marcuse, Herbert: 167
Marinetti, Filippo Tommaso: 245

Martin, Patricia Yancey: 35, 220
Martin, Ruth: 95
Martin, Thomas: 95
Marx, Karl: 253
McClary, Susan: 19, 20, 24, 26, 29, 31, 32, 33, 35, 36, 39, 60, 62, 64, 65
Meinhof, Ulrike: 196, 198
Melberg, Arne: 62, 65
Mellgren, Fredrik: 233
Merkel, Angela: 223, 229, 235
Midler, Betty: 98
Miller, Chloe: 188
Miller, Nancy C: 136
Miri, Behrang: 224, 231
Mitchell, Katie: 183, 187, 189
Mohanty, Chandra Talpade: 214, 216, 218, 220
Moi, Toril: 167, 168, 179, 181
Monnakgotia, Tebago: 233
More, Thomas: 11, 250
Morris, William: 11, 250
Morrison, Toni: 76, 77, 91, 94
Mortensen, Johan: 137, 138, 156, 164
Mouffe, Chantal: 201, 204, 207, 209, 214, 216, 217, 218, 220
Mozart, Wolfgang Amadeus: 2
Mukhin, Igor: 8, 234
Muñoz, José Esteban: 202, 203, 217, 220, 250 252, 253

N

Neuman, Ricki: 233
Nieder, Christoph: 65

Nielsen, Asta: 82
Nietzsche, Friedrich: 12, 15, 16, 108, 111, 113, 131
Nilsson, Birgit: 82
Nochlin, Linda: 251, 253
Nordin, Lissa: 179, 180, 181
Nussbaum, Martha: 129, 132
Nyström, Anna: 203

O

Obama, Barack: 119
Olsson, Ingela: 8, 192
Olsson, Henry: 147, 159, 164
Ono, Yoko: 194, 248
Österberg, Frida: 7, 18
Ostermeier, Thomas: 167, 171, 183

P

Pahlen, Kurt: 23,
Palm, Helga Maria: 47, 50, 63, 65
Palme, Olof: 204, 205, 206
Parly, Nila: 63, 65
Pearce, Lynne: 179, 181
Petri, Thomas: 8, 166
Peraino, Judith A: 20, 25, 32, 33, 36, 164
Pettersson, Anna: 184, 185, 186, 189
Phelan, Peggy: 238, 251, 253
Piaf, Edith: 82
Pinochet, Augusto: 124
Plath, Sylvia: 194
Plato: 19, 139, 140, 141, 142, 157, 164
Plozovin, Nikolai: 249

Poizat, Michel: 20, 32, 36, 59, 63, 65
PomoDori: 231
Poppius, Kristoffer: 217, 220
Proust, Marcel, 135
Puar, Jasbir K: 94, 224, 233
Puccini, Giacomo: 7, 13, 38, 69, 95, 70, 73, 74, 75, 78, 79, 90, 95
Puchner, Martin: 244, 253
Pueblo, Carlos: 122
Pussy Riot: 8, 14, 234, 235, 236, 237, 238, 240, 242, 243, 244, 245, 248, 249, 250, 251, 252, 253, 254
Putin, Vladimir: 235, 236, 242, 243, 244, 251, 252, 253

Q

Queerinstitutet (Gothenburg): 205
Queer Nation: 245

R

Ralf, Klas: 35, 36, 65
Rapace, Noomi: 8, 192
Räthzel, Nora: 10
Reagan, Nancy: 212
Reik, Theodor: 118, 119, 123, 128, 129, 130, 132
Reilly, Maura: 251, 253
Reitala, Heta: 9
Remi, Georges (Hergé): 224
Remmets, Anna: 253
Resnick, Sarah: 252
Rezler, André: 253
Rieger, Eva: 65

Richter, Sonja: 8, 166, 176
Ring, Lars: 190
Riot Grrrls: 241, 242
Robinson, Lea: 186
Rolf, Ernst: 81
Romberg, Bertil: 156, 163, 164
Rombo, Elin: 7, 24
Rosaldo, Michelle Z: 177, 180, 181
Rose, Tricia: 132
Rosenberg, Tiina: 1, 2, 4, 15, 19, 39, 69, 92, 93, 95, 97, 111, 113, 117, 129, 130, 132, 135, 156, 159, 160, 164, 167, 183, 193, 198, 201, 218, 220, 223, 235,
Roth, Nathan: 129, 132
Rudström, Johanna: 2, 7
Rytel, Joanna: 185, 209

S

Said, Edward: 73, 74, 76, 90, 91, 95
Sager, Maja: 10
Samutsevich, Yekaterina: 237
Sandell, Kerstin: 10
Sandlund, Fia-Stina: 8, 14, 182, 185, 189, 209, 211, 219
Sandqvist, Mona: 163
Sarkozy, Nicholas: 223
Sauter, Willmar: 164
Sboui, Amina: 245
Scherle, Arthur: 62, 65
Schneeman, Carolee: 247
Schneider, Rebecca: 238, 251, 253
Schor, Naomi: 28, 33, 36
Schottenius, Maria: 233
Schueler, Kaj: 220
Schück, Henrik: 164
Scott, James C: 239, 251, 253
Scott, Joan Wallach: 246, 251, 253
Scruton, Roger: 179, 181
Sedgwick, Eve Kosofsky: 23, 32, 36, 101, 102, 110, 111, 113, 151, 152, 154, 160, 165, 180
Segal, Lynne: 28, 33, 36, 179, 181
Seiler, Paul: 7, 14, 96, 98, 99, 109, 110, 112, 114
Senelick, Laurence: 92, 95, 159, 165
Sernhede, Ove: 129, 132
Shakespeare, William: 138
Shnookal, Deborah: 130
Sirk, Douglas: 107
Sjöberg, Alf: 163
Sjöberg, Birthe: 163
Sjöblad, Christina: 163
Skawonius, Betty: 217, 221
Smart, Mary Ann: 35, 36, 163, 165
Smith, Patricia Juliana: 20, 21, 32, 33, 35, 36, 62, 65, 92, 93, 159, 161
Smith, Patrick: 65
Söderling, Fredrik: 231, 233
Söderbaum, Kristina: 97
Söderman, Johan: 129, 132
Solanas, Valerie: 5, 8, 10, 14, 192, 193, 194, 195, 196, 197, 198, 238, 245, 254

Solomon, Robert C: 108, 111, 114
Sontag, Susan: 125, 130, 132
Spivak, Gayatri Chakravorty: 91, 95
Stacey, Jackie: 179, 181
Steen, Paprika: 8, 166, 176
Stein, Gertrud: 178, 194, 210
Stenberg, Roger: 8, 134, 192
Stenström, Johan: 163
Stéphany, Anna: 7, 22, 24
Streisand, Barbra: 82
Stern, Susanna: 2, 7
Stjernö, Steinar: 221
Strauss, Richard: 7, 22, 24, 32, 37, 60, 149
Strauss, Tilman: 187
Stridsberg, Sara: 8, 14, 192, 193, 194, 195, 196, 197, 198
Strindberg, August: 14, 169, 171, 174, 183, 184, 185, 186, 187, 189, 190
Svanell, Adam: 231, 232
Svedjedal, Johan: 158, 165
Swidler, Ann: 170, 179, 181

T
Templeton, Joan: 167, 179, 181
Thackeray, William Makepeace: 12
Tolokonnikova, Nadezha: 237, 249, 252, 254
Turner, Victor: 224

U
Unnar, Olaf: 205

V
van de Pol, Lotte: 32, 35, 159, 162
van Gelder, Sarah: 251, 254
Vang Nyman, Ingrid: 225
Vetter, Emma: 7, 22
Vicinus, Martha: 148, 159, 165
Vill, Susanne: 63, 65
Volkova, Violetta: 249
Voss, Egon: 63, 66

W
Wagner, Richard: 5, 7, 9, 12, 13, 14, 15, 16, 39, 40, 41, 42, 43, 44, 45, 47, 48, 49, 50, 51, 52, 53, 55, 56, 57, 59, 60, 61, 63, 64, 65, 66, 68, 105, 108, 111, 113, 123, 131, 132
Walby, Sylvia: 217, 221
Walsh, Michael: 62, 66
Warhol, Andy: 193, 194, 195, 198
Warner, Leo: 183, 187
Warner, Michael: 99, 110, 114, 224, 231, 233
Weer, Robert Lawrence: 34
Weigel, Sigrid: 62, 66
Weiler, Christel: 10
Weinius, Michael: 7, 52.
Westman-Berg, Karin: 137, 156, 165
Wieringa, Saskia E: 94
Wilke, Hanna: 247
Williams, Linda: 25, 32, 37, 59, 63, 66, 121, 129, 132
Wilson, Elizabeth: 248
Wolfram, Louise: 187

Wood, Elizabeth: 29, 30, 33, 34, 35, 37, 98, 103, 110, 111, 114

Woolf, Virginia: 154, 161, 165, 187

Werkmäster, Barbro: 203

Z

Zern, Leif: 175, 180, 181, 188, 189, 190

Zine El Abedine Ben Ali: 120

www.ingramcontent.com/pod-product-compliance
Lightning Source LLC
Chambersburg PA
CBHW050857160426
43194CB00011B/2193